Searching for the Patient's Presence in Medical Case Reports

Philologica Wratislaviensia: From Grammar to Discourse

Edited by Zdzisław Wąsik

Volume 5

PETER LANG
EDITION

Magdalena Zabielska

Searching for the Patient's Presence in Medical Case Reports

PETER LANG
EDITION

Bibliographic Information published by the Deutsche Nationalbibliothek
The Deutsche Nationalbibliothek lists this publication in the Deutsche Nationalbibliografie; detailed bibliographic data is available in the internet at http://dnb.d-nb.de.

Library of Congress Cataloging-in-Publication Data
Zabielska, Magdalena, 1982- , author.
Searching for the patient's presence in medical case reports / Magdalena Zabielska.
p. ; cm. – (Philologica Wratislaviensia: from grammar to discourse, ISSN 1866-699X ; volume 5)
Includes bibliographical references and index.
ISBN 978-3-631-65211-4 (print) – ISBN 978-3-653-04676-2 (e-book)
I. Title. II. Series: Philologica Wratislaviensia ; v. 5. 1866-699X
[DNLM: 1. Linguistics. 2. Medical Records. 3. Attitude of Health Personnel. 4. Paternalism. 5. Patients. 6. Physician-Patient Relations. WX 173]
R118
610.1'4–dc23

2014031805

The publication was partly sponsored by
the Faculty of English, Adam Mickiewicz University in Poznan.

Cover design by Beata Opala

ISSN 1866-699X
ISBN 978-3-631-65211-4 (Print)
E-ISBN 978-3-653-04676-2 (E-Book)
DOI 10.3726/978-3-653-04676-2

Peter Lang Edition is an Imprint of Peter Lang GmbH.
Peter Lang – Frankfurt am Main · Bern · Bruxelles · New York · Oxford · Warszawa · Wien

This publication has been peer reviewed.

www.peterlang.com

Contents

Introduction

It is a truism, yet universally acknowledged, that medicine has played a fundamental role in people's lives. Medicine concerns their health which conditions their functioning in society. It is medical professionals and their expertise that patients trust their lives with when they are ailing. That communication between doctors and patients is the key to success of treatment seems another truism, especially in the light of the recent substantial body of research into health communication. These issues appear to be of particular relevance in the era of European citizenship and mass migration of people. Yet, there is another type of communication, possibly less prominent but not less interesting to analyze. It is restricted to medical community and it aims at sharing medical knowledge. This communication may seem to exclude patients but it does not mean it does not concern them. They are written about and it appears critical how this is done.

The present work seeks to examine how patients are portrayed in professional medical texts. In more detail, the research question is whether patients are presented as subjects or objects of medical study and practice, or, in other words, whether they are imaged as whole persons and experiencing individuals in the descriptions of diagnosis and treatment. To this aim, a corpus of medical case reports from British and American journals available online has been analyzed paying special attention to the textual presence or absence of patients in the accounts of diseases and medical procedures, and possible explanations for these modes of reference. On the one hand, linguistic means used in patient imaging have been studied from a pragmatic perspective, i.e., their function in mediating particular information. On the other hand, the historical background of case reports has been taken into consideration as well as the present context of their production as factors instrumental in shaping this particular genre in form and content. Moreover, to give a detailed explication of the examined aspect, the analysis has drawn on a number of concepts from the sociology of medicine and medical semiotics. Furthermore, an attempt has been made to determine whether the researcher's interpretation of the texts at hand is shared by other readers. To this end, the results of the textual analysis have been confronted with the opinions of a group of respondents who have been asked to read selected fragments of the texts from the examined corpus.

The results appear to be of great importance, as what distinguishes medicine from other scientific areas is that it does not only study diseases and develop new ways of their treatment but also manages patients who suffer all the consequences of being ill. Following this argument, it the present author's belief that the writing about methods of enhancing patients' treatment should still refer to patients as beneficiaries of these methods, not only as those to whom these methods apply. This particular commitment situates the present work in a broader body of research postulating a patient-centered approach in medicine. What is more, patient presentation and its interpretation appear to be issues of concern in the light of the fact that texts written by the already established members of the profession not only acquaint novices with particular attitudes and values but also promote discipline-specific modes of writing.

The present work is based on the author's PhD dissertation entitled "Is there a patient in the text? A discourse study of patient imaging in case reports from British and American medical journals", defended in the School of English at Adam Mickiewicz University in Poznań, Poland. Only selected fragments of the dissertation have been published in linguistic journals and edited collections. The work consists of six chapters. While the first four present the theoretical and methodological background for the study, the remaining two are empirical in nature. In Chapter One, the key notions are explicated such as discourse, discourse analysis, text, etc. Moreover, theoretical background is discussed which includes various approaches to the relation of language, thought and reality, studies of scientific discourses in the context of their production as well as genre theory. The chapter also gives an overview of various genres subsumed under the label *medical discourse*. The aim of Chapter Two is to demonstrate the beginnings and evolution of the case report genre against the background of changing intellectual thought-styles and developing medicine of the nineteenth century. The chapter points specifically to those events in the history of medicine which affected medical discourse in general and case reports in particular. Chapter Three looks at the genre of case report from a contemporary perspective. The current mode of reasoning in medical practice and selected facts about medical education are presented as contextual factors influencing production and reproduction of medical discourse. Analytical tools and notions used in the empirical part of the work are listed and explicated in Chapter Four. In Chapter Five, patient imaging in the corpus of case reports is analyzed and discussed, whereas in Chapter Six, the reception of some of these results in the sample of students of medicine is demonstrated.

Poznań, July 2012 *Magdalena Zabielska*

Chapter One: Theoretical background

Drawing on a useful classification of various approaches to discourse analysis proposed by Nelson Phillips and Cynthia Hardy (2002), the present work is located in the area of social linguistic analysis which can be characterized as being constructivist and text-based in nature. According to the above authors, the aim of this framework is "to undertake a close reading of the text to provide insight into its organization and construction, and also to understand how texts work to organize and construct other phenomena" (Phillips and Hardy 2002: 22). This methodological choice excludes critical discourse analysis with its ideological commitment, which will be reflected in the decision of how the term *discourse* is understood in the present work. Moreover, it is constructivist in that it views the texts as shaped in the course of the history of the development of medicine. At this point a distinction should be made between distal and proximate contexts of the production of the texts. Distally, the evolution of the case report genre against the background of the history of medicine is taken into consideration. Proximately, the focus falls on the present context in which case reports are written, i.e., the current model of medical practice with its methodologies and modes of reasoning. The reflection of these factors in contemporary case reports will be demonstrated in the empirical part of the work where the linguistic selections used to write about patient diagnosis and treatment have been analyzed. Additionally, these choices have been investigated in the light of their potential to influence readers' perception. It is to be seen whether specific modes of writing about patients can be constitutive of certain modes of interpretation.

With reference to the basic distinction between quantitative and qualitative tradition, introduced by Zoltán Dörnyei (2007), both empirical chapters of the present work will be based on a mixed methodology and will follow the sequence of quan/QUAL → quan/QUAL (see Dörnyei 2007: 169). In the textual analysis of the corpus of medical case reports, the qualitative discussion of patient imaging will be supported by the quantitative data, i.e., the statistical analysis of patient reference. The two methodologies will also be used in the study of the reception of the texts by a wider audience, in which the conclusions from the analysis of the case reports are tested. Here the respondents' answers will be presented in percentages and discussed further. The use of lower and upper case in quan/QUAL → quan/QUAL underscores the gradation of importance of each stage in the two parts. It should also be noted that the study of the case reports – Chapter Five – is more extensive whereas the administered questionnaire – Chapter Six – has been designed to complement the results of the textual analysis. Lastly, the arrow denotes the sequence of the studies. Most important, the key concepts in the work will be discussed.

1. Discourse and discourse analysis

It seems that the terms *discourse* and *discourse analysis* are ubiquitous in contemporary linguistic literature which runs a gamut of definitions. The choice of the appropriate definition as well as the type of the analysis on the part of a researcher is dictated by the aims of the specific project and the data that are to be examined. Zoltán Dörnyei (2007: 30) refers to such an approach to methodology as "situationalist". In the present work, two understandings of discourse will be adopted, namely Norman Fairclough's (2003) definition which is more general and Kieran O'Halloran's (2003) which is more specific.[1] According to Fairclough (2003), generally, discourse may be understood as language which stands in relation to and is part of social reality (2003: 3, 26). This relation is manifested in a threefold manner – as ways of being, acting and representing. Firstly, ways of being constitute modes of linguistic behavior characteristic of individuals as well as of communities. Fairclough (2003) calls this phenomenon a *style*, for instance a style of a doctor. Secondly, discourse may be realized in various written and spoken forms, e.g., in newspaper articles and speeches respectively which are, at the same time, specific modes of mediating information. Thirdly, discourse may be representational in the form of particular discourses constituting different viewpoints from which reality can be approached (Fairclough 2003: 26).[2] These different vantage points correspond to various domains of people's lives which have their inherent modes of referring to reality, for instance medical discourse, legal discourse, political discourse, etc. Therefore, while discourse pertains to any form of symbolic representation, discourses are concrete realizations inherent to the contexts in which they

1 According to O'Halloran (2003: 12), these definitions of discourse differ from Michel Foucault's treatment of the term (2002 [1969]) in which he focuses on how knowledge is mediated and later reworked in the context of institutions (this aspect is also discussed by Erica Burman et al. 1997 and Norman Fairclough 2003).

2 The claim that discourse (language) is representational goes back to the numerous approaches to functions of language, e.g., Karl Bühler's (1990 [1934]).

are produced. Gunther Kress (1985: 7) explains that "[a] discourse provides a set of possible statements about a given area, and organizes and gives structure to the manner in which a particular topic, object, process is to be talked about". In Michael Karlberg's (2004: 14) words, discourses are ways of talking about specific things, as "[t]hey provide the productive scaffolding for human talk, thought, and practice".

Moreover, Fairclough's (2003) ways or representing are closely linked to the other definition of discourse adopted in this work, namely O'Halloran's (2003) who views it as the reader's comprehension of a text. The author points to various aspects which are instrumental in the process of understanding and emphasizes the context to which discourse is inextricably linked (2003: 12).[3] Consequently, while the former definition (Fairclough 2003) binds discourses to their contexts, the latter (O'Halloran 2003) focuses on the interpretation of discourses, for instance of texts.[4] What is more, the representational relation corresponds to the representational function of language, whereas the relations of being and acting are conversant with the main tenets of social constructionism which will be discussed later in this chapter.

2. Text

Texts are arenas for discourses. They may include only one type of a discourse or they may be collages of many. "Texts are the sites of the emergence of complexes of social meanings" (Kress 1995: 122), which makes them a unique source of information about particular realizations of discourses, embedded in contexts. Although it remains a challenge for researchers to capture this elusive relation between texts and social reality, nevertheless text analysis should be an essential part of discourse analysis. As Fairclough (2003) argues, "any analysis of texts … has to connect with theoretical questions about discourse (e.g., social 'constructive' effects of discourse). On the other hand, no real understanding of the social effects of discourse is possible without looking closely at what happens when people talk or write" (2003: 3). In the present work, I take Michael Alexander Kirkwood Halliday's (1979) view on language and text. As regards the former, according to Halliday (1979), language offers an array of choices how meaning can be expressed, i.e., a *meaning potential*, which is manifested in the

3 The very idea of examining discourse in its context comes from Foucault (2002 [1969]: 28).

4 The choice of the second definition was dictated by the aims of the second stage of the empirical part of the present work, i.e., the administration of the questionnaire among students of medicine (cf. Chapter Six).

lexico-grammatical system (1979: 122). Halliday's (1979) approach, therefore, focuses on the many ways in which a speaker/writer is able to phrase his/her thoughts. With respect to the latter, a given text is the *actualized meaning potential* (Halliday 1979: 122), a semantic content encoded in the lexico-grammatical system (1979: 138). As Niklas Luhmann (1990) observes, "[m]eaning always involves focusing attention on one possibility among many. ... Meaning is the link between the actual and the possible; it is not one or the other" (1990: 83). Consequently, every piece of information can be phrased in a variety of ways, thus, conveyed in a particular mode, and any choice in language that is made should always be viewed with reference to other options that could have been possible. Therefore, pertinent is the question whether the choice of words as well as what is present/absent in a text may affect the reader's interpretation of this text. This question will be addressed in Chapter Six.

3. Genre

It has been said that one of the manifestations of the relation between discourse and social reality are ways of acting, e.g., types of communication which have certain functions (see section 1.). These are called genres and they stand in a symbolic relation to social reality. On the basis of Foucault's (1994) very similar distinction, Fairclough (2003: 29) presents the scheme of a dialectic relation between discourse and genre in which "discourses (representational meaning) [are] enacted in genres (actional meaning)". What is also characteristic of genres is that they always serve a particular purpose. Consequently, Fairclough (2003) refers to them as "ways of Acting and Relating" (2003: 29). This dynamic element also reverberates in John Swales's (1990) widely acclaimed definition of genre, when he refers to it as an event. The definition has it that genre is a

> ... recognisable communicative event characterized by a set of communicative purpose(s) identified and mutually understood by the members of the professional or academic community in which it regularly occurs. Most often it is highly structured and conventionalized with constrains on allowable contributions in terms of their intent, positioning, form and functional value. These constrains, however, are often exploited by the expert members of the discourse community to achieve private intentions within the framework of socially recognized purpose(s) (Swales 1990: 58).

Firstly, according to the definition, the essential part of a genre is its aim. Although there are other factors which may influence the form of a genre, for instance audience, channel or medium, the goal of a genre seems to take priority. This view is also shared by Fairclough (2003) when he observes that the analysis of a chosen genre presupposes the question: "what are people doing [discoursally]?"

(Fairclough 2003: 70). This question will also be posed in the analysis of the corpus where the aims of particular sections of the texts under examination will be of great importance. Secondly, the definition draws attention to the high degree of structuring and conventionalizing of a genre. At this point, Swales (1990) uses the concept of *discourse community*. Later in his work he defines it as a group which utilizes in communication one or more genres that are known to its members (Swales 1990: 26). David Barton (1994) provides an even more detailed definition:

> A group of people who have texts and practices in common, whether it is a group of academics, or the readers of teenage magazines. In fact, discourse community can refer to several overlapping groups of people: it can refer to the people a text is aimed at; it can be the set of people who read a text; or it can refer to the people who participate in a set of discourse practices both by reading and by writing. … More generally, discourse communities are defined by having a set of common interests, values and purposes (Barton 1994: 57).

Discourse communities may comprise particular occupational groups or scientific circles which employ specific genres to achieve their communicative goals. Barton's (1994) definition explicitly states that although these people may not know each other, what they have in common is that they understand the chosen means of communication. What is more, the activities of discourse communities require constant reproduction of the conventions of speaking and writing which are often discipline-specific. Therefore, the mastery of selected genres is the required skill on the part of specialists. This aspect will be particularly relevant in Chapter Six when determining the potential of the examined texts to influence the novices' reception. Moreover, a genre is characterized by certain standards of writing. It follows that while it is generally desirable to make creative use of its linguistic resources, such creativity has its limits. There are salient features beyond which a writer cannot go, because this is what makes a given genre unique. As a result, as Vijay Bhatia (1993) points out, it is easy not only for specialists but also for competent speakers to differentiate between a business letter and a personal letter. Particular genres are associated with specific grammatical features, the organization of ideas and characteristic expressions which make these genres distinguishable from others (Bhatia 1993: 14). Therefore, although users are relatively free in their linguistic creativity, they have to remain within the scope of a number of rules and conventions determining a given genre.[5]

---

5 Another essential aspect of genres acknowledged by Swales (1990) is power, yet it is outside the scope of this work.

Furthermore, genres can be analyzed at various levels and which levels will be considered and how deep the investigation will be, will be determined by the subject of the study as well as its objectives. The first and the most basic level of the analysis considers the linguistic plane of texts. These analyses constitute the predominantly quantitative studies of texts, in which lexis and syntactic features are investigated. A classical example would be here the study conducted by Charles Barber (1962) where he considered three fragments from scientific textbooks of various domains in order to inspect quantitatively the characteristics of these texts. The variables Barber (1962) chose were the following: sentence-length, clause-types, verb-tenses, and the use of non-finite verbs. The next level in the analysis is text arrangement, the so called "text-patterning or textualization" (Bhatia 1993: 26). According to Bhatia (1993: 26), depending on the importance members of given communities attach to a specific use of language, a text will have a different structure and form. Bhatia (1993) stresses that the significance of this particular plane lies not so much in the quantitative study of texts, but in the explanation researchers attempt to provide, i.e., the rationale behind a given language use (1993: 27). What is more, it is often the case that one linguistic means may perform different functions in different genres.

The third level of analysis is the so-called "structural interpretation of the text-genre" (Bhatia 1993: 29). Utilizing the cognitive approach to genre-analysis, researchers are interested, on this particular level, in the way ideas are logically organized in a text. In sum, there are three basic platforms on which the analysis of genre is possible, each inquiring into its different aspects. One may, thus, investigate the linguistic structure of texts, additionally providing the rationale for a specific language use, as well as the organization of ideas. An example of such an approach is Swales's (1990) seminal work in which he offers a textual picture of a research article (RA for short) by dissecting the genre into its constituent parts and their aims. Swales (1990) concentrates particularly on Introduction and proposes CARS model (the name standing for "Create a research space") which describes moves and steps representing what happens there "discoursally" (Fairclough 2003: 70). According to this model, the author (1) establishes a territory (clams centrality and/or makes topic generalization(s) and/or reviews items of previous research), (2) establishes a niche (counterclaims or indicates a gap or raises a question or continues a tradition), and (3) occupies a niche (outlines purposes or announces present research or announces principal findings or indicates RA structure) (adapted from Swales 1990: 141). Each of these moves consists further of particular steps which mean particular information included therein. Admittedly, this model proved to be an invaluable contribution to the teaching of academic writing but also informed significantly the studies of genres. The keynote of a substantial body of this research was to demonstrate how certain generic requirements are fulfilled linguistically by authors (e.g., functions of marked themes – John Gosden 1992, and of subjects – 1993; hedging – Ken Hyland 1996, 1998a, functions of metadiscourse – 1998b; the structure of medical research paper – Kevin Nwogu 1997). Also in his book, Swales (1990) refers to numerous studies of particular linguistic aspects used across sections of RA. For example, Gregory West (1980) found that *that-clauses* occurred most frequently in Introduction, as this section is characterized by the reference to the already existing body of knowledge. In comparison with Introduction, Methods has the smallest frequency of *that-clauses*, due to the focus of this text-part on the description and course of a study/experiment (West 1980: 486–487). Jeanne Heslot (1982) concentrated on tense, Voice and 'person markers' and reported that, for example the Methods section is written primarily in the Passive Voice which, together with Results, are also characterized by the past perspective (Heslot 1982, cited in Swales 1990: 135).

Diana Adams Smith (1984), on the other hand, centers around author-comment, which is most extensive in Discussion and is achieved with the use of modal auxiliaries (1984: 33). Consequently, Swales's (1990) perspective on genre has the advantage in that it allows to approach linguistic choices the authors make from a pragmatic perspective. It means that particular selections can be studied with respect to the aims of the constituent parts of the genre under study in which these selections appear. This way, the use of given resources can be interpreted in terms of their functionality in a text. In other words, knowing the requirements of a particular genre. i.e., what sections it contains and what these sections are meant to convey, researchers may study the author's linguistic choices which are supposed to fulfill these aims. This perspective will also be adopted in the empirical part of the present work where patient imaging in sections of the case reports will be investigated.

All in all, what makes Swales's (1990) definition of genre stand out among others is its multidimensionality. Swales's (1990) approach to the notion of genre takes into consideration not only (seemingly obvious to analyze) linguistic features of texts, but also the conventions guiding its production. These are shared by the members of scientific communities and are used to organize activities in which genres are utilized. This way, Swale's definition (1990) emphasizes the social bottom of genres pointing to various social practices that genres are part of (cf. Kress 1985: 19). This view is also shared by Carolyn Miller (1994: 68) who claims that genres are "cultural-linguistic phenomena" in which meaning and form have a rule-governed structure with symbolic power.

Charles Bazerman (1988) goes even further maintaining that "genre is a social construct that regularizes communication, interaction, and relations" (1988: 62).

These features appear to be vital, as the present work in its analysis of the case reports will attempt to delve into the nature of this particular genre, both in its linguistic and organizational features as well as the specific practices around professional medical texts which perpetuate certain modes of writing. It is precisely this issue that underpins the social bottom of genres and it will be discussed in the following section.

4. Social constructionism and language

Assuming that discourses provide various lenses through which people see the world, discourse analysts seek to uncover the relation between discourses and reality. To this aim, discourse analysis does not approach a given discourse in isolation but places it against other discourses and emphasizes the importance of the corresponding context (Fairclough and Wodak 1997: 277). With these words, Norman Fairclough and Ruth Wodak (1997) underscore that discourses differ from each other, as they mediate different, context-specific perspectives. Moreover, the focus on the web of relations among discourses manifested in texts, their backgrounds and other discourses situates discourse analysis in social constructionism. According to Ian Parker (1992), "discourse constructs 'representations' of the world which have a reality almost as coercive as gravity …" (1992: 8). This citation emphasizes the common thread linking discourse, discourse analysis and social constructionism. Although the last element is not a uniform theory but a series of viewpoints (Gergen and Gergen 2003: 2), its main tenet is an attempt to establish how social phenomena come into existence. According to the authors, the body of pioneering literature concerning social constructionism can be divided into two groups. The works belonging to the first group address the issue of how scientific knowledge is constructed, while the second group contains the works regarding the social construction of everyday reality (Gergen and Gergen 2003: 3). Consequently, both everyday and scientific "realities" are believed to be social constructs that develop in the course of meaning negotiation in various forms of communication.

As regards social construction in science, it is assumed that science does not mirror reality but produces a version of it with selected elements only. As Karin Knorr Cetina (1981) puts it:

> Rather than view empirical observation as questions put to nature in a language she understands, we will take all references to the 'consitutive' role of science seriously, and regard scientific inquiry as a process of production. Rather than considering scientific products as somehow capturing what is, we will consider them as selectively carved out, transformed and constructed from whatever is. And rather than examine the external

relations between science and the 'nature' we are told it describes, we will look at those internal affairs of scientific enterprise which we take to be *constructive* [original emphasis] (Knorr Cetina 1981: 1).

Following the above-given quotation, researchers' or scientists' job involves, in John Potter's words, "tinkering" (1996: 35), by means of which they experiment with whatever is at their disposal in order to achieve the desired effect. The results of this tinkering, in turn, need to be accepted by other members of the community.[6] Consequently, science does not provide people with the reflection of the external world but with scientific constructs of reality upon which consensus has been made. This is exemplified well in Ludwik Fleck's (1979 [1935]) discussion of the evolution in the understanding of two diseases, namely syphilis and tuberculosis. While the former was firstly conceived of as "a punishment for sinful lust", the latter was regarded as "the 'romantic' disease ... of the poor". As Geraldine Van Rijn-Van Tongeren (1997: 40–45) argues, the diseases were seen rather as social events associated with people's living conditions or particular circumstances, and only later did they receive a more biomedical explanation.

Regarding everyday reality, Harold Garfinkel (1984) maintains that it is created in the course of continuous communication and action. It is through everyday activities constantly being talked about and discussed that people construct their experience and understand the world around them (Garfinkel 1984: 9–11). Such practices are referred to by the author as "endless, ongoing, contingent accomplishment" (Garfinkel 1984: 1). According to Garfinkel (1984), elements which are constitutive in language are, for instance, indexical expressions. They refer to particular people, objects or phenomena and give discourse a specific meaning, as they orient it to a given context (Garfinkel 1984: 5).[7] This way, according to Alain Coulon (1995: 17), Garfinkel (1984) points to a constitutive role of language. Also Peter Berger and Thomas Luckmann (1991 [1966]) observe that "[t]he language used in everyday life continuously provides ... [people] with the necessary objectifications and posits the order within which these make sense and within which everyday life has meaning ... (Berger and Luckmann 1991: 35–36).

Yet, the potential of language to reflect the external world and create meanings is not a new idea. On the one hand, it appears as one of the functions of language which were addressed by numerous linguists. For Karl Bühler (1990 [1934]), the

---

6 For more information about how scientific facts are constructed in medicine see section 7. in Chapter Three.

7 Cf. also the work by Harold Garfinkel and Harvey Sacks (1970).

representational function of language is the one of referring to things. According to the author, a language has an inventory of "the names" both in the lexical stock and syntactic rules. Next, "the names" are transmitted by means of "phonetic images" that correspond to their referents (Bühler 1990: 37). This function, according to Bühler (1990), could be traced to Plato (428/427 BC–348/347 BC)[8] and his *Cratylus* in which he defines language as an "organum" that conveys information about objects and states (1990: 30ff.). Roman Jakobson (1960) terms this function 'referential' and defines it as the one pointing to the context (1960: 353), for instance by means of the already mentioned indexical expressions (cf. Garfinkel 1984 above).

Michael Alexander Kirkwood Halliday's functions of language (1976) also include a representational one. His understanding of the function is very close to its counterpart in Bühler's theory, i.e., when language is treated as a means of conveying information, "of expressing propositions" (1976: 16). Also Halliday's more recent formulation of the metafunctions of language within The Functional Grammar framework includes an ideational metafunction, i.e., "interpret[ing] and represent[ing] experience" (Halliday and Mathiessen 1999: 569; see also Halliday 1979: 48–49).

Another attempt to shed light on the reflecting and creating character of language was the idea of a language-game (Germ. *Sprachspiel*) as proposed by Ludwig Josef Johann Wittgenstein (1889–1951) in his *Philosophische Untersuchungen. Philosophical Investigations.*[9] It could be defined after Roman Kopytko as "a custom, a socially constrained pattern of interaction" (2007: 794). In other words, language-games are modes of how individuals handle specific situations by means of language. Kenneth and Mary Gergen (2003: 4) explicate that language-games are realized not only in how something is said (the choice of grammatical resources) but also in what is actually said. Yet, what Kopytko (2007) underscores is the "rule-governed" character of language-games. It follows that they become meaningful only when they appear in an appropriate situation, as their use is functionally and contextually conditioned. What is more, they are viewed as dynamic linguistic phenomena, with new games appearing and other being abandoned (Kopytko 2007: 794–795). This way, they help to refer to and define the surrounding reality (Gergen and Gergen 2003: 4). According to

---

8 Cf. Plato 1998 [ca 390 B.C.] or (1975 /1793/).

9 As mentioned by Elżbieta Wąsik (2007: 189), the concept *language-game* refers to *game theory*, which was introduced for the first time by John [Johann] von Neumann (1903–1957) in 1928. Cf. Neumann (1959 [1928]), and Wittgenstein (1958 /1953/: § 2]) – editor's note: ZW.

Kopytko (2007: 807–808), such reasoning, in turn, allows to refer to Wittgenstein as a social constructionist as his ideas questioned the truth of the philosophical knowledge. Following Gergen and Gergen (2003: 4), with language-games Wittgenstein suggested that objective knowledge and meanings people make of things are linguistically constructed and become part of social practice.[10] Yet, as Kopytko (2007: 795) observes, although Wittgenstein acknowledges the role of context in the use of language-games, their "rule-governed" nature excludes any other factors which may affect the course of interaction, for instance speakers' creativity or spontaneity.

Yet another perspective in this ongoing debate over the potential of language to construct social reality is the question whether language influences the thought. In this context another prominent character needs to be mentioned, namely Benjamin Lee Whorf, who is called by Potter (1996) "the best known linguistic constructionist" (1996: 99). Whorf was an American linguist and his name is associated with the Sapir-Whorf hypothesis, which concerns the relation between language and thought. Interestingly enough, as Werner (2001) observes, despite the name of the hypothesis, while Whorf was its strongest advocate, it was Sapir's version that gained more popularity (Werner 2001: 65). Sapir (1951 [1929]) believed that language reflects the culture in which it is immersed by means of the lexicon which serves the purpose of naming things. At the same time, he underscored that rather than referring in different terms to the same things, the available lexicon conveys the underlying variety of cultures (Sapir 1951: 162). i.e., different understanding of phenomena, concepts or things. [11] Whorf, on the other hand, favored the claim that it is the differences in grammar that could affect the understanding of the world. According to John Carroll (1956), the studies of American Indian languages enabled Whorf to formulate the hypothesis that "differences between languages would be found to correspond to differences in ways of reporting events, and that we can feel intuitively the grammatical and behavior forces underlying the linguistic phenomena" (1956: 30). In other words, Whorf claimed that there is a relation between a given culture and the grammar of a language whose categories mediate culture-specific modes of reasoning. Interestingly enough, as O'Halloran (2003) points out, Whorf's works (1956) do not contain the explicit phrasing of what is widely thought as Sapir-Whorf hypothesis. The famous quote refers rather to the already mentioned grammatical

10 The issue of objective knowledge in the context of medicine will be touched upon in Chapter Three.

11 In a similar vein, Ludwig Wittgenstein, as emphasized by Kopytko (2007: 795), argued that the meaning of words depends on their use and not on their referents.

categories: "We cut nature up, organize it into concepts, and ascribe significances as we do, largely because we are parties to an agreement to organize it in this way – an agreement that holds throughout our speech community and is codified in the patterns of our language" (Whorf 1956 [1940]: 213). This quotation echoes Wittgenstein's understanding of language-games as ways of expressing meaning which are understood only when used according to certain rules.

As a result, two versions, i.e., Sapir's and Whorf's, were merged in what became to be known as the Sapir-Whorf hypothesis.[12] What is more, it is also possible to isolate two lines of thought in the hypothesis. It may be assumed that the influence of language structure directs speakers into a certain way of understanding a message. Such line of reasoning is based upon the premise that languages differ in how they relate to the surrounding reality that is roughly the same to their users. The differences are encoded in the lexico-grammatical systems which, in turn, contribute to different shades of meaning given to objects, phenomena, notions, etc. in a given language. This hypothesis is referred to as linguistic relativism. In the following one, Whorf (1956 [1940]) postulates that language determines thought:

> The agreement is, of course, an implicit and unstated one, but its terms are absolutely obligatory; we cannot talk at all except by subscribing to the organization and classification of data which the agreement decrees (Whorf 1956 [1940]: 213–214) … the forms of a person's thoughts are controlled by inexorable laws of pattern of which he is unconscious (Whorf 1956 [1941]: 252).

In other words, if different languages have different means of describing the same concepts, then it can be assumed that these different modes of description affect the way people think about these concepts because the structure of a language influences the thought. Yet, it seems that the extreme versions of both linguistic relativity and determinism are difficult to ascertain. On the one hand, as Roger Fowler (1996) notes, it cannot be said that different languages make it impossible for people to see the world in the same way if things from one language can be translated to another and people are able to understand these renditions. Instead, a weaker version can be adopted in which languages direct speakers to perceiving things in terms of specific notions and concepts that are available in

12 As Werner (2001) observes, the two sides of the hypothesis may stem from the difference in the understanding of the concept of language among linguists and anthropologists. While for the latter the lexicon belongs to language, the former devote less attention to it as opposed to syntax and phonology which display a particular structure (see Werner 2001: 66ff.).

a given language system. "Language and other codes ... have a cognitive role: they provide an organized mental representation for our experience. Whatever the 'natural' structure of the world ... we handle it mentally, and in discourse, in terms of the conventional meaning-categories embodied in our society's codes" (Fowler 1996: 3).

It needs to be added that, according to Fowler (1996), one of the later extensions of linguistic relativism assumes not only diversity *across* languages, but also *internal* diversity of languages which offers different means of expression within the same system (1996: 29–30). This allowed to approach the Sapir-Whorf hypothesis from a different angle. It may be said that a "language helps people to sort things, encourages them to think of the world in terms of artificial categories tacitly felt to be 'common sense'" (Fowler 1996: 30). At the same time, having a multitude of means of expression at one's disposal, a person "can see through and around his semantic system; but he is aware that, in doing so, he is seeing reality in a new light, like Alice in Looking-Glass House" (Halliday 1971: 332–333). Consequently, Halliday's view on the issue attributes more agentivity to a speaker who decides how he/she wishes to phrase a given piece of information, which, in turn, enables him/her to "see reality in a new light". What is more, Halliday (1971) points to the fact that the availability of various modes of expression on the part of a speaker/writer and his/her awareness of this diversity of meaning underscores the relation between language and thought, regardless of its nature (cf. Knowles and Moon 2006: 67).

Derek Edwards (1994; 1997) points to another shortcoming of the hypothesis. He observes that such an approach treats language as insensitive to contextual factors of communication. It disregards the fact that the apparent differences in means of expression of what is shared by two different cultures may stem from the specific conditioning of a speech situation and speakers' intentions. These may dictate for instance that the same message may be conveyed in different manners, depending on the circumstances in which an interaction takes place. Having said that, Edwards underlies the role of language which does not only communicate things but also takes part in the process of shaping of what is communicated (Edwards 1994: 217; Edwards 1997: 205–206).

Yet another approach to the Sapir-Whorf hypothesis which merits attention is the one proposed by George Grace, which Potter (1996) referrers to as "the most ambitious" (1996: 101) one. According to Grace (1987), language constructs reality in a three-fold manner, i.e., what is communicated needs to be specified ("conceptual events"), incorporated into a communicative event ("contextualization") and modalized ("modality"). While the second step consists in the specification what is referred to, e.g., by means of a definite article, the first and the third are executed with the help of grammatical structures, terms, and different speech modalities (question, assertion, etc.) respectively (Grace 1987: 32–38). Although, as Potter (1996) maintains, this approach describes different stages at which a message is shaped through linguistic resources, it still does not acknowledge "practices of actual language use" (Potter 1996: 101).

The above-given accounts of Wittgenstein's, Sapir's and Whorf's linguistic contributions are meant only to acknowledge the landmarks of research into language, thought, and reality (see the title of Whorf's book 1956 [1941]); hence the brevity of the accounts. Yet, as the subsequent approaches testify, these contributions have continued to inspire numerous researchers. In Michael Stubbs' (1997) view, from a sociolinguistic point of view, the relation between language, thought, and reality could be viewed from the perspective that it is "not language structure, but language use in discourse [and] not grammar, but systematic selections from the grammar" (1997: 365) that matter in communication. This formulation is in line with a more contextualized approach to linguistic relativism (as discussed by Edwards 1994, 1997) and with the potential of the variety of means of expression within a language respectively (as discussed by Halliday 1971). With regard to the climate of present day research, the Sapir – Whorf hypothesis still invites the reflection on how people's language choices may affect other people's interpretation of texts, whereas Wittgenstein's notion of language-games emphasizes the social and context-bound nature of people's linguistic behavior. Sapir, Whorf and Wittgenstein pointed to the lexicon and grammatical categories as constitutive elements of language. Also social constructionism, with its particular focus on language, according to David Cooperrider and Diana Whitney (2003), maintains that "alternations in linguistic practice … hold profound implications for changes in social practice" (2003: 177).

Consequently, following the main tenets of social constructionism, discourse analysts aim to determine the potential of language to create social reality (as maintained by Fairclough 2003: 8–9, and Phillips and Hardy 2002: 12–13). Just as Wittgenstein emphasized the "rule-governed" use of language-games (Kopytko 2007: 795), conditioned by their function and context, discourse analysis focuses on social practices. For Fairclough (2003) social practices "can be seen as articulations of different types of social element which are associated with particular areas of social life" (2003: 25). The reason why social practices are so important for discourse analysis is that they "articulate discourse" and impose certain ways in which a participant should behave linguistically, depending on the context in which he/she finds himself/herself (Fairclough 2003: 25). In other words, the context dictates what ways of acting, representing and being should be chosen (genres, discourses and styles respectively) according to social practice. Teaching in contemporary British education with all its participants, how they relate to each other, what kind of language is used there, etc. is given by Fairclough (2003) as an example of such social practices. From the perspective of this work, medical consultation may also be termed a social practice with its context-specific types of interaction, topics, power relations, etc. The question whether these aspects are instrumental in affecting people's perception of reality reverberates in numerous discourse analyses, ranging from the studies of media discourse (for example Kress and Hodge 1981; Fowler 1996), politics (Fairclough 1995, 2001), and institutions (Sarangi and Roberts 1999). Although varying in their research domains, the studies share the underlying aim of determining whether the change in the form of a message may affect its comprehension. They also pose a question of further influence of form on modes of thinking, talking and writing which develop in the course of participation in social practices.

Summarizing the basic premises of discourse analysis, James Gee (1999) argues for "a reciprocity between language and 'reality': language simultaneously reflects reality ('the way things are') and constructs (construes) it to be a certain way" (1999: 82). These words orchestrate with Potter's metaphor of construction yard (1996). For Potter (1996), language is not a mirror which renders reality as it is but a construction yard in which reality is constructed. In this sense, linguistic means constitute materials that can be combined in various proportions in order to obtain constructs of different patterns. Therefore, while language as a mirror is supposed to copy reality faithfully, in the construction yard, images, i.e., descriptions of reality, are constructed. At the same time, it needs to be stressed that "human practices, and descriptions could have been otherwise" and that "the world is constituted in one way or another as people talk it, write it and argue it" (Potter 1996: 98). The approach of "descriptions as constructions and constructive" enables to examine the process of their production, namely what resources are used, how they are combined and what happens with them (Potter 1996: 98). Although, following Norman Fairclough (2003: 8–9) and Bernard McKenna (2004: 12), the claim that language affects the way the world is perceived by individuals is fraught with difficulties in ascertaining it, it has not discouraged researchers from further attempts to substantiate it. As the present work focuses on one of the varieties of scientific discourse, its interaction with reality will be addressed in the following section.

5. Scientific discourse and its relation to reality

Originally proposed by Michel Foucault (1969), the importance of the corresponding context in the analysis of discourse has been addressed also by other researchers (e.g., Fairclough and Wodak 1997; O'Halloran 2003). The authors claim that discourses are anchored in concrete circumstances of their use and linked to various domains of people's lives. It is these circumstances that dictate what and how is communicated as well as what kind of practices of production and reproduction of discourses are adjacent to texts at hand. Moreover, James Gee's (1999) claim has been emphasized that the relation between contexts and texts is dialogic, in that the first affect the other and vice versa. This twofold relation has also been addressed by Charles Bazerman in his influential work *Shaping Written Knowledge. The genre and activity of the experimental article in science* (1988) in which his research focus fell on scientific discourse. As has been stated in section 1., discourse relates to social reality representationally in the form of individual discourses which are grounded in specific contexts. Consequently, scientific discourse may comprise modes of talking and writing about objects, phenomena, notions, etc. dealt with in numerous scientific areas. In his work, Bazerman (1988) demonstrates how knowledge-mediating is socially constructed, i.e., conditioned by the intellectual atmosphere of the time and various accompanying practices (cf. Fye 1987). The claim about scientific discourse is validated by the analyses of individual genres. Before that, however, Bazerman (1988) acknowledges the underlying tension between form and the meaning of language by examining three problematic aspects of this issue (1988: 19).

Firstly, it can be argued that the meaning of words transcends them and language is believed only to point to specific referents, while the remaining information can be added by the recipient of a message. Consequently, it is believed that meaning resides in speakers who try to best capture it with the help of available linguistic resources. Bazerman (1988) agrees that when people use language, they put a lot of effort to get the meaning right. Nevertheless, he claims that communication must take place in given social and linguistic contexts and that it is a creative process (Bazerman 1988: 19–20; see also Potter 1996 and section 4. above). Such reasoning also runs counter to Wittgenstein's understanding of language-games, which excludes any creativity on the part of speakers. The second argument is a reversed version of the first and it says that meaning is a matter of the composition of words (Bazerman 1988: 20). They can mean anything because they are not anchored in the outside world. Following this premise, reality is constructed solely by language. Bazerman (1988) concedes that language is a powerful means of creation and literary works are good examples to confirm that. However, he observes that "ways of perceiving and knowledge-making emerge out of sociolinguistic processes", pointing to the relation between language and social reality. Moreover, although some categories are not common to all cultures, it is possible to translate from one language to another, while some concepts remain the same across cultures and time. What is more, linguistic processes are usually dynamic and accommodate to the changing reality (Bazerman 1988: 20–21). Bazerman's (1988: 21) third argument accepts language as "a structured social creation" but assumes that any changes may take place exclusively in spoken language. On the basis of this premise, it can be argued that written language is devoid of any context and social meaning, whereas spoken language emerges as an immediate reaction to the current interlocutors' needs. In response to this, Bazerman (1988) exposes the centrality of social context and argues that also "writing is social action ... enmeshed in social activities" (1988: 22). Bazerman (1988) focuses particularly on scientific discourse, which, he argues, is shaped by a given discipline (1988: 47). It follows that the ways authors give account of their scientific activities are influenced by modes of reasoning, methodologies and objectives of a given area of study, because "authors also subordinate themselves to scientific knowledge as currently constituted" (Bazerman 1988: 30; see also Fye 1987). In Bazerman's treatment (1988), context means the object under study, the literature of the field, the anticipated audience, and the author's own self (Bazerman 1988: 24), yet they may differ depending on the type of analysis.[13]

In his study of scientific discourse, Bazerman (1988) demonstrates that the changing modes of giving account of experiments may eventually affect the way experimental procedures are performed. This influence, in turn, may help to yield expected results which then need to be validated by a scientific community (1988: 22). The author analyses the development of the experiment report genre on the basis of the corpus of texts from the *Philosophical Transactions of the Royal Society of London* from 1665 to 1800.[14] Interestingly, the first texts referred to as experimental accounts were food recipes. Later periods saw the genre developing which meant shifting modes of description and argumentation.

Also Dwight Atkinson (2001) has traced the progressive changes in scientific discourse on the basis of the papers published in the *Philosophical Transactions*

---

13 There exists a large body of research addressing different ways in which medical knowledge is mediated to other professionals as opposed to lay people (see Dubois 1986; Fahnestock 1986; Gilbert and Mulkay 1984; Koskela 1997; Myers 1990; Ventola and Mauranen 1992).

14 The *Philosophical Transactions of the Royal Society of London* was created in 1655 by the Royal Society of London. The journal played a significant role in the development of science with many great scientists publishing there (e.g., Newton, Franklin, Faraday, Kelvin, etc.) (see Atkinson 2001). According to Bazerman (1988), its first editor is credited to have invented the modern scientific journal in English (1988: 129).

of the Royal Society of London, yet the time frame of the texts in his corpus was the period between 1675 and 1975. As the author points out, the features of texts shifted from one pole to the other, namely from involved, author-centered and narrative-like to informational, object-centered and abstract (Atkinson 2001: 61–63).[15] Consequently, Atkinson's study (2001) demonstrates a significant progress within scientific discourse which brought it closer to the form known to contemporary readers. Moreover, Atkinson (2001) seeks to relate these changes to the social and historical contexts in which science was developing.

Philosophical Transactions of the Royal Society of London were also studied by Ellen Valle (1997), yet she limited her corpus only to life sciences, i.e., biology, botany, zoology, human or animal anatomy and physiology, and theoretical applied medicine. The time frame she investigated ranged between 1711–1870. There were three aspects Valle (1997) was particularly interested in: subject matter (*paradigmatic* index), implicit or explicit addressee (*pragmatic* index) and presence/absence of the statement of the purpose of the text (*rhetorical* index) (1997: 77–78). Examining the corpus in ten-year blocks at fifty-year intervals allowed the author to show that the texts gradually began to address clearly defined topics (1st parameter), aim at the scientific community (as opposed society in general, 2nd parameter) and develop a more and more explicit purpose of the text.

Yet another research attempt which had the same underlying aim as Bazerman's study (1988) is the project *Scientific thought-styles: The evolution of English medical writing*.[16] The research question Irma Taavitsainen and her colleagues asked themselves was "What can linguistic analysis really tell us about the underlying currents in the history of science?" (2002: 251). Consequently, assuming that language variability reflects extralinguistic reality, the aim of this undertaking was to examine the stylistic development of medical English from a diachronic perspective and against the socio-historical background.

The novelty of the project was to take into account the history of science as another conditioning factor in the study of texts. To this aim, the authors, inspired by Alistair Crombie (1994: 5–6), introduced the concept of *scientific thought-styles* which "can be defined as the underlying scientific concepts, objects of enquiry, methods, evaluations and intellectual commitments, which are mediated to us through language" (Taavitsainen et al. 2002: 253). The examined corpus

15 Similar results were yielded also in the study of the nineteenth century case histories from gynecology by Nowell-Smith (1995; see section 4. in Chapter Three).

16 The project *ScientificTthought-Styles: The evolution of English Medical Writing* is one of the projects carried out in the Research Unit for Variation and Change in English at the Department of English, University of Helsinki (see Bibliography).

contained medical treaties from the period between 1375 and 1750. The analysis revealed significant development in the texts with respect to the level of involvement, modality and rhetorical structure. Specifically, the authors drew the distinction between scholasticism and empiricism which gave rise to different writing styles. While the former was based on heavy reliance on authorities, the latter contributed to the development of rational thinking and inductive reasoning.[17]

Quite recently, also Britt-Louise Gunnarsson (2009) studied medical texts from the eighteenth, nineteenth and twentieth centuries using a multimodal methodology. This methodological commitment allowed her to examine changes in the texts from cognitive, societal and macrostructural perspectives and to relate the results to the stages of the development of medicine, as well as to the changes in the medical community and society in general. At the cognitive level, it meant that researchers progressed from giving accounts only of their own studies through collecting and referring also to other researchers to utilizing the knowledge gathered in the creation of theories. This, in turn, meant that from a societal and macrostructural perspective, researchers functioning individually and solely in their respective societies turned first into groups and then into developed scientific communities (Gunnarson 2001: 117–119). She concluded that at the level of the text, those from the eighteenth century can be characterized by a direct and personal style of writing, whereas the ones from the twentieth century are impersonal and detached (cf. Salager-Meyer and Zambrano 2001). In more detail, Gunnarsson (2009: 64) observed that content-wise, there was a gradual shift from "external world" to "scientific world". As regards evaluation, researchers moved from mere describing of the findings to the analysis. What is more, they ceased criticizing other researchers and began to evaluate their studies, which meant a shift from explicit to implicit criticism. Formally, the texts became homogenous with marked sections and headings (referring to regular constituents), "catalogue" (Gunnarsson 2009: 66) style of writing and increasing reference to other studies which clearly points to the authors' growing identification with the scientific community (Gunnarsson 2009: 53–71).

Coming back to Bazerman's influential work (1988), it is based upon the premise that discourses and genres are shaped by socio-historical contexts which set *thought-styles* and modes of reasoning. Consequently, the intellectual climate affects the ways in which objects, facts, phenomena, etc. are reflected linguistically, and these ways, in turn, become endorsed by the members of scientific communities. This allows Bazerman (1988) to conclude that science is socially

17 These issues will be discussed in detail in section 1. in Chapter Two.

created (see also Knorr Cetina 1981).[18] In this perspective, scientific writing is an "accomplishment", which orchestrates with Harold Garfinkel's (1984: 1) treatment of spoken language. What is more, according to Bazerman (1988: 13), "[t]o view writing from the prospect of language users is to consider the benefit of some choices over others" (see section 3.). Yet, such a view goes against the claim that scientific writing copies the natural state of things (Bazerman 1988: 14). On the contrary, science creates its own modes of reasoning and discourse which are grounded in a discipline-specific context and act as vehicles of scientific thought:

> Science, responding to its own dynamics and activities within its particular social circumstances winds up structured differently than other social systems, equally constructed out of their situations and activities, and developing their own appropriate symbolic systems. As a sociolinguistic system science has emerged through the socially situated language choices of language users. (Bazerman 1988: 149)

The above-presented studies demonstrating that scientific discourse reflects current intellectual atmosphere support the claim that discourses stand in a representational relation to social reality (Fairclough 2003; see sections 1. and 3.). Instead of mirroring nature in an objective manner, discipline-specific discourses convey modes of reasoning practiced at a given moment through selected linguistic resources.

What is more, as both Fairclough (2003) and Bazerman (1994) postulate, social construction of science is achieved through ways of acting, i.e., genres. According to Bazerman (1994), "[b]y using these typified texts we are able to advance our own interests and shape our meanings in relation to complex social systems, and we are able to grant value and consequence to the statements of others" (1994: 79). In the last two sections of the present chapter, a particular discourse and genre will be discussed as ways of representing and acting respectively.

6. Medical discourse

Following Fairclough's (2003) definition of discourse and social practices, medical discourse can be characterized as a social practice of relating to the broadly understood people's health. Moreover, medical discourse itself comprises different discourses which patients, physicians, other medical professionals as well as medical academics avail themselves of. Consequently, various discourse communities are formed by virtue of the fact that they participate in numerous spoken and written

18 This issue in the context of medicine will be discussed in detail in section 7. in Chapter Three.

practices, shared by and meaningful to the members of particular groups. These activities in Fairclough's definition (2003) are called *genres*. Moreover, the knowledge of genres characteristic of these groups is a requirement for membership in such a discourse community.[19] The most basic divisions of medical discourse can be either into spoken and written medical discourse, or into doctor-patient and doctor-doctor communication. If the former is adopted, one can give such examples as history-taking, patient interviews, case presentations during ward rounds (Anspach 1988; Atkinson 1995; Lingard et al. 2003; Schryer 2003), etc. On the other hand, written genres include case reports, research papers, reviews, etc. These examples can be grouped in a slightly different fashion if the latter categorization, focused on the participants of communication, is adopted. While history taking and interviews take place between a physician and a patient such genres as case presentations, case reports or research papers circulate among the members of the medical community. One more differentiation should be made at this point. Apart from spoken/written and doctor-patient/doctor-doctor distinctions, medical genres can be divided into those connected with practical medicine and those linked to medicine in the academia (discussed by Kjell Berge 2003). In this respect, just as research papers and reviews have more to do with sharing knowledge with academics, history-taking, case reports and interviews are used by medical practitioners.[20]

7. Studies in medical discourse – form vs. content

According to Suzanne Fleischman (2001), there is not as much research on medical discourse as one would think. Yet, it might be said with confidence that "the occupational register of a tribe of white-coated speakers" (2001: 473) has recently attracted keen interest. A substantial number of studies of spoken discourse have been devoted to the broadly understood communication in medical settings (e.g., Sarangi and Roberts 1999; Barton 2006; Candlin 2006; Heritage and Maynard 2007). Some part of this research examines discourse practices with reference to impressive technological advancement, specialization of knowledge, progressing systematization and the withdrawal of management (e.g., Iedema 2006; cf. Souba 2002). Other studies address the issues of communication in multicultural settings (Guido 2006; Roberts 2006). These are challenges that medical practice

19 This particular issue will be discussed in detail in Chapter Three, in which the influence of medical discourse on novices in the medical community will be addressed.

20 Further discussion about the distinctions can be found in works by Margaret Van Naerssen (1981), Catherine Schryer (1994), Lars–Christer Hydén and George Mishler (1999), and Suzanne Fleischman (2001).

has been facing recently and the aim of such research undertakings is not only to help clinicians in their work but also to improve the quality of their encounters with patients. The need for cooperation between medical professionals and linguists originates from the pivotal role of language in medical activities.

As Michel Foucault (2003 /1973/ [1963]) observes, almost every aspect of patient management is accomplished by means of language, from an interview, through the description of the patient's condition to instructing him/her. Therefore, a separate body of literature comprises interdisciplinary research which demonstrates that sociolinguistic knowledge and experience may support the process of medical assessment and treatment in cases of various speech-language pathologies, hearing-impairment and other disorders where the ability to communicate is an issue of concern (see Ball 2005).

The studies of written discourse can be divided into two groups addressing the following two issues: (1) the art of writing in medicine (language) and (2) the relation between form and content (language vs. subject). It may seem that the bulk of studies on written medical discourse are the quantitative investigations into specific lexical and grammatical features (be it modality – Vihla 1998; hedging – Salager-Meyer 1994; collocations – Luzón Marco 2000; noun phrases – Salager-Meyer et al. 2006; conditionals – Ferguson 2001 and collocations – Méndez-Cendón 2009) and their respective roles as well as how writers organize and present ideas in specific text-parts (as studied by Myers 1990; Salager-Meyer 1994 and Koskela 1997).[21] The other group of studies examines linguistic features of texts and the effect they produce. For example, as observed by Kenny and Beagan (2004: 1072), it has become a common practice to perceive the language of medical texts as neutral, economical and depersonalized, to a large extent due to the notorious use of the Passive Voice (see also Albert 2004). In a similar vein, the notion of authorial presence has received significant attention either in larger projects (the KIAP project 2006) or in separate research papers (e.g., by Grice and Kramer-Dahl 1992; Hyland 2001; Martinez 2001; Harwood 2005; Rundblad 2007 and Williams 2010).

Yet, a substantial body of research has centered around the broad term of patient imaging in written medical discourse. These are studies devoted to the linguistic presentation of patients and diseases (by Anspach 1988; Grice and Kramer-Dahl 1992; Donnelly and Hines 1997; Fraser 2003; Kenny and Beagan 2004) or to metaphors (e.g., by Hodgkin 1985; Sontag 1991; Becker 1994; Van Rijn-Van Tongeren 1997; Wallis and Nerlich 2005; Catenaccio 2006; Lopez 2007;

21 For more studies concerning both lexico-grammatical and rhetorical features of medical texts see Gotti and Salager-Meyer (2006).

Rundblad 2007; Semino 2010). In this particular literature researchers have investigated how patients are depicted by examining, primarily qualitatively, selected linguistic choices. A number of these undertakings have drawn on the theories from the neighboring disciplines such as the sociology of medicine, medical ethics or philosophy of medicine. Many is the time this interdisciplinary cooperation has proved effective in revealing not only how professional identities are reflected and enacted in language but also how scientific discourse images patients. The contribution of the aforementioned disciplines has pointed to essential contextual factors influencing the production of medical texts. One type of such texts will be introduced in the following section.

8. Case report as a medical genre

As has been concluded in section 3., genres are structured ways of acting by means of which people achieve their discoursal aims in socially meaningful ways. In the present section, the genre of case report will be described: its subject matter, structure and mode of presenting information.

Irma Taavitsainen and Päivi Pahta (2000) define the genre of case report in the following way:

> In its typical form, the case report records the course of a patient's disease from the onset of symptoms to the outcome, usually either recovery or death. The background and a commentary on the disease are also given, but their scope may vary. Often a limited review of the literature is added and the number of known cases stated (Taavitsainen and Pahta 2000: 60).

Taavitsainen and Pahta (2000: 73) add that sometimes case reports appear in sequences (two or more) in a given article.

The aim of this genre is to describe a new disease or a disease which is already known but which has unusual manifestations. According to Edward Huth (1982), only those case reports should be published which concern "the unique, or nearly unique, case that may represent a previously undescribed syndrome or disease; the case with an unexpected association of two or more diseases or disease manifestations that may represent unsuspected causal relation; the case with an unexpected evolution suggesting a therapeutic effect or an adverse drug effect" (1982: 58). Kathryn Hunter (1991: 93) explains that these strict requirements stem from the fact that the status of case reports has decreased significantly due to the standardization of medical education and studies.[22]

---

22 This issue will be discussed in detail in Chapter Three.

As regards their structure, case reports are "the briefest and simplest category of article" (Adams Smith 1984: 27) and usually consist of three parts: "a short Introduction, a more detailed Case Report body, and a brief Comment or Discussion section" (Rowley-Jolivet 2007: 185), yet it is not a unified composition (see Chapter Five). This structure can be compared with the arrangement of a narrative as exemplified by William Labov (1979), who divided narratives into Orientation, Complication, Evaluation and Result.[23] Consequently, case reports start with Orientation (Introduction) which, as the name suggests, orients readers to the patient whose case is described. This section, which may also include some demographic facts about the patient such as sex, age, sometimes occupation or ethnic origin, briefly explains the reason of his/her presentation. What follows next is Complication (Case Report body). It is the most extensive part, as it features not only the descriptions of diagnostic procedures of various kind but also the very treatment. Lastly, Evaluation and Results (Comment or Discussion), which, often combined, evaluate the actions performed by a physician and discuss the outcomes and effectiveness of treatment. The section may also include implications for further assessment and treatment procedures. According to James Calnan and Andras Barabas (1973), it is important that these types of information follow the same sequence in which they were given in the patient's case notes (1973: 8).

Rhetorically, the presentation of information in case reports renders them "descriptive and expository" (Salager-Meyer 1989: 155), which is in keeping with the primary aim of this genre. What underlies the content and form of case reports is well explained by Schryer (1994). In her paper (Schryer 1994), she compares the structure and rhetorical organization of two types of texts – those utilized in academic settings and those in the institutions of medical practice. The study enabled her to demonstrate how two scientific communities – researchers and clinicians – convey information in ways meaningful in their occupational activities. Yet, although both groups are members of the academia, the research traditions they differ in their goals as well as modes of mediating knowledge. According to Schryer (1994), while researchers seek to reconstruct a research process and prove its validity, clinicians' aim is to record how a particular problem is solved and examine the effectiveness of a solution. Consequently, experimental genres

23 The present comparison of case reports to a narrative was inspired by Paul Atkinson (1995) who examined case presentations and observed that their structure was similar to a story. Case presentations are highly conventionalized oral descriptions of patients and their diseases, which are performed by clinicians or medical students in clinical settings (see Atkinson 1995).

(for instance research papers) used in laboratories are argumentative, whereas recording genres (for instance case reports) used in clinics are descriptive.

The choice of a particular genre on the part of these two groups is dictated by two different activities they are engaged in but also by the socialization into two different modes of giving account of these activities (Schryer 1994: 113). Schryer (1994) rightly points out that case reports (recording genre) are all about problem solving. This fact is also well captured by Hunter (1991) when she refers to them as "reportage, a piece of scientific puzzle" (1991: 94), which, after being solved by a physician, is recorded for other members of the medical community with a view to sharing a new piece of information. Yet, with the development of medical practice the status of case reports decreased significantly. Firstly, as Dwight Atkinson (1992) observes, the introduction of modern diagnostic equipment and procedures rendered case reports less credible due to the subjectivity of the material presented there. Essentially, they are physicians' accounts based on their observation and their interpretation of signs of a disease. Secondly, also the growing importance of the genre of research article in medicine, which is often based on statistical analyses, devalued case report as a valid source of information. Consequently, nowadays, case reports are usually published to increase the knowledge of the medical community about rare cases (Taavitsainen and Pahta 2000: 61; Hunter 1991: 93) and to serve pedagogical purposes in medical training. The fact of the progressive devaluation of case reports in the history of medicine seems to confirm Charles Bazerman's theses (1988) (which were also developed later on in the *Scientific Thought-Styles* project) that genres and scientific discourse in general are conditioned by the current status of science and its attendant modes of reasoning. It is precisely because of the rapid progress in diagnostic procedures and heavy reliance on statistical analysis that the role of case reports changed.

The consequences of this process have been presented in Tavitsainen and Pahta's diachronic study (2000) of case reports from two periods – 1850–1900 and 1965–1995. In their paper, Taavitsainen and Pahta (2000) demonstrate that case reports were subject to similar changes as scientific texts in general (see also Atkinson 2001). Firstly, the case reports from the nineteenth century are characterized by two levels of narration, the former is the writer's narration in the first person, i.e., from his point of view, while the latter gives account of the patient's disease in the third person and foregrounds his/her symptoms. On the other hand, although contemporary case reports concentrate on the second level, they give priority to the description of clinical facts (not the patient's symptoms) in an effaced manner. Secondly, the texts from the first investigated period are characterized by a more involved style underscoring the presence of an author, whereas the texts from the latter period appear more impersonal and detached.[24] Taavitsainen and Pahta (2000) attribute this transformation to changes in the scientific community in that it grew more numerous as education and knowledge in general became more accessible. Thirdly, the intellectual climate needs to be emphasized as well. In the case reports from the nineteenth century essential was how a physician decided on treatment on the basis of the diagnosis. On the other hand, the emergence of new diagnostic tools, statistical analyses and studies based on larger populations affected the writers' choice of the presented data (Taavitsainen and Pahta 2000: 72–73). According to Taavitsainen and Pahta (2000), consequently, the compelling narratives about the incredible were transformed into concise and conventionalized accounts based on scientifically verifiable facts.[25] In sum, the above-presented study demonstrates that "[s]uch diachronic changes of text-internal generic conventions can be related to changes in society, in the discourse community, or in scientific methods" (Taavitsainen and Pahta 2000: 60; see also Bazerman 1988; *Scientific Thought-Styles*).

The aim of Chapter One was to define key notions such as discourse, discourse analysis, text and genre in order to situate the present work in the particular research tradition and point to the areas of interest. What is more, an attempt has been made to describe the type of data that will be studied in the empirical part, i.e., medical case reports. In the following chapter, the origins and evolution of the genre will be presented against the background of developing medicine which exerted influence on the way disease and patients were described.

24 See section 6. in Chapter Three.

25 For an interesting account of how recording genres sought to document the incredible see Nowell-Smith (1995).

Chapter Two: Medical discourse and case reports from a historical perspective

Anyone temped to study the history of medicine from the early beginnings to its current status will be impressed by its progress and what it has to offer to humankind at present. There are milestones in the history of medicine which made its development possible. However, this section will be restricted only to those facts which are relevant to the aims of the work. In detail, account will be made only of those events which directly or indirectly exerted influence on patient imaging in medical discourse generally and in case reports specifically, as, following Bazerman (1988), scientific discourses are conditioned by given disciplines. Consequently, it will be demonstrated how scientific discoveries and intellectual trends in medicine shaped the modes of patient presentation.

1. From Hippocrates to the seventeenth-century medicine

The practice of recording cases of diseases has its roots in Hippocrates' (ca. 460 BC – ca. 370 BC) medical writings. Harriet Nowell-Smith (1995: 49–50) and Brian Hurwitz (2006: 219–220) note that his case histories dealing with diseases in individual people were finely composed and followed the sequence of events. Moreover, as Hurwitz (2006) observes, Hippocratic case histories were characterized by close attention to detail when it came to describing the patient's body. "Hippocratic preoccupation with external appearances, signs, surfaces, and colors created a visual primacy that eventually culminated in our own times in the capacity to visualize the body from remarkable new technological vantage points" (2006: 218). Furthermore, Roberto Margotta (1996: 27) observes that it was Hippocrates' belief that doctor's duty is to relieve patient's suffering. Consequently, the account of a patient's illness in a form of a story was meant to prove the healing powers of a doctor. According to Nowell-Smith (1995: 50), the novelty of Hippocrates' case histories was that in giving account of a particular disease they combined medical theory and practice. Maurice Pigeaud (1988) claims that in so doing, Hippocrates' case histories laid the foundations of Western medicine (1988: 5–7, cited in Nowell-Smith 1995: 50). Quite different are Galen's (AD 129–200) case reports. In comparison to Hippocrates, Galen used to give a thorough account of patient's details as well as his/her experience of illness (Hurwitz 2006: 222–223).

According to Roger French (2003: 1–2), the form and content of case reports from the Middle Ages in turn were heavily influenced by the philosophical movement of scholasticism. For medicine this meant favoring ancient authorities as the ultimate source of knowledge. As a result, a doctor from the Middle Ages was called The Learned and Rational Doctor – *learned* meaning possessing the ancients' knowledge and *rational* meaning he could prove his right with appropriate arguments. In medical texts scholasticism was marked by direct references to authors – to ensure the quality of information – as well as by prescriptive phrases (Taavitsainen and Pahta 1998). Taavitsainen and colleagues (2002) note that the aim of these means of expression was emphasizing "the reliability and correctness of the information and the necessity of having confidence in knowledge that was handed down as axioms" (2002: 258).

As regards case reports, they played a central role in medical teaching for a very long period, as they served as the primary source of medical knowledge and the basis for diagnosis (Taavitsainen and Pahta 2000: 61; Hunter 1991: 93). According to Maurizio Gotti and Françoise Salager-Meyer (2006), it was not until the early fifteenth century that medicine rejected the unquestionable status of the ancestors' teachings as the ultimate authority (2006: 9; cf. French 2003: 9). "In a well-known dichotomy, science that relies on authorities is contrasted to empirical investigation and rationalistic views" (Taavitsainen et al. 2002: 253). With these words, Taavitsainen and colleagues (2002) point to the growing importance of observation in the second half of the sixteenth century (2002: 256). As noted by Albert Kyper (1654), more and more people realized that "repeated sensory observation can add up to a universal statement of truth" (cited in French 2003: 189). This, in turn, led to the development of anatomy which was based on visual inspection (French 2003: 190). Thomas Sydenham (1742) stresses that the underlying change in reasoning followed that constant observation of diseases could accumulate information (cited in French 2003: 191) necessary for their comparison and classification. In this respect, the recording nature of case reports seems to have served the purpose well (French 2003: 191–192).

According to Hurwitz (2006), the seventeenth-century case reports, on the other hand, recorded patient's internal experiences, at times spiced up with "considerable existential drama and a strong sense of the operation of fate" (2006: 225). Also Stanley Reiser (1981) observes that in case records from that period doctors gave more prominence to patients' accounts (1981: 4–5). This was probably the result of the lack of diagnostic possibilities on the part of doctors who could rely on nothing more than what a patient said. In the seventeenth century, in order to diagnose, doctors interviewed and observed their patients. First, they listened to patients' accounts of symptoms, i.e., how they felt. Second, doctors observed physical appearance and looked for any signs of a disease. They scrutinized "facial expression, posture, tongue, skin color, and manner of breathing" (Reiser 1981: 2). Apart from that, they also inspected patients' fluids and stools. Physical examination, however, was rarely used (Reiser 1981: 2). Yet, that state of affairs was about to be changed. On the one hand, autopsies shed light on the mystery of the human body. On the other hand, such advances in medicine as anatomical pathology, stimulated by technological inventions, made observation part of medical practice. As a result, the late eighteenth and early nineteenth century brought about fundamental changes in medicine.

2. Pathological anatomy

Just before significant changes in medicine took place, case reports had still been different from the ones written now. On the basis of volumes of *Philosophical Transactions* and, subsequently, *Medical Transactions of the Royal College of Physicians*, Hurwitz (2006) observes that the eighteenth century case reports very often contained the accounts of incredible ailments which were plaguing patients. These accounts, which were meant to be thrilling, "enable[d] readers to position themselves at the threshold of intimate details of the lives of strangers – their private, domestic situations and bodily details sometimes bordering on the immodest" (2006: 226; see also Gunnarsson 2009: 58). Yet, as the nineteenth century approached, there appeared voices in favor of an unemotional and detached style of writing (Hurwitz 2006: 227). This might have been the influence of several important discoveries. Firstly, according to Margotta (1996), it was François Xavier Bichat (1771–1802) who found that organs are built of smaller components, i.e., tissues. He also described them in the state of health and disease (1996: 138). For Bichat, tissues were "the analytical building blocks of anatomy, physiology and pathology". As Roy Porter (2003) observes, the most important conclusion he drew from his discovery was that "diseases must be seen as *lesions* of specific *tissues* rather than ... of *organs* (2003: 74; see also Reiser 1981: 19; Armstrong 2002: 58). Undeniably, that was a powerful conclusion which directed physicians where to look for a disease.

What is more, Bichat openly advocated dissecting dead bodies and examining pathological changes with the following words: "Open a few bodies, this obscurity will soon disappear, which observation alone would never have been able to have dissipated" (Bichat 1822, quoted in Reiser 1981: 19). Bichat's discovery marked the beginning of the era in medicine which was to unveil the secrets of the human body. As Porter (2003) points out, "here was the medicine with the all-powerful gaze ... [and] [t]he anatomizing eye was pressing on still further" (2003: 74).

According to Marsden Blois (1984), Bichat's works found its continuation in the studies of Rudolf Karl Virchow (1821–1902), one of the greatest pathologists. Virchow repeated after Bichat that disease targets not whole organs but tissues and added that tissues' reaction to disease causes their dysfunction. This led Virchow to the claim that disease is the altered condition of tissues and cells (1984: 110), which, in turn, as noted by Margotta (1996: 158), resulted in the explosion of microscopic studies of bodily constituent parts. Moreover, Nowell-Smith (1995) emphasizes that Virchow's scientific activity influenced medical case writing in a number of respects. According to the pathologist, content wise, only relevant information should be included. Consequently, banning unnecessary facts and deliberations from medical texts, Virchow paved the way to empiricist and inductive medicine. His anatomical-pathological model, which soon began to be utilized in the recording of ailments, presupposed also a certain way of describing patients. With the underlying assumption that it was tissues and cells where illness was to be sought, "organs assumed center stage, and patients' views were retained as prefatory material" (1995: 52). Also the publication of John Warter's *Observation in Medicine, Or The Art of Case Taking* (1865) contributed to the conventionalization and impersonality of the genre. Just as in Virchow's autopsies, Warter (1865) explained in a form of a checklist how to write a case report. Eventually, authors were instructed to focus on providing necessary information in an organized manner, which, in turn, limited the information about the patient's experience of illness.

As Nowell-Smith (1995) comments, from that moment, "[a]n ill person is thus processed and stretched out upon the axes of medical inquiry ... [while] [t]he infinite number of pains and fears of which they are made up have been tidied into a small and finite number of categories" (1995: 53). Nowell-Smith (1995) also draws attention to the fact that the concerns about the dehumanizing portrayal of patients were voiced as early as that. Regarding the style, describing autopsies required precise execution of the cause and effect sequence as well as the appropriate ordering of material. What is more, clear language and specialized vocabulary were also prescribed. "The dream of a transparent language of pure representation, in which the world can be rendered exactly and precisely, has been part of the empirical sciences since their inception" (Nowell-Smith 1995: 56). This vision became real with the establishment of the clinic, which will be the topic of the next section.

3. The birth of the clinic

Frederick Cartwright (1977) gives account of one more major event in the history of medicine that the eighteenth century witnessed, namely the birth of the clinic.

The novelty of the institution was that treating patients was at the same time an opportunity to educate medical professionals through the so called bedside teaching. The first clinics were established by Herman Boerhaave, a professor of medicine and botany at the University of Leyden. Because at the time university education did not offer any clinical training to its students, Boerhaave decided to teach them while performing his duties in a local hospital (1977: 47–48). This way regular hospital care became a means of passing knowledge, which paved the way to a new form of medical service. Yet, according to Blois (1984: 110), such teaching practices required a totally different approach to disease. Before the pathological anatomy, symptoms themselves were perceived as diseases and had to be elicited from a patient. As Newman notes (1957: 30), this understanding changed with the advent of observation, Bichat's and Virchow's discoveries and performing autopsies, all of which agreed with the idea of the clinic, i.e., of "the physical examination of the patient". Physicians needed to be taught how to obtain information about the signs of disease as well as other abilities necessary to diagnose a condition (Newman 1957: 30). Therefore, as Paul Atkinson (1997) points out, "[t]he space of the patient bedside thus became a new locus of inquiry and research as well as treatment and instruction" (1997: 4) where new investigative means played a significant role. Furthermore, the institution, combined with the procedures employed there, gave rise to a new medical discourse which is thoroughly dealt with by Michel Foucault (2003 [1963]).

To demonstrate the novelty, Foucault (2003) provides fragments of two medical texts, from the mid-eighteenth and mid-nineteenth century respectively. While in the first text "membranous tissues like pieces of damp parchment ... peel away ... [and] were passed daily with the urine" (Pomme 1796 [1762]: 60–65, quoted in Foucault 2003: ix), in the second one, the layers of membranes are described as "transparent", "tenuous", "buffy" (Bayle 1825: 23–24, quoted in Foucault 2003: x). Other attributes referred to in the second fragment include location, shades, thickness and texture, which reflects close attention to detail. The striking difference in the precision of the chosen vocabulary as used in the two texts is attributed by Foucault (2003) to the growing knowledge of the human body and its ailments. It is not only that the whole new area of the unknown was revealed to physicians but also that intellectual advancement changed the way they perceived disease. In Foucault's (2003) words, "the language of fantasy" (2003: x) which described "the silent world of the entrails, the whole dark side of the body" (2003: xi) became a "loquacious gaze" (2003: xii). This "mutation in discourse", as Foucault (2003: xii) labels it, came to reflect the growing importance of observation, the recognition and understanding of symptoms and the emerging classification of diseases (2003: 4–12). One of the manifestations of these trends were Bichat's and Virchow's works in pathological anatomy which enabled to define the nature of disease and its location (see section 2.). Consequently, careful scrutiny, which Foucault (2003) terms as *medical gaze*, coupled with medical expertise, allowed a doctor to track a disease and identify it respectively. The two processes are referred to as reading (Foucault 2003: 71; cf. Walsh 2004) and deciphering (2003: 72).[26]

In the clinical environment, the process of decoding symptoms and assigning preconceived disease labels was continuously performed during patient's observation. Furthermore, accumulating knowledge enforced faithful linguistic representation. As a result, saturated with descriptions of shades, size, texture, etc., medical discourse became to function in Foucault's (2003: xii) view at the level of *spatialization* and *verbalization* "of the pathological". Foucault (2003) emphasizes this merger of observation and language when he claims that seeing means saying (2003: xii–xiii). This transformation is also well captured by Rita Charon (1992), who claims that "medicine unfolds in its language – its incantations as well as diagnostic imagery" (1992: 115).

In his exploration of factors triggering the change of medical discourse, Foucault (2003) also makes mention of the patient's status. As Foucault (2003) points out, in order to recognize a disease, a doctor had to scrutinize the body for the signs and symptoms. Yet, as not all of them are indicative of pathology, he had to separate the wheat from the chaff and consider only those pertinent ones. Therefore, disease began to be inspected in abstraction from a patient as he/she "is only an external fact … [and] the medical reading must take him into account only to place him in parenthesis" (Foucault 2003: 7), through syntactical methods of disengaging patient from physician" (Charon 1992: 115). What is more, in the very clinic, "the patient is the accident of his disease, the transitory object …" (Foucault 2003: 71).

While Foucault (2003) draws attention to the above-given perception of a patient in a loose relation to medical discourse, Harriet Nowell-Smith (1995) has examined specific texts which already reflect the phenomena in question.

---

26 According to French (2003), the idea of reading the body goes back to Galen's times when the argument that the "body was intelligible" (2003: 38) was voiced by the proponents of human dissection and vivisection. They believed that it would provide information about the human anatomy. In the modern clinic, it is common practice to read the body as if it were a text in order to interpret the signs of a disease. This is also referred to as somatography (Rawlison 1982: 71; see also Hunter 1991: 8 and Kenny and Beagan 2004).

4. The nineteenth century

In her study of the nineteenth century Canadian gynecological case reports, Nowell-Smith (1995) demonstrates how the above-discussed innovations in medicine were reflected in language. The use of the Passive Voice, a well-known feature of scientific discourse in general, was supposed to render the facts in an objective way, regardless of who presented them (cf. Grice and Kramer-Dahl 1992: 73). Although authorial presence is out of the focus of this work, it needs to be mentioned at this point, as it had some consequences also for patient imaging. Nowell-Smith (1995) maintains that patients as objects of sentences are not imaged as active participants. She also adds that in Hippocratic writings this was not the case (Nowell-Smith 1995: 85; cf. section 1.).

Another novel feature of the nineteenth-century gynecological case reports is that the texts are entitled, usually naming the illness that the patient under study underwent. Absent in Hippocratic case reports, this characteristic enables the author to state the cause of a problem with a single label which locates the patient's condition along the axis of normal/abnormal (Nowell-Smith 1995: 54; see also French 2003: 191–192; Hurwitz 2006: 229–230). This procedure, in turn, was possible thanks to repeated observations of patients and, consequently, the accumulation of knowledge about diseases (cf. section 1. in Chapter Three).

Yet another feature of those case reports is the use of statistics. According to Nowell-Smith (1995), the end of the nineteenth century saw the introduction of numerical information concerning "birth, death, and disease" (1995: 59). Apart from their primary function which was to add credibility to a document, they contributed to the order of information which was presented (1995: 59–61). As will be shown in the following section, the development of new diagnostic procedures in medicine will make statistics and other measurable medical data an essential element of medical records. This is in line with Nowell-Smith's observation (1995) that already at that time doctors faced the challenge of precise and objective writing, having in mind that they wrote about humans. Although based solely on Canadian gynecological case histories, this study draws attention to the important facts in the development of the case report genre, which is presented against its historical backdrop. Considerations regarding language mentioned by Nowell-Smith (1995) were a sign that medical discourse was about to change (Foucault 2003). The next two sections will address the nature of this change, dealing with a number of technological inventions, which indirectly exerted influence on the language of medicine.

5. The advent of technology

According to Reiser (1981), "the practice of dissecting bodies to find physical evidence of disease began to transform some eighteenth-century physicians from word-oriented, theory-bound scholastics to touch-oriented, observation-bound scientists" (1981: 19). Also a number of technological innovations which made diagnosis more and more precise, contributed to this change. The novelty lay in either quantifying or examining capabilities of new tools, i.e., offering far more than mere scrutiny (cf. Scambler 2003). At the beginning of the nineteenth century the stethoscope was discovered which added sound to the previous very limited methods of observation or patient's accounts. This "'seeing' into the chest'" (Reiser 1981: 45) enabled physicians to determine the presence or absence of disease on the basis of the auditory stimuli coming from the inside of the body.

Apart from the sense of hearing, also physician's sight became more powerful. The ophthalmoscope made it possible to inspect the interior of the eye, while the laryngoscope looked into the larynx, to name but a few instruments. Even more possibilities were offered by the X-ray, which not only detected chest diseases more effectively than auscultation but also enabled doctors examination without intervention into the body. Yet, while these devices explored gross anatomy, another invention unveiled "the cellular universe" (Reiser 1981: 69). Initially used for observing tissues, cells, and humors (e.g., phlegm, blood), the microscope contributed to other medical achievements such as Robert Koch's[27] discovery of bacteria (Resier 1981: 82). All these inventions sharpened human senses in that they laid bare not only the interior of the body but also its basic constituents, enabling more and more accurate diagnosis. At the same time, as Reiser (1981) observes, while the stethoscope or speculum were used in the patient's presence, the diagnosis by means of the microscope did not require the patient to be present. What is more, as Condrau (2007) notes, many physicians, amazed by the possibilities of new equipment, considered these machine-obtained data more credible than the ones gathered directly from a patient (2007: 529).

Yet another group of devices allowed to study with exact precision the main functions of the body such as breathing, pulse and temperature. The advantage of such machines as the spirometer, electrocardiograph or thermometer was "the translation of physiological actions into the languages of machines" (Reiser 1981: 91). This allowed more objective measurement in comparison to a subjective

---

27 For his (1882) isolation of tuberculosis bacteria, Heinrich Hermann Robert Koch (1843–1910), a German physician, was granted the Nobel Prize in Physiology or Medicine [Swedish: *Nobelpriset i fysiologi eller medicin*] in 1905 (editor's note: ZW)

and impressionistic diagnosis made through feeling and hearing (Reiser 1981: 121). While "the anatomist and the microscopist used as a yardstick the visual configuration of the elements in a tissue … [,] [t]he chemist sought a fixed record of a similar kind through the proportional relations of the elements in a liquid, stated numerically" (Reiser 1981: 130).

It is impossible not to appreciate the role of chemistry in medicine. It allowed to study chemical components of body fluids in order to detect changes in their content, which, in turn, signal a disease. At the same time, chemistry heralded the beginning of era when a large amount of medical facts were "technologically generated" (Reiser 1981: 166). As Scambler (2003) points out, "the physical examination [was] undermined by the molecular processes underlying normal physical functioning" (2003: 183–184). This, consequently, as Reiser (1981: 166–167) notes, made many physicians voice their worries about patients being objectified in the process of laboratory examination.

What is more, also the practice of interviewing patients was gradually being devalued due to the subjective nature of the patient's accounts and doctors' belief that technology would handle it better and quicker (Reiser 1981: 171). According to Reiser (1981), "[t]he numbers generated by the thermometer, the graphs drawn by the electrocardiograph, the pictures created by the X-ray machine, the images captured by the microscope, [and] the diagnostic judgments rendered by the computer" (1981: 229) undeniably sharpened physician's senses and made diagnosis more precise. Yet, looking at a patient merely "through a screen of machines", as Reiser (1981: 230) puts it, contributed to his/her perception as an object of a medical enquiry, determined by and reduced to numbers and norms. "Machines inexorably direct the attention of both doctor and patient to the measurable aspects of illness, but away from the human factors that are at least equally important" (Reiser 1981: 229; cf. Shorter 1985).

Similar concerns have been voiced also by Nowell-Smith (1995) in the study of gynecological case reports from the nineteenth century. As Hurwitz (2006) notes, the calls for a more precise and effaced language (cf. section 6. in Chapter Three) were finally put into practice. The authors began to write in a more impersonal style, employing the Passive Voice and eliminating agency on the part of a patient (2006: 229). As a result, the texts dealt with "mindless bodies, depersonalized behaviors, and fragmentary body parts" (Crites 1966: 26). Patients were described with the help of the discourse about disease which "'analyzed', separated and shredded" (Arney and Bergen 1983: 4) them. The general trend of favoring machines and their objective measurements over patients' accounts is also reflected in the growing number of references to new diagnostic equipment, following the need to translate the clinical reality into a text as faithfully as possible (Hurwitz 2006: 228–230).

According to Hurwitz (2006: 228), the gradual devaluation of the patient's accounts due to the growing sophistication of the means of medical examination is also reflected in the case reports from that period. The trend is manifested through the separation of the initial demographical information about patients as well as their documented complaints from the subsequent descriptions of diagnostic and treatment procedures. Similar findings have also been reported by Tavitsainen and Pahta (2000) in their diachronic study of case reports from two periods – 1850–1900 and 1965–1995. As regards the former time frame, Tavitsainen and Pahta (2000) demonstrate that the case reports are characterized by two levels of narration – the first one which is the author's narration in the first person and from his/her point of view, and the second one which gives account of a patient's disease in the third person and foregrounds his/her symptoms (2000: 63–64). The patient's part "is told in a vivid style with illuminating details such as remarks on the patient's looks, frame of mind, and expectations, evaluating attributive adjectives such as *judicious* [original emphasis] and similes depicting the symptoms of the illness" (Taavitsainen and Pahta 2000: 65), which points to the fact that authors had not ceased using unusual vocabulary. Yet, though both written by a physician, the two parts differ in the mode of writing with the doctor's narrative more effaced. What is also important is that the patient's level of narration is less prominent and it serves as an addition to the account of physician's judgements and decisions (Taavitsainen and Pahta 2000: 64, 66).

All in all, the turn of the nineteenth century marked an important moment in the history of medicine. Thanks to the introduction of autopsies and, subsequently, pathological anatomy, disease came to be understood as changes in the patient's body that could be directly observed. It was then when doctors' diagnostic procedures turned from speculation, partly based on the patient's accounts, to observation which entailed the recognition of the signs of disease.

The invention of the stethoscope and other revolutionary diagnostic methods gradually made the process of medical assessment more and more precise. Moreover, the observation of signs of disease also lay at the heart of a new medical institution, namely the clinic. As regards medical texts, the above-presented studies of the nineteenth-century case reports corroborate the general trend of the diminishing role of the patient in the context of diagnosis and treatment due to the changes in modes of medical reasoning and technological progress. The trend found its textual representation both in the style of narration as well as in specific linguistic features of the texts. Yet, these are just one aspect of the transformation of medical discourse, which was associated with the clinic. Further technological advancement brought about a new model of medical practice which shaped not only medical profession but also its discourse. These issues will be discussed in the next chapter.

Chapter Three: Medical discourse in the modern context

So far two important stages in the history of medicine have been discussed. The first period, "the era of dogma" (Flexner 1990: 52), was characterized by the strong adherence to the teachings of ancient philosophers and thinkers. Doctors followed these dogmas uncritically, treating them as the core of medical knowledge. The end of scholasticism brought about observation as means of getting to the nature of things (cf. section 1. in Chapter Two). This resulted in several important discoveries (cf. section 2. in Chapter Two) and the adoption of a new concept of disease which was further corroborated by various technological inventions (cf. section 5. in Chapter Two). These not only made diagnostic procedures easier and more precise, but also affected the development of medicine as an area of study and practice. Furthermore, these contextual factors had a bearing on the form and content of medical case reports.

Consequently, Chapter Three will present selected events from the history of medicine from the twentieth century onwards and their impact on the status of the patient in the discipline which, by definition, is meant to serve his/her needs. Furthermore, the account of the currently practiced medical model will be given as well as a brief characteristic of medical education as the context of production and reproduction of modern medical discourse. The traces of the present-day intellectual climate in medical discourse in general and in medical case reports in particular will be exemplified as well.

1. The reign of technology continued

According to Fritjof Capra (1985), the developing medicine of the nineteenth century refocused the physician's eye from the patient to disease. The fact that "pathologies were located, diagnosed, and labeled according to a definite system of classification" (1985: 126) was possible thanks to new diagnostic devices and growing medical knowledge. The twentieth century saw the continuation of the era of discoveries with antibiotics and other modern drugs, which was a direct consequence of the advances in molecular biology (Capra 1985: 127–129). On the other hand, technology was offering more and more devices that diagnosed patients, treated them and sustained their lives. Developing disciplines such as: "physics, chemistry, electronics, computer science and other related fields" made it possible to produce computerized "blood analyzers and tomography scanners, machines for renal analysis, cardiac pacemakers, [and] equipment for radiation therapy" (Capra 1985: 147–148). A substantial part of these inventions enabled doctors to establish a more precise diagnosis. Paul Atkinson (1995) points to a specific group of devices that scrutinize every little element of the human body: "X-rays, ultrasound, computed tomography; magnetic resonance imaging; nuclear tracing" (1995: 62). The knowledge about the patient's condition, once accessible to a physician solely through observation, palpation, auscultation and percussion, came to light in various shades and magnitudes.

All these innovations constitute an extension of the medical gaze from the turn of the nineteenth century. As a result, the "epistemological break" (Atkinson 1995: 60) that took place redefined disease and its existence in the human body. The innovative reasoning prescribed scanning the body for pathological changes which had to be interpreted by those equipped with medical expertise. After decoding the signs, they were associated with specific organs or systems and assigned a label denoting a condition or illness.

Consequently, "the patient's body became legible" (Atkinson 1995: 60; cf. Lupton 1994). Yet, according to Cecil Helman (1994: 103), this legibility was even finer as, apart from visual observation and physical examination, it was possible to check the body with the help of various tests. Their aim was to translate the condition into indices of quality (visualization) and numbers (measurement). As regards the former, such medical documents as X-rays, blood smears or echocardiography could be visually assessed. In the latter case, "weight, height, circumference, blood count, hemoglobin level, levels of electrolytes or hormones, blood pressure, heart rate, respiratory rate, heart size or visual acuity" could be measured. These, in turn, depending on their quality and value respectively, determined the patient's condition (Helman 1994: 103). However, as Atkinson (1995) points out, the visual inspection does not appear to be straightforward. It rarely allows either a black or white option and is based on convention (Atkinson 1995: 65; cf. section 7.).

At the same time, modern technology made this reading an extremely complex process, which breaks down the human body into its basic constituents. Graham Scambler (2003) notes that present day diagnoses explain patient's conditions in terms of chemical processes – cellular or molecular ones (2003: 29). What is more, according to Atkinson (1995), "[t]hese diverse technologies mean that the body of the patient is no longer localized in the discrete, integral body of the actual patient". "[T]he clinical gaze is no longer anchored to the bedside itself [and] … is now dispersed" (Atkinson 1995: 61).

What Atkinson (1995) has in mind regards the scope of medical gaze as well as its object. As far as the former aspect is concerned, certain diagnostic procedures are not performed in patient's presence, either at his/her bedside or during a consultation, but in other places such as specialized departments, laboratories, etc. These "multiple sites of investigation" (Atkinson 1995: 61) are the result of the progressing specialization of medicine with various branches forking and concentrating on increasingly smaller objects of study. As regards the object of clinical gaze, it is not only patient's body-parts and organs that are diagnosed at the real time but also various samples of fluids, tissues, etc. that are taken and then analyzed elsewhere. As a consequence, subject to separate diagnostic procedures, the patient's body "may be read and interpreted *in abstentia* [original emphasis]" (Atkinson 1995: 62).

Atkinson's observation (1995) draws attention to two important respects in which modern technology influences the patient's status in medicine. For one thing, it renders his/her bodies interpretable, offering various means that visualize and measure biological processes and conditions. Moreover, thanks to the amazing capacities of modern technology, attention can be drawn to individual fragments of the body, abstracting away from the person. "The [fragmented] body is thus transformed into a series of signs and representations, by means of a complex array of technologies of inspection" (Atkinson 1995: 62). Atkinson (1997) also notes that the beginnings of the clinic (cf. section 3. in Chapter Two) were marked by the emerging perception of "the individual … [as] a field of medical-clinical investigation" (1997: 6).

While the newly established clinic came to treat the human body as the locus of its attention, the subsequently developing technology caused "the fractionation of patients into organ systems", as Watts (1985: 545) puts it. "The discursive space of the body" (Atkinson 1995: 61) is therefore composed of pieces, each being separately observed, assessed and treated. As will be shown in the empirical part of the present work, this phenomenon, which is under the investigation of the sociology of knowledge, manifests itself linguistically in the studied texts.

The next section will give account of how the impressive pace with which medicine was developing in the twentieth century, contributed to the formation of a medical model which has been practiced for over a century now.

2. The biomedical model

Chapter Two and the previous section have addressed two watersheds in the history of medicine. On the one hand, it was pathological anatomy, which shifted doctor's attention to constituent parts of the human body and connected bodily changes with the presence of disease. On the other hand, developing technology enabled physicians to look deeper and inspect more carefully, which meant not only finer distinctions but also greater knowledge of the matter studied. Yet, there was a flip side to it. Supported with the capabilities of new equipment, at many occasions medicine was reduced only to studying and interpreting "X-ray photographs, scans, printouts of blood tests, or the strips of paper from an electrocardiogram" (Lupton 1994: 105) representing body-parts or biological processes by means of numerical and visual signs.

As a consequence, the application of modern diagnostic/treating devices and broadening medical knowledge directed medical practice to a particular path which has come to be known as *biomedicine* or *Western medicine*. The following section will present some of its underlying premises which have a bearing on the way in which medicine is practiced in Western societies.

The disciplines that have been particularly involved in studying the biomedical model are the sociology of medicine and the ethnography of medicine. As Peter Conrad (2005: 1) explains, while the former deals with medicine in the context of society, e.g., doctor-patient communication, the status of the medical profession, etc., the latter concentrates on medicine in the contexts of its practice. The disciplines approach medicine critically, which means that they do not treat medical knowledge as given but as the product of social and cultural practices (Atkinson 1995: 25). Consequently, biomedicine is "a product of western society and culture" (Gordon 1988: 20). It is a "collective representation of reality" (Hahn and Gaines 1985: 6), a version of medical knowledge and reasoning. By this is meant that, firstly, it is a mode of practicing medicine associated with western societies and, secondly, that it is based on a certain body of established knowledge. As regards the former, biomedicine draws on technological development and the possibilities offered by its application. Regarding the latter, the biomedical model presupposes certain modes in which medical practices are executed and interpreted.

Consequently, according to Robert Hahn and Atwood Gaines (1985: 6), there is a dialogic relation (cf. section 5. in Chapter One) between medical practice and the biomedical model in that the latter affects how medicine is practiced, which, in turn, strengthens the model. Yet, although biomedicine can be contrasted with other medical systems outside the Western realm, for instance humoural medicine in Latin America and China (discussed by Logan 1975 and Macdonald 1984), it is not unified and it varies across cultures and countries (Hahn and Gaines 1985: 17; Lupton 1994: 106; Atkinson 1995: 27).[28] Additionally, what is

28 In these countries, humoral medicine is based upon the premise that human health is conditioned by the balanced body temperature.

generally understood as biomedicine has also been referred to in various sources as *medical model, scientific model* (Lupton 1994) or *Western medicine*. Nevertheless, it is possible to isolate after Derick Wade and Peter Halligan (2004: 1398), several assumptions from the biomedical mode of reasoning:

(1) All illness and all symptoms and signs arise from an underlying abnormality within the body (usually in the functioning or structure of specific organs), referred to as a disease;
(2) All diseases give rise to symptoms, eventually if not initially, and although other factors may influence the consequences of the disease, they are not related to its development or manifestations;
(3) Health is the absence of disease;
(4) Mental phenomena, such as emotional disturbance or delusions, are separate from and unrelated to other disturbances of bodily function;
(5) The patient is a victim of circumstance with little or no responsibility for the presence or cause of the illness;
(6) The patient is a passive recipient of treatment, although cooperation with treatment is expected.

Points (1), (2), (3) and (4) assume that disease results solely from cellular or biochemical changes in the body, ignoring their psychological, sociological and cultural conditionings. On this reasoning, biomedicine is believed to be reductionist (cf. Scambler 2003: 104; Hahn and Gaines 1985: 3; Gordon 1988: 19; Pellegrino 2001: 83) as it excludes any other factors conducive to the etiology, course, and treatment of disease. In other words, a treated person is defined by and, therefore, reduced to biological processes taking place in his/her body, barring any other sources of influence.

This reductionist stance is thought to originate from Cartesian[29] separation of body and soul which should be dealt with by science, and philosophy and religion respectively. As researchers observe, in the course of the specialization of medicine into numerous branches and sub-branches the mind was taken over by psychology and psychiatry while the body by science (Helman 1994: 104; cf. Capra 1985: 122; Gordon 1988: 20; Suchman and Matthews 1988). As

29 Adjectival form derived from Renatus Cartesius known as René Descartes (1596–1650), French philosopher and mathematician. The most known *dictum* of Descartes "I think, therefore I am" [*je pense, donc je suis;*] is rendered by some contemporary translators with the statement "I am thinking therefore I am", which seems to reflect the understanding of its original propositional content more precisely. Cf. Descartes 2006 / 1980/ [1637], page 28 and the translator's commentary on page. (editor's note: ZW)

a result, medicine began to have a lot in common with science. According to Edmund Pellegrino (2001), drawing on physics and chemistry, medicine started to unveil processes taking place in the human body (2001: 31). Moreover, as technological advancement in medicine progressed, various inventions helped to fulfill this aim. Certain phenomena became visible, audible and measurable, which allowed physicians to concentrate on smaller and smaller constituents of the human body, abstracting away from the whole person. As Ruth Wodak (1996: 35) observes, the question 'Why does it hurt, what happened?' evolved into 'Where does it hurt?' What is more, Deborah Lupton (1994) notes that what could be observed and measured was treated as objective (1994: 102). Therefore, physicians sought the confirmation of certain disease phenomena in medical tests or physical examination, excluding the emotional and social aspects of patients' lives. As researchers point out, as a consequence, focusing on the body, biomedicine distanced it from the experience of illness (see Mishler 1984: 192; Kirmayer 1988: 60; cf. Jaye 2004: 41). Armstrong (2002: 58) claims that "[t]he real development of the new pathological medicine … was the development of techniques that allowed the clinician to bypass the patient's self report and attempt to identify the exact nature of the lesion from the tell-tale indicators or signs it left within the body" (see also Baron 1985: 607; Hunter 1991: 52 and Hofmann 2001: 14). This meant that the reliability of the patient's account continued to decrease (cf. section 5. in Chapter Two).

Furthermore, as Atkinson (1995) observes, such a mode of reasoning engendered certain sets of oppositions that now underlie biomedicine, namely disease/illness and signs/symptoms. The first pair originates from medical anthropology and follows that disease is a concept of a state conditioned by the presence or absence of the manifestations indicating a given pathological change.[30] What is more, definitions of diseases, their course, and treatment are agreed upon by medical professionals. Illness, on the other hand, is defined by researchers in terms of its subjective perception by a patient (see Bond and Bond 1986: 200; cf. Gordon 1988: 25; Lupton 1994: 93; Radley 1997: 57; Fleischman 1999; Boyd 2000; Armstrong 2002 and Conrad 2005: 5). In Anglo-European medical education, students are taught to treat diseases and not illnesses (cf. subsection 4.2. and section 5.).

The other pair – signs/symptoms – is closely linked to and built upon the first set of oppositions, as it also distinguishes between medical – objective – and lay – subjective – perspectives in the context of disease manifestations. While

30 Cf. also Young (1982) and Kleinman (1973; 1980).

signs are, according to Deborah Gordon (1988), "objective indications in the patient's body" (1988: 25), as they can be discerned by a physician (directly or through reading medical tests), symptoms constitute the way a patient experiences disease, i.e., "the patient's complaints" (1988: 25; cf. Atkinson 1997: 164). The differentiation can be illustrated with the following excerpt from the record of a patient encounter in which there is a clear division between the subjective and objective:

> 1/8/99, 06:30
> SUBJECTIVE: Twenty-four-year-old woman presents on her first day of surgery rotation with complaints of anxiety, agitation, and apprehension
> OBJECTIVE: VS (vital signs): afebrile, tachycardic
> Gen (general): well-nourished woman, no acute distress
> HEENT (head, ears, eyes, nose, throat): pupils (Ghosh 2004: 154).

As can be seen in the above-given example, following Kenneth Boyd (2010), what is termed as subjective "is a feeling, an experience of unhealth which is entirely personal, interior to the person of the patient" (2000: 10). On the other hand, objectivity is guaranteed when a disease lends itself to sensorial observation or measurement (2000: 10).

The above distinctions exemplify how the development of medical thought and the subsequent incorporation of new diagnostic means contributed to a new mode of reasoning. Before the advent of pathological anatomy and the reign of technology the doctor's knowledge about the patient's condition came straight from the diseased and the body was impenetrable for the human eye. In contrast, as Flexner (1990) notes, "[s]cientific medicine has its eyes open" (1990: 53) in that, supported by modern technology, it sees even invisible diseases (cf. Fredriksen 2002). The evolution in thinking about disease and diagnostic machines offered a precise and objective account of the patient's health which rendered his/her input less credible. The medical gaze was redirected to the constituent parts of the body where a disease was supposed to be sought. As a consequence, medicine began to separate the objective from the subjective and the visible/the tested from the guessed. Yet, such a separation allowed only categorical understanding of health and disease. A person who complained about certain ailments but these could not be diagnostically assessed was treated as healthy.

Points (5) and (6) above introduce another important aspect of the biomedical model, namely the passive role of a patient. The already mentioned devaluation of the patient's account relegated him/her to the role of a passive participant in the process of diagnosis and treatment. Barring both the external and mental factors affecting the patient's health – points (2) and (4) above – a patient has become "coterminous" (Armstrong 2002: 82) with the body, "a passive site of disease manifestation" (Atkinson 1988: 180) where signs and symptoms are to be decoded by a physician. In biomedicine, as Gordon (1988) notes, the focus falls primarily on the body, "nature's representative in human beings" and "a physical object" (1988: 29–30; cf. Armstrong 2002: 82). It can be objectively observed/tested with the help of technology, and described by means of the language true to nature, i.e., numbers (1988: 20, 30). This goes in line with Cartesian dualism of body and soul and the biomedical dichotomies of signs of disease which are objectively found in the patient's body, and symptoms of illness which are subjectively experienced by an individual. At this point, also the biomedical concept of disease needs to mentioned. In this model, a disease is an entity and is referred to as "it" (as discussed by Blois 1984: 97; Hunter 1991: 135; Lupton 1994: 19; Fleischman 1999: 8–9 and Woods 2006: 129; see also a metaphor approach to this conceptualization in section 4. in Chapter Four). What is more, diseases have their names under which subsumed is a certain body of information about causes, progress and treatment. Yet, referring to diseases as things and not as states which change eradicates the perception of disease as being experienced by patients (cf. Woods 2006: 19).[31]

What further contributes to the passive image of the patient's body is the already discussed process of its fragmentation in the era of modern diagnostic devices. The representing of his/her constitutive parts by means of visuals and numbers in various places of investigation is part of the "biomedical disaggregation or distribution of 'the body'" (Atkinson 1995: 109). As Atkinson (1995) observes, the application of the advanced diagnostic procedures and the specialization of medicine called to existence "disembodied body" (1995: 89). It is the body whose fragments are inspected and described separately, as if "units on an assembly line" (Souba 2002: 140), from different perspectives of individual observers (referred to by Radley 1997: 54 as a "field crisscrossed by the various discourses of patients, doctors and healthy people") and without reference to its owner (Atkinson 1995: 89). Such imaging of a patient and his/her body is possible within the framework which focuses its attention on disease in abstraction from a patient.

In short, the biomedical model is based upon the reductionist premise that restricts the concept of disease to pathological changes, "molecular derangements", as Wiley Souba (2002: 142) puts it, thus, excluding the psychological and social aspects of its manifestations and development. It has been also demonstrated that the biomedical model and its depersonalized image of a patient evolved in

31 Section 2. in Chapter Four will address in detail how the concept of diseases as entities is manifested in medical discourse.

the course of the development of medical thought and was supported by the advancement of modern technology. While these external conditions contributed to the formation of the model, the process of socialization of students of medicine and their subsequent practice ensure further existence of the biomedical approach. The following section will address this process.

3. "Boys in white"

The aim of the previous section was to introduce the model of medicine that originated from the developing medical thought and the increasing use of modern diagnostic devices in medical practice. Both new ideas and new equipment shed light on the human body in the state of disease and contributed to the formation of the biomedical model. As has been already mentioned, it is reductionist in its treatment of a patient, as it centers around his/her body and biological processes while abstracting away from the patient and social and psychological aspects of his/her illness. As will be shown, the process of medical education and further practice reproduces this model and strengthens its basic premises.

Medical studies and subsequent work as a physician of any specialization involves the complex process of socialization into medical culture. In the course of their education students not only acquire medical knowledge but also learn to behave in a way that is required from a medical professional. Various sources ranging from the ethnographic studies of medical communities to works about the structure of medical education give accounts of what this processes looks like (see Becker et al. 1977; Coombs 1978; Flexner 1990; Good 1994 and Atkinson 1997).[32] Firstly, the very nature of medical studies merits attention. It is interesting to note that apart from what is taught also how much and how it is done affects the future physicians' point of view. According to Kevin Takakuwa et al. (2004), "[m]edical school is, in many ways, like boot camp – patriarchal, militaristic, and designed to strip you of your individuality and turn you into a physician clone, devoid of personality, emotion, or creativity" (2004: xv). In this vein, the potential of medical studies to produce homogenized groups of doctors is explored by Brenda Beagan (2000). On the basis of the interviews with the third-year students of medicine and the facts from the history of medicine she demonstrates how people of different social and cultural backgrounds, with different gender identities and personalities, are molded into a unified body of physicians. This

32 The present account is based solely on the information considering medical education in the USA, Canada and the United Kingdom. Yet, it is believed that many aspects of this account of medical culture are true also for other western countries.

effect is achieved in two simultaneous processes. The first one is less explicit, as it results from the way how medical studies are organized. The students are required to learn loads of material and attend numerous courses. As a consequence, they lack time for any leisure activities and engagements outside the area of medicine, usually staying in each other's company. Such immersion in one subject only and restriction on contacts with other people may affect students' worldview and allow another one to dominate (cf. Berger and Luckmann 1991: 157:ff.; Hafferty and Franks 1994). Yet, this resocialization according to Beagan (2000: 1257) affects not only students' lifestyles but also their attitudes. Students should become neutral doctors who, by the same token, view all people as a homogenous group. It is assumed that only through neutrality are they able to become "undifferentiated physicians" (2000: 1260) – in terms of behavior and even clothes (white uniforms). A doctor is expected to be an "impartial knower, ... subject whom dispassionate science has enabled to transcend social particularities" (2000: 1262). What is more, medical uniformity claims the right to eradicate cultural differences also among students themselves.[33] Unfortunately, such an attitude results in their failure to recognize the diversity among their patients and its significance (Beagan 2000: 1265; cf. Poirier and Brauner 1988).

The other process discussed by Beagan (2000) involves explicit teaching of the same values, attitudes and patterns of behavior, which are part of the curriculum of medical studies. They are known for promoting depersonalized approach to patients which significantly affects the way people manage traumatic experiences and extreme situations (cf. Kenny and Beagan 2004: 1076; cf. Coombs 1978). This process takes place at various stages throughout medical education. As Howard Becker and colleagues (1977) describe, during the first, preclinical year students are taught the structure and functions of the human body on the courses in anatomy, neurology, physiology, biochemistry and the introduction to psychiatry. Their activities include dissection of cadaver, work in laboratory and studying resources (1977: 81). Attention should be drawn at this point to dissecting cadaver. As Flexner (1990) notes, from the scientific and educational point of view, it is an opportunity for students to see the body both as a whole and in its constituent parts (1990: 62). It is also one of the first highly stressful situations (see also Coombs 1978: 112; cf. Jaye 2004).

The theoretical knowledge gained during the first year is then applied during the second one, which includes pathology, microbiology and pharmacology, and

33 For an excellent book containing personal experience of medical students of various ethnic backgrounds see Takakuwa et al. (2004).

physical diagnosis. The three disciplines are considered to be part of the essential body of knowledge needed in the two subsequent clinical years (Flexner 1990: 61; Coombs 1978: 88–89). Becker and colleagues (1977) add that it is also the first time when students deal with patients. They spend time as apprentices in hospitals and clinics to learn further and to be trained under the watchful gaze of physicians (1977: 186). Clinical years are particularly important in the course of medical studies in that it is the time when students get a chance to put theory into practice (cf. Hunter 1991: 29). What is more, they develop the appropriate and prescribed approach to patients and profession, which, supposedly, should help them to tackle difficult situations. This appropriate attitude is understood as the lack of emotional involvement and concentration solely on the task of diagnosis and treatment. The latter is possible partly thanks to the significant role of modern diagnostic devices which enable to examine body-parts, tissues or samples in abstraction from their owners. According to Mohammadreza Hojat and colleagues (2009), who characteristically entitle their article *The devil is in the third year ...*, the latter is possible partly thanks to the significant role of modern diagnostic devices which enable to examine body-parts, tissues or samples in abstraction from their owners (2009: 1188). "In intensive care, coronary care, and neonatal units, it may be questionable where the patient leaves off and some mechanical apparatus begins. Since many of these patients are comatose, heavily sedated, asleep, or irrational, they may more easily be perceived as extensions of tubes, respirators, and signaling devices than as human beings" (Howard et al. 1977: 16).

Other socializing activities include contacts with patients' bodies which are "peered at, probed and felt" (Atkinson 1997: 99) and dealing with cadaver (Coombs 1978: 113). The ability to manage in such moments is taught both through the already mentioned detached attitude and the routinely nature of medical procedures. According to Laurence Kirmayer (1988), the very paraphernalia of the hospital, such as curtains, drapes or baffles, serve, apart from their original function, as the symbolic separators of the body. Additionally, the body itself is isolated from its owner by a hospital gown (Kirmayer 1988: 60–61). As regards cadaver experience, as Coombs (1978) notes, students are taught to separate the human element from cadaver, which helps them to manage stress in various tasks at dissecting bodies. What is more, the prospect of learning so many details about human anatomy may contribute to students concentrating more on a task than on their own feelings. Being reduced to the facts about its parts, the body comes to be perceived "as an object rather than a diseased person" (Coombs 1978: 113). Consequently, the fragmented body, the epitome of modern medicine (cf. sections 5. in Chapter Two and 1. in this chapter) serves as the depersonalizing device drawing students' attention away from the very patient.

This exemplifies a general clinical practice of reducing the emotional load attached to treatment activities, "view[ing] patients not as people with feelings, but as medical entities, specimens, or objects of scientific interest" (Coombs 1978: 262). As Capra (1985) maintains, with the disease/illness distinction, it is not an ill person who is treated but a disease (1985: 152; cf. Fleischman 1999).

Regarding the routinely character of medical procedures, young physicians tend to live their patients' lives and develop personal attachment to them. Yet, with time and the increasing number of treated patients, a doctor comes to accept his/her situation. He/she ceases to be emotionally involved and concentrates on the task, while "his or her feelings remain nicely controllable as frigid blocks of ice" (Hodgkin 1985: 1821). Emotional distance makes it easier to tackle witnessing dying patients, patients suffering from acute pain, and confronting them with the information about their condition (Coombs 1978: 127–128; cf. Hodgkin 1985). Atul Gawande, the author of *Complications: A Surgeon's Notes on an Imperfect Science*, which owns its success to the rising tide of popularity of such TV series as *House M. D.*, *Grey's Anatomy*, etc., also touches upon this issue. He refers to Carl Schneider (1998) who claims that medical culture imposes certain distancing practices and behaviours, which enable doctors to work more effectively (1998: 22).

Furthermore, according to Coombs (1978), the very stage at which medicine finds itself now, namely the heavy reliance on technology and science, contributes to the atmosphere of "restrained emotionality" (1978: 260; cf. Kirmayer 1988: 81). The fact that information about a patient is only partially supplied by him/her while the rest is obtained by means of tests weakens the direct contact between the parties. Constant resorting to machines which diagnose smaller and smaller body entities and concentration solely on the interpretation of the results drives doctors away from patients and their emotions. In such a reality patients become disembodied and their bodies fragmented in the course of diagnosis and treatment.

Clearly then, as medical profession means working under heavy pressure, medical studies teach students to deal with it, i.e., to refrain from emotional involvement and adopt an impersonal attitude. Also the routinely character of various medical assignments is conducive to the development of this behavior. This way, students learn to abstract away from the very patient and focus on the treated bodily element.

The above-presented "medical teaching model", which underlies the process of socialization into medical culture (Coombs 1978: 132–133), has been criticized for teaching emotional detachment towards patients and viewing them as objects of medical treatment (as discussed by Ashcroft 2000: 293; Beagan 2000; Coombs 1978: 264; cf. Freidson 1970; Lock and Gordon 1988). According to

Joseph Lella and Dorothy Pawluch (1988), concern has been also voiced about the objectifying practices when handling cadaver (1988: 125). Capra (1985) goes as far as to name this mode of training "macho value system" (1985: 163). At the same time, the "aloofness and detachment of the case-hardened doctor" (Coombs 1978: 127) practicing "cold medicine" (Atkinson 1997: 190) have become the epitome of a modern physician. Yet, beginning from the first half of the twentieth century, voices were raised against such a model of medicine, which resulted in alternative approaches postulating the empowerment of the patient and raising his/her status in medical treatment. Consequently, as O'Toole (1995) rightly observes, "the greatest challenge facing medical students today is not the mental incorporation of daunting volumes of biomedical information and scientific ways of thinking, but rather the need to remain humanized" (1995: 1387).

4. Alternative models of medicine

It has been demonstrated in the two previous sections that the biomedical model favors the pathological explanation of a disease, concentrating solely on its bodily manifestations. Such a mode of reasoning is partly being perpetuated by the advancing technology which makes it possible to study minuscule fragments of the human body. As a result, modern medicine abstracts away from the patient, directing medical intervention towards his/her body-parts affected by a disease (cf. Capra 1985: 158). Medical education also strengthens this objectifying perspective. Students of medicine must learn to commune with patients' bodies and cadaver, and to work under heavy stress. Viewing patients and their bodies only as objects to be studied and treated eliminates this emotional load from a medical assignment and makes it a mere task to be completed. Yet, from its formation, the biomedical model has been subject to criticism and gave rise to alternative strands in medical practice. The following section will address some of the issues voiced against the biomedical model and demonstrate how they contributed to the creation of new approaches. The section will also point to some examples of the application of these alternatives in medical practice and their consequences for medical discourse.

4.1. Patient-centered medicine

The innovative devices of the nineteenth century which visualized the human body and bodily functions immediately caused concern over the diminishing patient's role as a source of information (cf. sections 5. in Chapter Two and 1. in this chapter). The subsequent introduction of the equipment that tested smaller and smaller parts of the body with greater and greater precision (cf. sections 5. in

Chapter Two and 1. in this chapter) widened the gap, on the one hand, between a patient and his/her body and between a patient and a physician on the other. As regards the former, in modern clinics, patients became disembodied while their body-samples were to be studied in abstraction from him/her.

Concerning the latter, the biomedical model of medicine as well as medical education drew physicians away from their patients as treating their bodies came to be viewed not only as scientifically motivated (cf. section 6.) but also easily managed (cf. section 3.). Yet, as Armstrong (1984) observes, such one-dimensional perception of a patient has been changing from the fifties (1984: 739). Apart from the bodily sphere where diseases manifest themselves also the social sphere and its influence upon the patient's health came to be acknowledged. The author of this "boldest attempt" (Armstrong 2002: 66) was Michael Balint (1956) who maintained that localizing bodily manifestations was not enough to diagnose a patient. He claimed that what was missing was the elicitation of information about symptoms which then had to be placed against the background of the patient's experience (Balint 1956). Consequently, observation began to be accompanied by patients' interviews which were to "illuminate the dark spaces of the mind and social relationships" (Armstrong 1984: 739). While diagnosing, physicians examined patients' bodies to discern any signs of a disease and listened to the patients' accounts of symptoms. This way, although Cartesian dualism of mind and body (cf. section 2.) was not eliminated, the mind component was granted significance in the assessment of the patient's condition.

The separation of signs and symptoms as part of the biomedical model was also seen in a new light. While a sign was still associated with a lesion, a symptom received new meaning as it was linked to the patient's identity. As Armstrong (2002) observes, "[t]he patient was beginning to have a voice – and an existence – independent of pathological lesion" (2002: 65). Such a change in perception paved the way not only to the acknowledgement of the role of the patient's account but also to subsequent improvement in the quality of doctor-patient communication (cf. Armstrong 2002: 67–70). Eventually, the change gave rise to two conceptual frameworks, namely "illness-centered medicine and person-centered" approach which marked the shift from the treated illness and "a pathologically changed part of the body or a part-function of the body" to the treated patient and "expressions of patient's unique individuality, his tensions, conflicts, and problems" (Balint et al. 1984 [1970]: 26). This clear differentiation led to further formulations which, although in various forms, shared the underlying criticism of the biomedical model and advocated openness to the patient's experience. For example, according to Graca Pereira and Thomas Smith (2006), the biopsychological model by George Engel (1977) was based upon the premise that the diagnosis of a disease is incomplete without the consideration of the psychological and social aspects of the patient's life (2006: 455; cf. Hunter 1991: 21; Quill 1983). Such a holistic approach was in direct opposition to the reductionist biomedical model which took only biological facts as pertinent in the treatment of a disease (cf. Pellegrino 2001: 83).

In a study of the literature devoted to patient-centered medicine, Nicola Mead and Peter Bower (2000) enumerate five points in which this alternative model differs from the biomedical one: bio-psychosocial perspective, the patient-as-person, sharing power and responsibility, therapeutic alliance and the doctor-as-person. Firstly, the patient's condition should be considered with regard to a composite of biological, psychological and social factors of one's life, which is a reiterated assumption of the biopsychological model by Engel (1977). In other words, "illness and disease are [not] coterminous" (Mead and Bower 2000: 1088; illness/disease, cf. section 2). Secondly, the same illness can be experienced differently by different people. Consequently, while in the biopsychological model an attempt is made to understand the patient's illness in all its multidimensionality, "the patient-as-person" aims at determining "the individual experience of illness" (Mead and Bower 2000: 1089). Thirdly, following Mead and Bower (2000), patient-centeredness redefines the doctor-patient relation towards more cooperation and shared decision-making. This entails more active participation of the patient in the process of diagnosis and treatment. Fourthly, the physician's attitude towards the patient is believed to affect patient's compliance with doctor's recommendations and the overall result of a therapy. It follows that the fulfillment of this particular condition rests primarily upon a physician.

The last point can be treated as a supplement to the previous one in that it emphasizes positive features displayed by a doctor, which may also stimulate and streamline contacts with patients. While "therapeutic alliance" specifies the relationship between the two parties in terms of the success of treatment, "doctor-as-person" underscores doctor's personality traits which may contribute to the positive outcome of the interaction. Consequently, the new emerging model challenged the widely held assumption that treating dysfunctions or conditions was all that medicine should be about. According to Louis Dubertret (2006), patient-centeredness was "a therapeutic revolution with a strong impact on patient-doctor relationships, medical education, … as well as the awareness of the rights and the duty of patients" (2006: 73).[34]

34 In Dubertret (2006), the model is referred to as *patient-based medicine* and it is viewed from the perspective of the components of a medical encounter. However, the model has the same underlying principles as in Mead and Bower (2000).

Furthermore, the new model of medicine and its many formulations found its reflection in the works of philosophers and ethicists of medicine. They also focused their attention on patients' complex and multi-faceted backgrounds that have to be taken into consideration. On that reasoning, what needs treatment are not diseases but ill people. Doctor's actions cannot be restricted only to the eradication of disease, as attending to the patient's experience is equally important. The quotes from works dealing with the alternative approaches such as: "people are ill as wholes and not as parts" (MacWhinney 1975: 176) and "treat the patient not the lab" (Hahn 1982; cf. Anspach 1988: 366) illustrate well the new mode of reasoning.[35] According to Armstrong (2002), "[t]he interface between the doctor and the patient was no longer the gap between an observing gaze and the anatomical space of the patient. The new medical perception interrogated the patient as a social space, as a body inhabiting a specific social milieu, but more important, as a space of subjectivity" (2002: 69). In other words, the medical gaze refocused from a lesion, scar, fracture, etc. to a whole person who suffers all the consequences of being ill. At the same time, as Pellegrino (2001) observes, the experience of illness was seen as missing part of the biomedical model (2001: 83). Furthermore, it also transpired that patient management could be taught and that the appropriate attitude towards patients could positively affect the quality of the doctor-patient relationship. From the point of view of a physician, his/her ethical code is supposed to be intrinsic to this particular profession which serves the ill and not conditions (Pellegrino 1979: 127). The physician is "to restore the patient's humanity, which has been wounded" (Kestenbaum 1982: 18) or, in Pellegrino's terms (2001), to return "wholeness" (2001: 88) to a person. Consequently, what medicine should strive for is the use of both science and social sciences in "the lived reality" of the patient to treat the body and values (Pellegrino 1976: 17). This way, the patient would become according to Victor Kestenbaum (1982: 20) "a subject of experience" underlying the humanization "of medicine and health care". Following these assumptions, alternative approaches to medicine, regardless of their names, refocused attention from the diseased body to the treated patient. What is more, the change in the perspective meant the substantial involvement on the part of a doctor who attended the patient and his/her experience.

35 In a similar vein, in a recent advertisement, Unicorn, a polish association supporting oncology, calls for donations with the slogan "Widzimy całego człowieka, nie tylko jego chorobę" ("We see the whole person, not only his/her disease" [translation mine, MZ]).

4.2. Patient-centeredness in practice

Apart from scholars of various disciplines, also educational authorities acknowledged the alternative strands in medical practice. There is a substantial body of literature discussing new subjects and courses for the students of medicine as a response to the above-mentioned changes. Kestenbaum (1982) observes that the close scrutiny under which the biomedical model has come prompted medical universities and schools to supplement the curricula with courses in social behavioral sciences (discussed by Jaye 2004), medical ethics and humanities (discussed by Warren 1984; Herman 2001; McCarthy 2003 and Bub 2004). The aim of these courses is to teach students to develop professional values and the understanding of the patient's experience of illness, so that they, in Yanling Huang and Siouzih Lin's (2000: 134) words, "learn to be human before learning to be a doctor", but also to sensitize doctors to the role of patients' identities in the process of diagnosis and treatment. The new initiatives include problem-based learning (Kenny and Beagan 2004) and a community-based approach to medical humanities (Donohoe and Danielson 2004) as well as a variety of literature- or narrative-based courses. In the former type of courses, students learn from individual case stories and are given a chance to transfer their knowledge directly in the form of community service.

As regards the latter, the rationale behind such research strands as *narrative medicine*, *narrative-based medicine* or *narrative bioethics* is that narratives prove to be helpful both for medical professionals and patients (discussed by Greenhalgh and Hurwitz 1988; Miles and Hunter 1990; Hunter et al. 1995; Mattingly 1998, and Skelton et al. 2000). First, medical students may read literary texts or write their own ones in an attempt to develop compassion and respect towards patients (studied by Charon et al. 1995; Marshall and O'Keefe 1995; Mathiasen 1997: 1223; Brady et al. 2002; George et al. 2006; Kumagai 2008). Secondly, patients themselves can through narratives communicate their experience of illness and feed back crucial information (cf. Rabinowitz et al. 1994: 2008; Halkowski 2006), something that doctors aim at. As Cheryl Mattingly (1994) rightly points out, "[w]e make as well as tell stories of our lives and this is of fundamental importance in the clinical world" (1994: 811). From a slightly different perspective, following Jane Harden (2000), patient-centered narratives only can also be divided into *clinical*, i.e., those presenting the patient as a research participant to other researchers, with a view to developing "appropriate interpretation", and *theory-building*, i.e., those where the patient is presented as an individual and seeking "appropriate care" (2000: 56). Narratives can also be written by doctors themselves, in order to reflect upon their activities and share their experience with others (examined by Pellegrino 1982; Trautmann 1982; Coles 1986; Horowitz et al. 2002, and Wear and Aultman 2005: 1056).

Furthermore, the discussion led to the establishment of a number of journals related to medical ethics and humanities (Kestenbaum 1982: 8–10). However, Franz Ingelfinger (1976) expresses his concern over the possible impact of these publications on the actual physicians' work. He claims that in order for any of the theories to be put into practice, they need to reach journals aimed at medical practitioners (Ingelfinger 1976: 1318).

Yet another reservation regarding the potential of new holistic approaches is Hunter's (1991), who notes that "no one disagrees [with the biopsychological model], yet little changes" (1991: 21). The reason for this situation is, in Hunter's (1991) opinion, the fact that the biomedical model as such does not exist. The difference between the two models (biomedical and alternative ones) is largely exaggerated and practicing only the biomedical one would be dangerous for patients (Hunter 1991: 21). Others claim that although there are other approaches to clinical medicine, the biomedical model is treated as "normal medicine" (Atkinson 1988: 181). It is constantly reproduced through both teaching and training and, therefore, has achieved "the status of a dogma" (Capra 1985: 164). Yet, according to Capra (1985), its influence reaches further than medical community, becoming also "the common cultural belief system" (1985: 164, cf. section 2.). In other words, it is a natural mode of thinking and part and parcel of medical practice (Atkinson 1988: 181). An example of the entrenched biomedical perspective is imaging disease as "it". As Paul Hodgkin (1985) observes, it seems to be ubiquitous not only in medical discourse but also in everyday language and it is difficult to think about a disease in different terms (1985: 1821).

Joseph Bensman and Robert Lilenfeld (1973) postulate that such a firmly grounded position of the biomedical model appears to be possible thanks to *habits of mind*. They define the notion as "approaches to the world, ... attitudes towards everyday life, and specialized attitudes, ... extensions of habits of thought that emerge and are developed in the practice of an occupation, profession, or craft" (1973: 1). Specialized attitudes obtained "in the practice of an occupation, profession, or craft" are the key words in the definition, as they explicitly point to certain ways of thinking which are taught either through theory or through specific assignments. According to Kestenbaum (1982), these are "the backgrounds and horizons of meaning against which and through which ... scientific worlds take shape" (1982: 7). In light of this definition, the biomedical model as outlined above can be viewed as an example of such a habit of mind, which, although not explicitly mediated, is deeply entrenched both in medical schools and in clinical/hospital practice where students are immersed in medical culture. For instance, the model may affect the type of questions to be asked, modes of reasoning and interpretation, and treatment of data. In order to become habits of mind, these choices need to be continuously repeated, a condition to which clinical environment is conducive. As a consequence, habits of mind become "second nature", automatically triggered reactions which seem natural (Kestenbaum 1982: 7). The fact that the biomedical model has been subject to scrutiny and engendered alternative approaches confirms its status of the habit of mind. What is more, its deeply ingrained nature enables to understand its taken-for-granted status in medical reality.

5. Incommensurability of discourses

There seems to be, however, one more reason for this dominant position of biomedicine, namely the incommensurability of two discourses which can be associated with the biomedical and the alternative model(s) respectively (discussed by Rawlison 1982; Hunter 1991 and Atkinson 1995). To explicate the nature of the problem, Paul Atkinson (1995) refers to the notion of *voice* (originally developed by Brian Torode 1984, cited in Atkinson 1995: 111) to denote different worldviews orienting speakers towards reality in particular ways. In this context, Elliot Mishler's (1984) distinction between *the voice of medicine* and *the voice of the lifeworld* seems relevant. According to the author, while the latter refers to the patient's account of the experience of illness, the former is the doctor's perspective. In such an approach, physicians are regarded as "applied bioscientists", "collectors and analyzers of technical information elicited from patients", while patients are "passive object[s] responding to the stimuli of a physician's queries" (1984: 10). In his study of doctor-patient communication, Mishler (1984) points to the dominant position of *the voice of medicine*. In Mishler's (1984) own words, *the voice of medicine* can be compared to "the technical-scientific standpoint of the biomedical model" which interrupts *the voice of the lifeworld*, "the concerns of everyday life" (1984: 6). Atkinson (1995) refers to the former voice as decontextualized (1995: 129) and it seems to be a keyword, as what is focal in this viewpoint is a disease viewed as free from its milieu (cf. Mishler 1984: 192). He (1995) also offers other sets of opposites, namely *personal experience* and *textbook science* or *the voice of science* and *the voice of experience* which all seem to follow the underlying dichotomies of the biomedical model (cf. section 2.).[36]

36 As there are different voices, so are discourses. Fleck (1979) distinguishes *journal science*, *textbook science*, *vademecum science* and *popular science* whose modes of mediation depend on the audience to whom the knowledge is addressed.

Although Atkinson (1995) uses Mishler's (1984) voices in the context of interactions in the doctor-patient dyads, such a distinction seems to be universal in medical discourse in general, referring to texts and modes of behavior as well. Hunter's (1991) book also includes a subsection devoted to the issue of incommensurability of discourses. The title *One illness, two stories* illustrates well the yawning gap between patient's and doctor's discourses, which can be extended to *the voices of the lifeworld/science* and alternative/biomedical models respectively. The patient's account is, according to Hunter (1991), a personal story of an experienced ailment.

Consequently, illness is described here from the perspective of its influence on the patient's life. The other discourse, i.e., from the doctor's perspective, is totally different. It is the patient's account seen through the biomedical lenses which depersonalize his/her experience and select only necessary information pertinent to the diagnosis. What is more, the account is phrased in a specialized vocabulary. This way, the patient's perspective becomes "distorted and flattened" (Hunter 1991: 13; cf. Kleinman 1988; Poirier and Brauner 1988: 5; 1992: 116–117; Condrau 2007: 529; Kumagai 2008: 655).

All in all, although describing the same medical fact, the two discourses originate from two different underlying worldviews and have different aims. The patient's account is the story about illness, out of which a doctor constructs the story about disease. Yet, as Hunter (1991) observes, the patient's story is neither changed for the other nor translated. "Neither [of them] can be comprehended or satisfactorily reduced to other's terms" (1991: 124). "[T]he subjective experiential story and the outsider's objective, scientific interpretation" (Hunter 1991: 124) cannot be united because, as Lawrence McCullough (1989) claims, "medical language … [,] an abstract discourse about organs … is not about patients and their experience of illness" (1989: 103). Unfortunately, according to Hunter (1991), "[t]his difference, critical to the care of the patient, is seldom acknowledged in medicine" (1991: 14), which, in turn, perpetuates the taken-for-grantedness of the biomedical model. For Mary Rawlison (1982), however, it is not the incommensurability of the discourses but the fact that medicine uses "scientific language concerning itself only with observable and measurable physical findings … inadequate to its own practice" (1982: 83). This language deals only with the body and abstracts away from any contextualization of its primary subject.

Consequently, according to Rawlison (1982), medicine focuses on biological processes and pathological lesions but does not place them against the background of those whose bodies are affected (1982: 83). In Rita Charon's (1992) treatment of this problem, while doctors are said to "control, to contain, and to enclose ..., categorizing and reducing, patients enlarge and embroider". What Charon (1992) has in mind is that, for example, when, e.g., pain is discussed, the doctor will attempt at eliciting its details such as what kind of pain it is, how long it has been present, etc. whereas the patient will focus rather on its very experience. In other words, the doctor will try to use the available terms and notions to translate it into the language of medicine which will allow the diagnosis while the patient will, not limited by the discourse, focus on his subjective perception of the problem (1992: 116–117; see also Poirier and Brauner 1988: 5; Donnelly and Hines 1997: 1045–1046, and Kumagai 2008: 655). This view is also shared by McCullough (1989: 124), who notes that patients and physicians avail themselves of two different languages, of illness and disease respectively, and that neither party can employ the language of the other.

To summarize, according to the authors dealing with the incommensurability of discourses, medical discourse (be it the biomedical model, *the voice of science*, etc.) fails to acknowledge the fact that the aim of medicine is not to center exclusively around identifying and treating bodily dysfunctions but instead to view them against the background of a person and his/her experience. The focus of modern medicine should fall on the entirety of the patient as opposed to his/her fragmented body. In other words, when examining their bodies and biological processes, patients should be viewed not as objects of science but its subjects whose illness needs to be understood (cf. Pellegrino 2001: 31).

Due to the fact that the discourse of biomedicine comes as a natural choice, its reflections can also be found in medical texts (cf. section 6.). In this context, Hunter (1991) distinguishes between impersonalization and reification in the approach to a patient. By impersonalization Hunter (1991) understands a symbolical transformation of a patient into a medical narrative. It is a story that contains information about disease manifestations in a given patient and subsequent treatment which in medical community "comes to *be* [original emphasis] a patient" (Hunter 1991: 135). However, patients tend to be discursively equaled with a disease and there are several causes of such a state of affairs. Firstly, the incommensurability of the discourses appears to be part and parcel of Western medicine (Hunter 1991: 134). The biomedical model adopted there is conducive to the view of diseases as entities (cf. section 2.) and focuses solely on their manifestations in patients as opposed to their experience of illness. Secondly, it is claimed that in emergency, what counts is a disease or a condition to be treated and not the patient's experience. Thirdly, such objectification is supposed to help physicians to distance themselves emotionally from their task (cf. section 3.). As a result, treating disease and not the patient's suffering reduces the emotional load accompanying patient management:

> The person who becomes a case of bowel cancer is a problem in therapeutics to be addressed, but a person who has become the bowel cancer itself is a fait accompli. Bowel cancer is a congeries of qualities and events with a known course requiring physical attention but no investment of self (Hunter 1991: 137).

Yet, if modern medicine treats pathological changes exclusively, then it is only a step away from identifying patients with these changes. "Without a saving recognition of the reality and persistence of the patient experience and its incommensurability with its medical interpretation, the diagnosis replaces the case history as an representation of a patient" (Hunter 1991: 136). Therefore, turning the patient's account into a medical text about his/her disease exemplifies "abstraction", which is typical of medicine. What should not be allowed, however, is treating patients as disease entities (as discussed by Hunter 1991: 136 and Mead and Bower 2000: 1089). Unfortunately, as will be demonstrated in the next section, the language of modern medicine reflects the biomedical model. It is what the biomedical mode of reasoning forces on medical discourse, what sociologists of medicine question and what alternative models strive to change.

6. Contemporary medical discourse and case reports

The currently practiced model of medicine as well as the character of medical education are reflected in the contemporary medical discourse. As Kenny and Beagan (2004) claim, it has become to be widely recognized as neutral, economical and depersonalized (2004: 1072). Even the titles of papers devoted to the language of medical publications are indicative of the problem: *Why are medical journals so badly written?* (Albert 2004) or *The surgeon as a scientific writer* (Anaya-Prado et al. 2006). Some of the accusations leveled at medical discourse specify particular linguistic choices, e.g., to a large extent the notorious use of the Passive Voice (cf. Albert 2004; Kenny and Beagan 2004), as the resources to be blamed for the present situation. Renee Anspach (1988) and Nuala Kenny and Brenda Beagan (2004) observe that the authors tend to textually omit patients while describing biological processes taking place in their bodies and the treatment they undergo. The textual absence of those who are diagnosed and treated is also possible when technology is treated as the agent (cf. Anspach 1988: 366; Kenny and Beagan 2004: 1074f.). In her study of case presentations, Anspach (1988) found that medical equipment and diagnostic procedures are presented as "revealing" or "showing" particular results of studies.[37] In such a presentation,

37 Case presentations are highly conventionalized oral descriptions of patients and their diseases, which are performed by clinicians and medical students in clinical settings

it is not only machines or procedures whose role is underscored but also the data which, obtained in this way, are supposed to be credible and objective. The feature of emphasizing the role of data, i.e., it is data that "show", "prove" or "reveal", has been also attested in other varieties of scientific discourse (see Hyland 2001; Martinez 2001). To describe this characteristic Jonathan Potter (1996) coined the term "data primacy" (1996: 153). He claims that the fact that the Agent is deleted from the text contributes to rendering the information objective and independent from human involvement (Potter 1996: 153). Also Nigel Gilbert and Michael Mulkay (1984) hold that scientists "construct texts in which the physical world seems regularly to speak, and sometimes to act, for itself" (1984: 56). In case presentations (and medical texts in general), this feature is linked to another one, namely the removal of agency. In this case, the sentences in which diagnostic procedures and treatment are described do not include the Agent who performs these actions. Again, what is emphasized here are the performed actions and their correct choice but not the person who performs them. In general, the research on the use of various impersonal constructions in scientific discourse indicates that their aim is to focus on what is being studied (as studied by Bazerman 1988; Potter 1996 and Luzón Marco 2000). On the basis of the history of the development of medical practice, it may also be assumed that as the specialization of medicine progressed and the methods of treatment improved, illness (Dubertret 2006: 75) and various medical procedures rather than people who perform these procedures became more emphasized in texts (Ashcroft 2000: 288). That being said, the Passive Voice seems to serve its purpose, i.e., drawing attention to medical facts and treatment and hiding the "humble servants of the discipline" (Hyland 2001: 209; cf. section 3. in Chapter One).

Following the researchers' claim that the ways of speaking and writing to which medical students are exposed to during medical training dictate certain modes of reasoning concerning patients and medical knowledge (as discussed by Anspach 1988: 359; Donnelly and Hines 1995: 1045, and Kenny and Beagan 2004:1075f.), the central position of modern medical equipment, medical tests and the data they provide in textual representation may also be the consequence of the attitudes and values developed by students in the course of medical studies. As has been demonstrated, the activities and tasks assigned to students during hospital and clinical training are supposed to teach them how to handle difficult

---

(cf. Atkinson 1995). Although different from case reports in that they are delivered orally, case presentations bear significant resemblance to their written counterparts both in the form and content (see Anspach 1988; Hunter 1991 and Atkinson 1995: 90ff.).

and stressful situations through emotional detachment and various depersonalizing techniques. In the context of written medical discourse, the Passive Voice is regarded as an example of such techniques. Yet, as the researchers observe, the notorious use of this linguistic resource allows for such bizarre situations when there is no reference either to patients or to the very physicians and the only active participant in a description is *the chest tube bubbling* (Kenny and Beagan 2004: 1074). As Suzanne Poirier and Daniel Brauner (1988) observe, "a written and oral style that does not use „I" or active verb forms with which to discuss a patient discourages a sense of medicine as a personal, active, and interactive enterprise" (1988: 6). Another depersonalizing device is used when the results of the tests are given. These are reported either as "attributes" (Atkinson 1995: 107) of patients or the patients are even not referred to. Some authors of medical texts also tend to refer to patients as *cases*. In medical texts, the word *case* is used to denote an individual occurrence of a particular disease, but there are studies which document using the word to refer to patients, especially in spoken discourse (cf. Hunter 1991; Grice and Kramer-Dahl 1992: 73; Fowler 1996; Atkinson 1997). This suggests treating a patient as "the object of some disease entity" (Mead and Bower 2000: 1089) or reducing him/her to the disease he/she suffers. It may also lead to other naming practices of this kind used among health professionals (as studied by Anspach 1988). As Roger Fowler (1996) rightly observes, the impersonality of the *case* word or other objectifying terms referring to patients does not seem to be suitable for speaking or writing about such subjects as ailing patients and their experience. From such a perspective, they "lose his or her individuality, and … [are] subsumed in an aggregate of people", for instance in "the pseudo-locative phrase 'in the majority of cases'" (1996: 128–129). Even in guides to medical writing it is stated explicitly that "a case is a particular instance [while] … a patient is a person" (Matthews and Matthews 2008: 135, see also DeBakey and DeBakey 1983; Wodak 1996: 26, and McEwen 2009: 103) and that these two cannot be used interchangeably. Irene McEwen (2009) explains further that the case is "the patient's condition, including the therapeutic and personal consequences of that condition" (2009: 103). The word may also suggest identifying the patient with "a clinical problem rather than a human being who has an essential role in decision making and outcomes" (2009: 103). The last feature of medical discourse that is supposed to reduce the emotional load are acronyms. In this case, as Kirmayer (1988) notes, the whole meaning that the name of a disease encodes is reduced to a set of letters which may seem neutral in value to patients and physicians (1988: 61).

As regards case reports specifically, similarly to the case reports from the previous centuries, also those from the twentieth century have the hallmarks of the developing medicine as a field of study and profession. According to the definition of the genre of case report, it is composed of three parts, each of which with its own purpose (cf. section 8. in Chapter One). Following this structure, contemporary case reports begin with a brief introduction of a patient and his/her current condition presented in the third person. It needs to be emphasized that the patient's account of his/her state of health is reworked into the doctor's discourse (cf. section 5.), "adopt[ing] an objectified and technical lingo" (Hurwitz 2006: 231). Next comes the part dealing with the examination of a patient. As Hurwitz (2006) notes, this section is usually a description of the outcome of tests of various sorts, with pure observation (palpation, feeling, etc.) limited to the minimum. The dominance of such material reflects the widespread application of modern medical equipment, which allows to measure and/or observe every function and element of the human body respectively. This way, according to Hunter (1991), "[w]ith the advances of science, medicine ... has moved to the construction of pathophysiological plots" (1991: 172; see also Baron 1985: 607). Yet, even the textual representation of such a phenomenon merits some attention. In their diachronic study of medical case reports, Taavitsainen and Pahta (2000) report that what distinguishes the twentieth century case reports from those one hundred years older is the almost invisible authorial presence (2000: 67; cf. Hurwitz 2006: 236; Gunnarsson 2009: 60–61). Taavitsainen and Pahta (2000) note that in modern case reports, the authorial comments are restricted only to the beginnings and endings of texts. The middle part, which contains tests results, is presented in a "matter-of-fact" mode, excluding the presence of the author and relying on the objectivity of data rendered by machines (2000: 69). This view is also shared by Britt-Louise Gunnarsson (2009) when she observes that in the twentieth century medical texts "[t]here is an abundance of numbers and names of drugs and devices" (2009: 61) or, from a more general perspective, by Barbara Hoekje (2007), who refers to medical discourse as "based in supremacy of technology and science" (2007: 333).

Consequently, the twentieth-century case reports are characterized by a neutralized position of the author while the focus falls on the diagnostic procedures and the performed treatment. What is more, while other studies associated impersonality and objectivity with developing diagnostic possibilities (e.g., by Ashcroft 2000; Dubertret 2006) and the specificity of medical education (e.g., by Beagan 2000), here the researchers attribute these features to the growing medical community and the fact that the worldwide readership of the contemporary professional medical journals cannot be compared to the close community of scholars to whom the nineteenth century case reports were written. Therefore, as Taavitsainen and Pahta (2000) point out, nowadays, the mode of writing case reports is more detached and impersonal (2000: 72). These results have been also confirmed by Margaret Van Naerssen's study (1985) of medical records, whose structure and content are very similar to case reports. Among the features of this text-type Van Naerssen (1985) mentions specialized vocabulary, abbreviations and the low frequency of words referring to patients.

As regards case reports, the fragment with the greatest frequency of patient references is Introduction in which his/her symptoms are described. However, even here the account is presented either with a doctor slant or is scant (Hurwitz 2006: 235; cf. Van Naerssen 1985: 62–63), often being marked with the words: "the patient complained of…".[38] The reason of such a state of affairs, in Jane Macnaughton and Martyn Evans's (2004) view might be, apart from physicians' lack of time to write lengthy accounts, "a reluctance to contaminate the factually indisputable with the experientially unverifiable" (2004: 57). As Macnaughton and Evans (2004) observe, the patient's experience in medical records is a disputable issue. Nevertheless, the fact that medical records have become increasingly accessible to patients has eradicated some of the value-laden vocabulary contained there and has initiated the debate over the status of the patient's voice in these purely scientific accounts of medical facts (2004: 58).

Concluding the discussion on contemporary medical discourse, it must be stressed that the genre of case report underwent significant changes. Hippocratic case reports were highly focused on the subject of study and the author revealed no emotional involvement. On the other hand, Galenic case reports were characterized by verbosity and more focus on the patient's point of view.

The seventeenth and eighteenth centuries saw even more preoccupation with patients' accounts in case reports. What was also characteristic of that period was the propensity of the authors to write about curious medical phenomena to pique readers' interest. However, the discourse about diseases changed with the introduction of pathological anatomy at the turn of the nineteenth century. This was coupled with the growing importance of observation and developing technology, which offered more and more accurate images of the human body and recordings of its functions (cf. Hurwitz 2006). New diagnostic devices made the body transparent and allowed accurate assessment while medical sciences directed where the medical gaze should be focused. What is more, developing medical knowledge and modern equipment determined what counted as reliable data, which diminished the role of patients' accounts while the very patients became to be treated as "quantifiable material" (Gunnarsson 2009: 61). All these factors contributed to the establishment of the biomedical model, a certain viewpoint on diseases and patients.

---

38 This issue will be discussed in detail in the analytical part of the present work.

On the other hand, the specificity of medical education can also exert influence on how doctors mediate their knowledge, which is reflected in the content and form of medical texts. In this light, the genre of case report became an account of a disease as manifested in pathological changes whose presence is rendered visible by means of various diagnostic procedures. It does not, however, consider the patient's experience of illness. According to Hunter (1991), "the published case report make[s] no accommodation to the patient's experience and ignore[s] its incommensurability with the medical version ... [it] present[s] (1991: 144). Each developmental point of the genre of case report, characterized by the differences in the authorial stance, patient status and the understanding of disease, reflected changes in modes of reasoning in medicine and science in general. It follows that at certain points in the history of medicine, its crucial notions changed, i.e., were reconstructed and then further reproduced in medical practices until the next discovery.

Finally, the selected studies which have examined medical texts in general or case reports in particular merit attention. Although it can be said that they all concern the relation between form and content (rather than, for instance, focus quantitatively on particular linguistic features, cf. distinctions made in section 7. in Chapter One), the picture of medical discourse they reveal is rather one-dimensional. On the one hand, there are studies in which authors enumerate typical features of medical texts and add some impressionistic comments (e.g., Donnelly and Hines 1997; Albert 2004; Anaya-Prado et al. 2006). Their aim is not, however, to discuss thoroughly a given genre as conditioned by the context of its production but rather to outline some issues of concern and suggest possible solutions to the problems under examination. On the other hand, there are studies dealing with case reports specifically (or related genres) but from various perspectives. Hunter's (1991) description of the case report genre, though very detailed (accounting for its aims, structure and conventions of writing) and containing interesting observations, is not supported by any linguistic data. As regards Nowell-Smith's (1995) study, she does provide some examples of texts but only to illustrate the facts from the history of medicine she discusses. Anspach's (1988) study of case presentations, by contrast, includes the analysis of selected linguistic features of this speech genre. However, she comments only briefly on the contextual factors and their possible influence on the form and content of the examined case presentations. Yet another type of study is exemplified by the one by Hurwitz (2006). It offers a comprehensive account of the changes that the case report genre underwent and, though adopting a literary perspective, provides some valuable insights into the language of the said texts.

A separate body of research on medical discourse in general and case reports in particular constitute various studies from a diachronic perspective, for instance Taavitsainen and Pahta's (2000) study of case reports. This paper differs from the others in two respects.[39] Firstly, as opposed to Hunter's (1991) and Hurwitz's (2006) papers where specific modes of conveying information are examined, here particular linguistic means are isolated and analyzed with respect to the effect they produce. Moreover, in other papers, more attention was given to the intellectual atmosphere and development of medicine at particular points in time than to contemporary case reports and their contextual underpinnings. In Taavitsainen and Pahta's study (2000), both historical and present-day backgrounds receive equal amount of interest.

The last section of the present chapter will attempt to summarize the facts concerning medical discourse in its historical and contemporary perspectives with regard to the social constructionism theory.

7. Socially constructed biomedical discourse

Chapter Two and the present chapter, which deal with case reports against the historical and contemporary backgrounds respectively, have demonstrated how scientific discourse is shaped by a given discipline. It has been exemplified how a stage of development of a given field of study dictates certain modes of reasoning, classifying, naming etc. As Eliot Freidson (1970) rightly points out, "many of the today's medical conceptions of illness are not the same as they were in the "modern" medicine of yesterday and … at least some of tomorrow's medicine will contradict the today's" (1970: 210). Consequently, the change of form and content of medical case reports has been analyzed against the historical backdrop of discoveries and technological inventions which triggered the evolution of the perception and understanding of disease and the role of a patient. Two watersheds in the history of medicine are specifically pertinent to this work. The first one was the introduction of pathological anatomy which fixed the medical gaze on organs and tissues (cf. section 2. in Chapter Two). The other one was the birth of the clinic which, coupled with the modern diagnostic devices, defined the parameters of medical gaze (cf. sections 3. and 5. in Chapter Two).

According to Atkinson (1995), while "[t]he bedside remains as the original site of clinical understanding" (1995: 61), the modes of understanding were evolving with the advances of science and technology (cf. Foucault 2003: 54). As a result, each stage of the development found its manifestations in medical practice but also affected written medical discourse as a primary means of medical record. The genre of medical case reports underwent significant changes as well, both

39 Cf. also Taavitsainen and Pahta (1998) and Taavitsainen et al. (2002).

in how it was written and what it contained. This confirms Charles Bazerman's (1988) claim of the influence of a discipline on its discourse and tallies with other discipline- and genre-oriented studies (e.g., Atkinson 1992; Taavitsainen and Pahta 2000). Yet, apart from the fact that medical discourse reflects the present stage of development of medicine, it is also constructed and reproduced in everyday medical activities in which medical professionals are engaged. What is more, it is not a neutral discourse, but the one grounded in the current model of medical practice.

In section 1. in Chapter Two, a brief account of social constructionism has been given. According to Deborah Lupton (1994), although social constructionism has been present in sociological studies for quite a long time (e.g., Berger and Luckmann 1966), its application to research concerning the construction of reality and of the body has contributed to the growing popularity of the theory also among the sociologists of medicine (1994: 11). To reiterate, within social constructionism two main strands can be isolated, namely how scientific knowledge and everyday reality are constructed (cf. Lupton 1994: 93). Biomedicine lends itself easily to the analysis within the framework of these two.

As regards scientific knowledge, medicine claims to be science which records natural phenomena in a unbiased manner (cf. Bazerman 1988 in section 5. in Chapter One). Such reasoning is based on two pairs of opposites: (1) objective/subjective and (2) nature and the individual's perception of nature. Following these, nature is objective and exists independently of people, but they can perceive it subjectively, each in its own way (cf. Greenhalgh 1988: 25).

The biomedical distinctions such as disease/illness and signs/symptoms (cf. section 2.) are anchored in the above-given basic differentiations. According to Gordon (1988), in the biomedical framework, disease is viewed as a "natural phenomenon", the patient's body as a nature's manifestation, while medical knowledge is accumulated and validated through scientific rationality, a naturalist method (1988: 24). The method is based upon the premise that something may be treated as a medical fact only if it lends itself to test and verification. This assumption explains why biomedicine favors biological explanations over the social or psychological ones (cf. Helman 1994: 102). Yet, the argument in favor of scientific medicine has been accepted only partially.

Some researchers disagree that "'there is nothing there' independent of social actors" (Atkinson 1995: 41) and that the knowledge about the human body and its aspects are socially constructed (as discussed by Hahn and Gaines 1985: 6; Atkinson 1988: 179 and Atkinson 1995: 42–43). What is constructed, however, is, for example, the biomedical understanding of certain processes and conditions. If this understanding is constantly reproduced, it becomes entrenched in medical practice and treated as natural and unquestionable medical knowledge. This way, as Lupton (1994) notes, "medical knowledge is regarded … as a series of relative constructions which are dependent upon the socio-historical settings in which their occur and are constantly renegotiated" (1994: 11).

How medical knowledge can be socially constructed and how meaning becomes "endless, ongoing, contingent accomplishment" (Garfinkel 1984: 1) is successfully exemplified by Atkinson (1988, 1995, 1997). Atkinson draws attention to the difficulty and complexity of interpretation of the results of medical tests rendered by various diagnostic machines. In his exploration of the hematologists' work, Atkinson (1995) observes that the analysis of blood smears and traces requires more than mere theory mastered in the course of medical studies. "[S]eeing is not straightforward" (1995: 68) as the visualizations that hematologists interpret are far from being simple. Apart from referring to the gained knowledge, they have to know "how to 'see' and 'what to look for'" (1995: 68). The skill itself is often supported by image enhancers which actually enable to create an image to be studied (as discussed by Lynch 1985a, 1985b, 1990). What is more, as Atkinson (1995) observes, in the very process of reading physicians often resort to additional reference sources such as atlases. They contain models for comparison which aid the process of interpretation, i.e., identifying, classifying and naming (1995: 68). Having created the image and discerned what was sought for, hematologists use appropriate linguistic means to describe the obtained image as credibly as possible.

To this end, specific vocabulary concerning colors, shades, sizes and count is necessary. These are words and phrases from the everyday language but with additional meanings understood only in this particular context. The specialized lexis is usually mastered during hospital training when students have the opportunity to use it (Atkinson 1995: 73). Consequently, the interpretation of such diagnostic material can be treated as "perceptual and cognitive tasks" (Atkinson 1995: 69) aided by external devices.

Similarly, the reading of images (or any other forms representing human bodily parts or functions), which are themselves conventional (Atkinson 1995: 63; cf. also Yoxen 1990: 282), is by no means a straightforward task and requires a lot of practice. Before any diagnosis can be made, the very image has to be obtained and then read according to available knowledge and descriptive means. Only then can it lend itself to medical assessment. Good examples can be interpreting X-rays (as analyzed by Pasveer 1989) and echocardiography (studied by Daly 1989) to name but a few. According to Bernike Pasveer (1989), these are processes where visual material does not render the body/bodily functions credible but reworks them (1989: 361).

What is more, what Jeanne Daly's study (1989) demonstrates is that very often specific tests are performed not because they are necessary but in order to reassure a patient, "facilitating the social" (1989: 115), if the physician's diagnosis is not convincing. In this case, medical discourse is supported by technology that is believed to present data more objectively. Pasveer's study (1989), on the other hand, points to the fact even the process of interpreting X-rays has been changing with the evolution of the device itself, medical knowledge in general and the profession of radiology in particular.

The aim of the presentation of the above-given studies (Atkinson 1988, 1995, 1997; Daly 1989; Pasveer 1989) has been to illustrate the role of modern technology in medical practice. According to Bjørn Hofmann (2001), advanced diagnostic devices generate concepts which help to identify and describe diseases, enable physicians to acquire knowledge about them but also offer means for their management (2001: 10). What is more, the first type of the activities enabled by technology, i.e., identifying and describing, is linguistic in nature. As Paul Atkinson observes, "[l]ooking, seeing and describing are linguistically organized activities" (1995: 74) that take part in the construction of scientific facts (cf. section 4. in Chapter One).

While the work of hematologists and other specialists who handle the interpretation of medical tests exemplifies the process of the construction of science (cf. Bazerman 1988 in section 5. in Chapter One), the construction of medical cases is a good example of the social construction of medical reality. According to Hunter (1991), "[i]n medicine, the case is the basic unit of thought and discourse" (1991: 51).

A case commences the whole process of diagnosis and treatment through gathering information, its interpretation and presentation (Hunter 1991: 68). It frames the patient's account of a disease into a story and retells it in the physician's discourse. There are two modes of case management. The first one is *working up a case* which basically aims at gathering necessary information from a patient and examining him/her in order to arrive at the right diagnosis. The other mode is case presentation (cf. section 6.). "As a fundamental ritual of academic medicine, the narrative act of case presentation is at the center of medical education and, indeed, at the center of all medical communication about patients" (Hunter 1991: 51).

Case presentations demonstrate interesting occurrences of particular diseases as manifested in individual patients or are simply used to present new patients to other members of a medical community. As noted by Anspach (1988), although case presentations are also delivered at conferences, during the consultation with a specialist or may be part of case records (1988: 360), much has been written particularly about oral case presentations during hospital rounds, when new patients are presented by students of medicine (cf. Anspach 1988; Hunter 1991; Atkinson 1995). According to Anspach (1988), the ability of the skillful presentation of a case lies at the top of medical professional's skills (cf. Hunter 1991: 57). It is the ability to convey necessary information in an appropriate mode to which novices are socialized (Anspach 1988: 359). In other words, the socialization encompasses not only what should be included in this presentation but also how it should be given.

The body of information in such a speech act must be sequentially arranged to resemble a narrative (cf. section 8. in Chapter One) and must include: relevant demographic facts, patient's history and physical examination, medical tests and treatment (Atkinson 1995: 100). What is more, each element has its own typical mode of presentation encoded in lexical and grammatical choices (cf. section 6.). For instance, the part in which the results of medical tests are given does not contain many references to the patient described. Tests results are, according to Atkinson (1995), "the litany of medical facts", "a formulaic element of case construction" (1995: 107), rendering the patient's body fragmented into various numbers and values. This way, the part exemplifies "the biomedical disaggregation or distribution of the body" (1995: 107).

As Van Naerssen (1985) notes, the constant reproduction of the format ensures that novices acquire the skill of presenting a case. On the one hand, the acquisition includes the style of a particular speech act, namely the narrative-like structure, as well linguistic resources which all contribute to the presentation of the information in a required mode. On the other hand, regarding the content, the genre employs specific concepts and distinctions which comply with the current medical model regulating modes of reasoning. This makes case presentation "a very powerful means for the reproduction [in this case] of orthodox biomedicine" (Atkinson 1988: 201) as lexical and grammatical choices, which are part of the desired form, "reveal tacit and subtle assumptions, beliefs and values concerning patients, medical knowledge, and medical practice to which physicians in training are socialized" (Anspach 1988: 359).

Comprising all the minutiae of his/her condition, a case presentation unites the fragmented information into a whole, i.e., the story about a patient, which is a medical construct itself. Along with taking cases and other case-related oral genres, case presentation belongs to "the discourse of bedside teaching", i.e., modes of talking (and writing) acquired to be utilized in the context where they are understood.

While case presentation is an example of oral genre that students are socialized into, Catherine Pettinari (1988) gives an account of the socialization into a written genre, namely operative reports. In this case, the process takes place during the internship of the fifth year surgical residents and Pettinari (1988) traces the evolution of their styles.

The residents learn not only what such a report should include but also how it should be written. The linguistic elements that are supposed to be acquired include: describing actions instead of states to present a replicable procedure, procedural discourse with successive activities, and descriptive means to present findings including "'creative' complex noun phrases" (Pettinari 1988: 99).[40] The use of such linguistic resources allows to foreground the essential information from the insider's point of view and, consequently, present information in a manner that is understood in this particular community.

These two examples of the socialization into medical culture (Anspach 1988; Pettinari 1988) demonstrate how students of medicine are taught what to look for, what to include and how to conventionally describe it. This way they create oral and written constructs which function as understandable units in a currently practiced model.[41] The fact that these medical constructs are constantly recycled allows Atkinson (1995) to refer to them as "circuits of discourse" (1995: 59). While in the case of hematologists, the skillful use of vocabulary is additional to the ability to discern appropriate data, case presentation combines lexico-grammatical choices and sequentiality which foreground the right choice of information. This way, the current model of medical practice is reproduced.

The aim of Chapter Three has been to present the present-day context of production and reproduction of medical discourse. Firstly, the biomedical model of medicine was described which lies at the heart of medical practice in Western societies. The model was discussed from the perspective of the sociology of medicine, which allowed to approach this framework critically and to reveal the underlying assumptions of its discourse. Secondly, a short characterization of medical education was given with particular attention to the attitudes and values the students of medicine are taught, both towards patients and the profession. Thirdly, patient-centeredness was introduced as an alternative to the dominating biomedical model. The account included the premises of the model and the results of its implementation in the selected areas of medical culture. Also an

40 These are long noun phrases describing the patient's body and/or including author's comments on observation (Pettinari 1988: 99)

41 The current biomedical model may be contrasted with other non-Western models which are culturally constructed (cf. subsection 4.1.), as "[m]odern medicine is not absolute: it is a social institution dominant in our time and place but not in others" (Freidson 1970: 210)

attempt was made to contrast the discourses of the dominating and alternative models. Finally, contemporary medical discourse in general and case reports in particular were briefly described. Here emphasis fell on their patient imaging as conditioned by the present biomedical model. In the following chapter, the analytical tools for the study of the patient persona in the case reports will be presented.

Chapter Four: Theoretical aspects of the analysis of medical case reports

The empirical part of the present work is comprised of two chapters. Firstly, in Chapter Five, the analysis of the compiled corpus of medical case reports will be presented and followed by the discussion of the results. Next, in Chapter Six, an attempt will be made to determine whether patient imaging as revealed in the study of the corpus can be corroborated or refuted by other readers of the texts in question. Lastly, the discussion of the results yielded in both stages will be given. The following chapter will be devoted to the theoretical grounding, which served as the basis for the construction of the analysis in Chapter Five and will start from the macro- and move on to micro-perspective on the texts. Consequently, Chapter Four will give an account of the hierarchical levels of medical description, two modes of disease presentation (Blois 1984), its semiotics, the definition of metaphor and its types illustrated by relevant examples from medical discourse, as well as selected analytical tools necessary for the analysis of the corpus.

1. Hierarchical levels of medical description

According to Alan McKee (2003), textual analysis attempts to delve into how individuals understand reality, i.e., "to gather information about sense-making practices" (2003: 68). Consequently, medical discourse constitutes one of the many vantage points which dictate certain modes of thinking (2003: 128) and medical texts exemplify such "making sense" of the world in the medical context. On this reasoning, as Suzanne Fleischman (1999) observes, not only is disease a "biological event" but it is also a social construct of various medical and non-medical practices (medical texts among them), which reflect the past and current medical knowledge (1999: 11; cf. Rosenberg 1985, 1989). Therefore, the following three sections will be devoted to various aspects of how disease may be described, moving from macro- to micro-structures.

Marsden Blois (1984) demonstrates how disease can be presented in terms of the part/whole relation (cf. Van Dijk 1980 and section 4.). According to Teun Van Dijk (1980), employed in many cognitive processes, this relation can emphasize either parts as isolated from a whole or a whole as assembled of its parts (1980: 3). In this perspective, a disease can be analyzed at various hierarchical levels of medical description, depending on which constituent part of the human body is affected. Blois (1984) isolates the following stages in this description:

Table 1. Hierarchical levels of medical description (after Blois 1984: 113)

Level	Description
Level 0	Patient as a whole
Level 1	Major patient part: e.g., chest, abdomen, head
Level 2	Physiologic system: e.g., cardiovascular system, respiratory system
Level 3	System part, or organ: e.g., heart, major vessels, lungs
Level 4	Organ part, or tissue: e.g., myocardium, bone marrow
Level 5	Cell: e.g., epithelial cell, fibroblast, lymphocyte
Level 6	Cell part: e.g., cell membrane, organelles, nucleus
Level 7	Macromolecule: e.g., enzyme, structural protein, nucleic acid
Level 8	Micromolecule: e.g., glucose, ascorbic acid
Level 9	Atoms or ions: e.g., sodium ion

Following the description as demonstrated in Table 1, the departures in the patient's condition are features of diseases, which can be considered with reference to a patient in general or to the specific parts of his/her body affected by these changes. On this reasoning, while anxiety, fever or anorexia pertain to the whole patient's condition, the pain which occurs in angina pectoris can be felt in given body-parts (Blois 1984: 112). The levels in Table 1 start with the whole body, go through systems and organs where bodily sensations of various sorts can be experienced, and end with cellular, molecular and atomic levels at which biological processes can be inspected. These processes may not always cause directly observable or felt signs, yet very often certain bodily or mental reactions are the consequences of the abnormalities at these lower levels. Therefore, while at levels 0–4, the description may refer to specific symptoms or reactions which patients have, the other levels describe changes not directly affecting patients' experience (levels from 5 to 9).

Such a division is reflected in the ways patients describe symptoms, e.g., "I hurt (ache) all over" (Blois 1984: 113), and in the ways they are described in medical texts. What Blois (1984) also pays attention to is the generality and, consequently, validity of information provided at different levels. As the description at the upper levels considers a general constitution, for instance nervousness or dizziness, it serves as prefatory information. Lower levels, on the other hand, refer to certain biological changes measured and assessed by means of various tests that are believed to provide objective account of the patient's state (cf. Hofmann 2001: 12). This mode of reasoning goes in line with the biomedical model and, consequently, its separation of subjective symptoms from objective signs (cf. section

2. in Chapter Three). Following Leon Eisenberg (1977), it assumes that "patients suffer illness; physicians diagnose and treat 'diseases' ... [where] illnesses are *experiences* [original emphasis] of disvalued changes in states of being ... [while] diseases, in the scientific paradigm of modern medicine, are abnormalities in the structure and function of body organs and systems" (1977: 43). The phrase "disvalued changes" emphasizes the decreasing credibility of the patient's account in the history of medicine and, at the same time, constitutes the hallmark of the biomedical approach (Blois 1984: 118; cf. sections 2. and 4. in Chapter Three).

Yet, those levels which score lower on the scale of biomedical credibility cannot be removed altogether. It is because the process of diagnosis cannot proceed solely with its focus on the lower levels, but it must "trac[e] a causal chain" (Blois 1984: 119) from top to bottom. Therefore, the difference between the information given at particular levels appears to be not categorical, i.e., valid/invalid, but more or less objective (Blois 1984: 121), which has to do with the way this information has been obtained. The effect of this hierarchical description on patient imaging in the case reports under study will be demonstrated in the analytical part of the present work.

2. Modes of disease presentation

Apart from the division of medical description into levels pertaining to different constituents of the human body, Blois (1984) proposes two modes by means of which a disease can be presented, namely a *nominalist* and *psychological* mode.[42] While the former treatment describes a disease in terms of its "attributes" (Blois 1984: 92) which are enumerated in abstraction from the patient, the latter views it as a collection of changes as experienced by a particular individual.

Associated with Plato who attempted to classify diseases, the *nominalist* mode treats a disease as an "isolatable entity" (cf. disease as "it" in section 2. in Chapter Three; Pasveer 1989: 375) which manifests itself unchangingly in all patients. Moreover, it is viewed as a thing determined by a list if its attributes. Blois (1984) proposes the following schema for this mode: "(Disease A || symptom1, symptom 2,...sign1, sign2,...course,...)" (1984: 98) where all the elements make up a given disease.

42 The label *psychological* was originally introduced by Owsei Temkin (1968), but the mode is also referred to as *biographical* or *historical* (Cohen 1961). Eventually, Blois (1984) decides on the label *attributive* which should point to the patient's attributes making up a disease. This decision, however, appears to be confusing as Blois (1984) uses the word *attributes* also earlier while describing the other mode, i.e., the *nominalist* one. Therefore, in order to avoid misunderstanding, in the present work, the label *psychological* will be used to refer to the mode alternative to the *nominalist* one.

Consequently, the said mode allows to describe a disease as a purely abstract concept that is separate from its context, i.e., the patient (Blois 1984).[43] The *psychological* mode, on the other hand, which is attributed to Hippocrates, has a different perspective. Although he acknowledged the view of illness as a thing, his case histories gave the account of individual patients suffering from particular diseases. As a result, in such a treatment, a patient and his/her illness become the locus of attention. This approach can be presented in the following way: "(John Smith ill || change1, change2, change3,…)" (Blois 1984: 100). In comparison to the *nominalist* account, this mode does not center around a disease as abstracted from its context but a disease as occurring in a particular patient experiencing changes of his/her state, which should be referred to as illness if the distinctions from the sociology of medicine are adopted (cf. section 2. in Chapter Three). The difference between the two modes can be exemplified by the different ways in which doctors and patients may refer to the same medical condition. As exemplified by Gerhard Nijhof (1998), while a patient may talk about stomach ache, the doctor may refer to it as gallstone colic, thus, reducing the experience of a state to an entity carrying particular meaning in medical discourse (1998: 739). This entity can be enumerated and referred to in abstraction from the patient, as opposed to particular sensations, i.e., "attributes that constitute his illness" (Blois 1984: 100). Clearly then, the difference between the two modes appears to match the biomedical distinctions between signs/symptoms and disease/illness (cf. section 2. in Chapter Three), though Blois (1984) does not use these terms following the distinctions of the sociology of medicine. Table 2 below summarizes these distinctions with relation to the two above-defined modes of disease presentation:

Table 2. Disease presentation in the biomedical model

Subjective	**Objective**
illness – state experienced by the patient	disease – abstract concept described separately from the patient
symptoms – manifestations of an illness as experienced by the patient	signs – pathological changes in the patient's body
psychological mode – description of an illness from the perspective of the patient's individual experience	nominalist mode – a general description of a disease without reference to the patient

43 The underlying idea of the *nominalist* account of a disease is what in the theory of conceptual metaphor (Lakoff and Johnson 1980) is referred to as an ontological metaphor (cf. section 4.).

It has been already highlighted that contemporary case reports derive from Hippocratic case histories, as their aim is to describe individual occurrences of particular diseases in particular people. However, it will be demonstrated that the texts under study tend to present diseases in abstraction from those who undergo them. Yet, in the analysis, the acknowledgement of the structure of case reports (cf. section 1. in Chapter Five), hierarchical levels of medical description and modes of disease presentation is necessary, as patient imaging in these texts is not one-dimensional and the three aspects have a bearing on the form and content of the texts in question.

3. The semiotics of disease and illness

In section 2. in Chapter Three, the distinction between disease and illness has been made, which lies at the heart of the biomedical model. This differentiation is well illustrated by Fleishman (1999): "Illness incorporates our human perception and experience of somatic or mental disorders; disease removes the patient from the pathology" (1999: 7). In order words, while disease is a pathological change which can be analyzed in abstraction from the patient, illness is in itself an experience of the changed state and cannot be viewed as removed from its context. According to Fleishman (1999), such reasoning presupposes the separation of the suffering person from his/her condition. While disease can exist as an abstract, illness includes particular experience, hence "illnesses are personal and unique, [while] diseases abstract and cumulative" (1999: 7).

An interesting perspective of analyzing the concepts of disease and illness is proposed by Kathryn Staiano (1986). She explores how medicine is practiced among Black Caribs (also referred to as the Garifuna people) inhabiting the area from Belize to Nicaragua along the Caribbean coast of Central America. In her research, she draws on medical semiotics, which enables her to study the local system of signs of disease and illness and their interaction with the Western biomedical model. Staiano (1986) explicates medical semiotics as "the translation and interpretation of the physiological, behavioral, and linguistic signs which indicate health and illness" (1986: 1). She motivates the choice of the analytic framework by the interdisciplinary nature of semiotics. It provides researchers with metalanguage which enables them to study signs in various contexts as well as their forms and relations within or across systems (Staiano 1986: 7–8). Consequently, with regard to the process of semiosis, "illness functions as a communicative act" (Staiano 1986: 9) but the character of this communication is conditioned by its context.

Staiano's (1986) thorough analysis of the local medical practices is based upon the premise that they are cultural products grounded in the context of their production. Staiano (1986) adopts the Peircian approach to semiotics where the relation between signs and their referents is never fixed. It is a constantly changing process of semiosis (1986: xiii) in which signs of illness and disease are communicated, interpreted and negotiated. What is more, the signs function not in a straightforward but metonymic manner, i.e., " 'stand[ing] for' some greater whole" (1986: xi; cf. section 4.). Language wise, the signs may be studied with regard to their "expression" in broadly understood texts, for example their chronology and relation to other signs. The decision to use particular signs and not others depends on their availability in a particular medical system.

In the introduction to her ethnographic study, Staiano (1986) makes a number of comments about how the symbolism of disease and illness is reflected in language by means of syntax. According to Staiano (1986), it makes a difference if a person says "I am…" a diabetic, "I have" or "I suffer from…" diabetes.

As regards the first construction, such phrasing equates an illness with a patient, suggesting that the illness becomes his/her experience (Staiano 1986: 31; cf. Sayers 2002: 90). The second construction images a disease as possessed by a patient. It is in the patient, but it is not something that he/she experiences. Yet, according to Sue Estroff (1993), what these two constructions have in common is that they both suggest a "fusion of the self with the sickness, of diagnosis with identity …" (1993: 257). This view is also shared by Ewen Speed (2006), who studied discourses of mental health service users. For Speed (2006), the constructions in question image patients as "repositories of pathology" (Speed 2006: 30; see also Armstrong 1983 and Foucault 2003 [1973]). A similar example is also "to be diagnosed with" (cf. Fleischman 1999: 7), either from the patient's perspective, i.e., "she was diagnosed with…", or from the physician's, i.e., "we diagnosed…". Both these constructions point only to the presence of a disease in a patient but not to his/her experience. Additionally, regardless of whether a patient is textually present or absent, the two *diagnose*-phrasings exemplify the *nominalist* account of disease, treating it as an "isolatable entity" (cf. disease as "it" in section 2. in Chapter Three) located in a patient.

The last example, i.e., "I suffer from…" diabetes, explicitly refers to the fact that illness is experienced by a patient (Staiano 1986: 31). Yet, in contrast to the second construction, i.e., "I have", here the illness is not an entity, and as opposed to the first construction where the patient's identity and illness are merged. Therefore, as Fleischman (1999) concludes, "depending on the language employed, a person may be a suffering individual, possessor of a disease-object, or experiencer of a state of ill-health" (1999: 8). Furthermore, while the first and the third construction clearly acknowledge disease as the patient's experience, the second one portrays it as an independent entity (cf. section 2. in Chapter Three) analyzed outside the milieu of its existence.

Yet another semiotic mode of disease presentation is metonymic (cf. section 4.). It is when certain body-parts are coterminous with particular conditions of body or psyche., i.e., "I have too much blood" or "My blood is stagnating". For physicians these body-parts may often substitute patients, which is further encouraged by the biomedical model and its focus on localized biological changes (Staiano 1986: 27). Therefore, as Staiano (1986) concludes, "the human body is, at one and the same time, vessel of meaning and source of experience" (1986: 33).

4. Metaphor

It has been demonstrated in the two previous sections that the "the use of language to refer to something other than what it was originally applied to, or what it 'literally' means, in order to suggest some resemblance or to make a connection between the two things" (Knowles and Moon 2006: 1). In other words, metaphor describes a thing in terms of another thing, establishing a common ground between the two. According to Murray Knowles and Rosamund Moon (2006), there are three elements of metaphor: vehicle, topic and ground where a metaphor is the vehicle, its meaning is referred to as the topic, while the similarity between the two is the ground (2006: 7).

Following this distinction, in order to establish the link between the literal and the metaphorical a given metaphor should be studied with respect to its meaning. However, it should be noted that only when there is no doubt about the literal meaning can metaphorical meaning be determined (Knowles and Moon 2006: 3). Consequently, as Knowles and Moon (2006) explain, in the expression: "the white blood cells which help to fight off invading microorganisms" (2006: 7), the activity of microorganisms is compared to invasion. The common ground between the metaphor (invasion) and its meaning (the activity of a disease in a given location and manner, which damages health) is to appear and cause damage (2006: 7). What is more, imaging microorganisms as "invading" is an example of drawing on the vocabulary associated with war. This choice is by no means accidental as describing disease in military terms is widely used in medical discourse (cf. section 7. in Chapter One).

The publication of George Lakoff and Mark Johnson's book *Metaphors we live by* (1980) introduced a new perspective from which metaphors could be studied. The authors argued for the ubiquity of metaphors not only in language but also in people's activities and thinking, as "our conceptual system ... is fundamentally metaphorical in nature" (Lakoff and Johnson 1980: 3). This view is also shared by

Zoltán Kövecses, (2005) who claims that "metaphor is only derivatively a linguistic phenomenon" and that metaphors manifest themselves through language because they underlie the functioning of the brain (2005: 21). Knowles and Moon (2006) point to three important aspects of this approach. Firstly, although metaphors manifest themselves not exclusively in language, it proves to be a good material to study them. Secondly, metaphors are instrumental in conceptualizing certain abstract notions. Thirdly, while some metaphors might be characteristic of a given culture, others can be shared by different cultures. For instance, the above-presented phrase referring to microorganisms by means of military vocabulary is associated with Western societies (Knowles and Moon 2006: 25).

As far as the analysis of conceptual metaphors is concerned, instead of vehicle, topic and ground, source and target domains are identified. The former is where the metaphor originates while the latter is where the meaning is mapped on. Consequently, if the above-given phrase is considered again, here, the source domain is WAR, which is then drawn upon to describe microorganisms entering the body.[44]

In Lakoff and Johnsons's (1980) approach to metaphor, they isolate three types of metaphor – structural, orientational and ontological. Consequently, the example of microorganisms invading the body is an instance of the structural metaphor, in which "one concept is metaphorically structured in terms of another" (1980: 14). In other words, in order to make the activity of microorganisms more comprehensible, it is associated with something which is part of the human experience and with which a valid comparison can be drawn (cf. Knowles and Moon 2006: 31).

Another example of structural metaphor is metonymy, which concerns either referring to wholes in terms of their parts and vice versa or "naming by association" (Knowles and Moon 2006: 37). As exemplified by Knowles and Moon (2006), the former would be, for instance, referring to *workers* as *hands* while the later calling the *theatre* the *stage* (2006: 37). The difference between metonymy and the previously discussed metaphor is threefold. Firstly, while metonymy enables to refer to a thing in terms of the whole/part relation, according to Kövecses (2005), metaphor explicates "a more abstract concept (the target domain)" by means of "a more concrete one (the source domain)" (2005: 29).

In other words, in metaphor, the source domain offers specific lenses through which the target domain is viewed. Secondly, metaphor consists of two domains as opposed to metonymy which has only one domain of relation, i.e., between a

44 Conceptual metaphors are written using capital letters and the metaphorical concept comes first (Knowles and Moon 2006: 24).

whole and a part. Thirdly, the fact that in metonymy there is only one domain makes the relation between the elements "conceptually 'close'" (e.g., workers and hands) (Kövecses 2005: 29). In the case of metaphor, they are "'far' from each other in conceptual space", yet, as a result of the metaphor, they are brought together by some shared aspect (Kövecses 2005: 29).

Orientational metaphor, on the other hand, "organizes a whole system of concepts with respect to one another" (Lakoff and Johnson 1980: 14) using some form of spatial configuration. Here referring to patients as containers which draws on the container metaphor as introduced by Lakoff and Johnson (1980), would be a good example. In this metaphor, concepts are viewed as having an inside and outside and as containing other concepts/things. As Lakoff and Johnson (1980) explain, "[w]e are physical beings, bounded and set off from the rest of the world by the surface of our skins, and we experience the rest of the world as outside us. Each of us is a container, with a bounding surface and an in-out orientation" (1980: 29).

When the container metaphor is used in medical discourse, the source domain CONTAINER is mapped onto a patient who "contains" a disease. The concept of disease in a patient is utilized to describe a number of medical procedures or to give account of medical facts.[45] On the one hand, the patient's body tends to be viewed as a container in which diseases are localized and particular treatment performed. The skin, on the other hand, is the "bounding surface" which is crossed by a doctor in an attempt to get from the outside to the inside and manage the diseased site. A pathological lesion may also be identified on this" bounding surface", e.g., a skin condition, which may not necessitate surgical intervention. Language wise, the container effect is achieved by placing the words referring to patients in the position of complements of prepositional phrases which together function as adverbials of place, here with the meaning of a container. As a result, they serve as the background modifying the topic of a sentence. What comes to the fore is either an instance of a disease that has been localized in a patient (cf. Hodgkin 1985) or specific treatment that is performed.

This textual effect is also referred to, though indirectly, in one of the guides to medical writing (cf. Zeiger 2000). In this guide, scientific authors are advised to make the topic of a sentence its subject. Consequently, if the topic is a particular medical procedure performed on a patient, the procedure and not the patient should be moved to the position of the sentential subject (cf. Zeiger 2000: 22). As a result, sentence (1) should be changed into sentence (2):

45 For specific examples cf. Chapter Five.

(1) The children with arteriovenous shunts **had** the shunts opened, heparin injected, and the arterial and venous sides of the shunt clamped.
(2) In the children who had arteriovenous shunts, the shunts **were opened**, heparin **was injected**, and the arterial and venous sides of the shunt **were clamped**. [original emphasis] (Zeiger 2000: 22)

In sentence (2), the patient is moved to the prepositional phrase and functions as the location where treatment is performed. This way, in certain sentences, the advice contributes to using the container metaphor.

Finally, it has been said in Chapter Three that one of the defining characteristics of the biomedical model is its conceptualization of disease as an isolatable entity. This conceptualization is an example of the third type of metaphor, i.e., ontological metaphor, which, by "understanding our experiences in terms of objects ..." helps to describe them in a variety of ways (Lakoff and Johnson 1980: 25). In medical discourse, this conceptualization allows to present decontextualized information about diseases (cf. *nominalist* account of a disease in section 2.).

As regards the research on metonymy in scientific discourse, it is scarce (Rundblad 2007) and Gabriella Rundblad's (2007) study of impersonality in medical discourse is a rare exception. Rundblad (2007) demonstrates how the authors of the examined texts employ metonymy to position themselves against other medical professionals. For instance, this metaphorical tool allows the writers to refer to the participants of the described procedures as *the answers*, to the other doctors as *the hospital* (2007: 253) and to the other researchers as *the studies* (2007: 251).

While the study above concerned the use of metonymy with reference to other authors or participants of medical procedures, from the perspective of the present work, of interest is the use of metonymy in the presentation of patients. Here referring directly to patients' body-parts can be given as an example which is pervasive in medical discourse (cf. section 3.). This mode of reference aims at drawing attention to the affected body-part or the treated pathological change. It follows that the body-part does not stand for the patient, but represents him/her metonymically when it is his/her body is referred to. Such a reference is called by Blake Howald (2008) *metaphorical extension*. To this aim, the whole/part relation is used, which is demonstrated for instance in Joan Emerson's (2004) study of gynecological encounters.

According to Emerson (2004), sensitive as gynecological consultations are, they require tact and carefulness on the doctor's part, which manifests itself also in his/her linguistic behavior. Emerson (2004) observes that while referring to women's genitals, personal pronouns are exchanged for definite articles, i.e., *your vagina* for *the vagina*, so as not to make the direct link between the person and his/her body-part (2004: 173). This way, the body-part is figuratively separated from its owner, which should contribute to the impersonal character of the encounter, and, in turn, lessen possible embarrassment on both sides. As Suzanne Fleischman (1999) claims, through metonymy "the sufferer is excluded from the ensuing treatment, which is directed toward the synecdochic sign ... [and] from the health professional's perspective the patient becomes the affected body part" (1999: 22). Such a type of part-whole relation is classified by Madelyn Iris and colleagues (1988) as *functional parts*, where "[t]he part ... contributes to the whole, not just as a structural unit but as essential to the purposeful activity of the whole" (1988: 272). With this explication in mind, as exemplified by Elżbieta Górska (1999), the sentence below describes the part of the body and its condition which affects the functioning of the larger structure, i.e., the whole body (1999: 78–79):

(3) *The left eye had* 3+ *anterior vitreous cells, an engorged disk, and cystoid macular edema.* NEJM5

Patient imaging of the type demonstrated above, i.e., drawing attention to disease or treatment, is in line with the biomedical model of medicine. Yet, in order to determine how patients are imaged, apart from what the texts center around, i.e., their content, also how this imaging is achieved linguistically needs to be explained. Therefore, in the following section, the selected grammatical notions and cognitive concepts will be described which will enable the analysis of the form of the case reports at hand.

5. Analytical tools

5.1. Sentence constituents from three perspectives

As will be demonstrated in the analytical part of the present work, the words referring to the patients described in the examined texts appear in various sentential positions, which affects the prominence and functions of these words. First, the analysis necessitates a short overview of the notions which are to be used therein. These include the definition of the subject and the object (examined from three perspectives), the Active and Passive Voice, thematic roles as well as nominalization.

Traditionally and from a syntactic point of view, a sentence is thought to consist of two parts, namely the subject and the predicate, the latter comprised of object, complement and adverbial. As regards the subject and the object, position wise, they precede and follow the verb respectively (in the case of a declarative sentence) (Greenbaum and Quirk 1990: 207). Functionally, the subject is "prominent positionally" in that it is a "perspectival center" and "the starting of the communication of a sentence" (Smith 2003: 192–193). Supporting evidence for the prominence of the subject can also be found in psychological studies (e.g., Paivio 1979 and Brennan 1995). Wallace Chafe (1976) compares the structure of a sentence to a package of information which is "unwrapped" step by step by a reader. Although it consists of many elements, "knowledge directly attached to the subject may be most immediately accessible" (1976: 44). While the subject constitutes "what is talked about", the predicate is "what is said about it" (Palmer 1994: 2). This simple definition tallies with Michael Alexander Kirkwood Halliday's (1994) functional definition of Subject as what is predicated about (1994: 76). In other words, the predicate provides the information on the "subject referent" (Smith 2003: 189). Halliday's (1994) perspective is an example of the pragmatic approach to grammar which presupposes particular communicative functions that sentence constituents perform.

According to Carlota Smith (2003), a sentence is characterized by a certain "dynamism" (2003: 187) with a bipartite mode of the presentation of information. In this sense, the subject and the predicate can function as theme and rheme, containing known and new information respectively (2003: 189).[46] In Smith's (2003) words, "a sentence makes a comment about the sentence referent, and the comment is expressed by the predicate" (2003: 189). Such an understanding of theme/rheme is based on "position and familiarity status" (2003: 196).[47] In the vast literature devoted to this particular area, the functions can also be referred to as datum and novum or topic and focus/comment (cf. e.g., Hasan and Fries 1995; Smith 2003). While the latter pair pertains to their anchoring in the context (Duszak 1998: 68), the former one is explicated by Anna Duszak (1987: 127) in terms of pragmatic perspectivization. "[B]y topic selection the speaker relativizes what is being said to a particular point of reference, i.e., he chooses a certain camera angle on the state of affairs described" (Duszak 1987: 127–128). This comparison is reminiscent of Halliday's (1970: 161) definition of theme as "the

46 To avoid confusion between the function of theme and the thematic role of Theme, throughout the work, the latter will be spelt with a capital T. The use of the former, on the other hand, will be marked with reference to theme/rheme distinction, so as to differentiate it from the sense of a subject of a particular section, fragment, etc.

47 The functions of theme and rheme originate in Functional Sentence Perspective developed by the linguists from the Prague School (cf. De Beaugrande and Dressler 1981; Halliday and Hasan 1976).

peg on which the message is hung", which is also quoted in Duszak (1987). In this light, a sentence has two poles whose status is functionally defined.

Semantically, depending on the meaning of a verb, a sentence may consist of a different number and type of arguments. As Bas Aarts (1997) phrases it, "[a] rguments are participants in what one linguist has called 'the little drama' that a proposition expresses. To be a participant in a drama you must be playing a role" (1997: 88). To put it differently, a clause may image a situation which stars participants (Greenbaum and Quirk 1990: 209). According to Robert Van Valin (2001), these participants play various roles and every verb is characterized by a number of arguments with their own semantic meanings, which is referred to as "argument structure" (2001: 23). The said roles, on the other hand, are called thematic roles and they constitute "the syntax-semantics interface" (Van Valin and Lapolla 1997: 139), linking syntactic positions with semantic content. Although there is no absolute agreement on the number of possible thematic roles, the following list seems to be a compromise based on the many versions:

Table 3. Thematic roles (after Aarts 1997: 88)

Role	Description
Agent	The 'doer', or instigator of the action denoted by the predicate
Benefactive	The entity that benefits from the action or event denoted by the predicate
Experiencer	The living entity that experiences the action or event denoted by the predicate
Goal	The location or entity in the direction of which something moves
Instrument	The medium by which the action or event denoted by the predicate is carried out
Locative	The specification of the place where the action or event denoted by the predicate is situated
Patient	The 'undergoer' of the action or event denoted by the predicate
Source	The location or entity from which something moves
Theme	The entity that is moved by the action or event denoted by the predicate

Following the above-presented roles, the verb *devour*, for instance, selects the Agent who devours something and the Patient/Theme who/which is the object of devouring (Aarts 1997: 89).[48] Moreover, it is possible to describe the circumstances in which the aforementioned "little drama takes place". This is done by

48 In order to avoid confusion between the thematic role of Patient and the patient as the subject of the present work, the former one will be written with a capital letter.

means of adverbials included in the predicate group which, for instance, may specify the location of the action denoted by a verb. In this case, this element plays the role of Locative (possibly Source and Goal), which can also be referred to as a *circumstantial role* (Halliday 1970: 149) or *setting* (Firbas 1975: 319). As will be shown in the following chapter, the words referring to the patients in the case reports receive different thematic roles, depending on the meaning of the verbs which take them as their arguments.

It has already been stated that the subject and the object appear before and after the verb respectively. Yet, this position holds only for a sentence in the Active Voice and, if passivized, the order of the constituents as well as the allocation of prominence will be affected. This change can be observed in the following two sentences:

(4) *The surgeon operated on two patients yesterday.*
(5) *Two patients were operated on by the surgeon yesterday.*

In (4), the subject (*the surgeon*) is the Agent and the objects (*patients*) are the Patients. In (5), however, the Patients occupy the subject position while the Agent is moved to the object position, obtaining "a peripheral status" (Palmer 1994: 16). As a result, (5) is said to promote the Patients and demote the Agent of the active sentence to the subject and object positions of the passive sentence respectively (cf. Givón 1990: 567–568). These foregrounding and backgrounding operations, as Edward Keenan (1985: 243) calls them, shift the sentential perspective, changing the sequence of "what is being talked about" and "what is said about it" (Palmer 1994: 2; cf. Smith 2003: 189). The terms 'promotion' and 'demotion' already suggest a hierarchical relation between the two (Palmer 1994: 16). Indeed, if a given situation with participants involved is described, "they rank on a scale according to their importance" (Givón 1984: 137).

Consequently, the subject and the direct object are primary and secondary clausal topics respectively (Givón 1984: 138; cf. Smith 2003: 193). Also Jeanne Van Oosten (1984), who proposes a list of features of a prototypical topic, mentions perspective, "salient" participation and agency (1984: 325, quoted in Duszak 1989: 116). This pragmatic perspective has repercussions for the already discussed passivisation, influencing prominence given to particular sentence constituents/participants. In this view, given a prototypical Active Voice sentence, the Agent is "the most topical participant", "the apex of the topic hierarchy", being the first candidate for the subject position. In contrast, in a prototypical Passive Voice sentence it is the Patient who/that is granted the title of "the most topical participant" and the position of the subject (Givón 1990: 566).

Clearly then, grammatical relations have their pragmatic consequences for the prominence of specific participants with their thematic roles (cf. Van Dijk 1980: 95–96). Underlying this reasoning is the approach to a sentence introduced by the linguists of the Prague School – Functional Sentence Perspective – in which semantic, grammatical and functional levels are considered (cf. Firbas 1974; De Beaugrande and Dressler 1981; Halliday and Hasan 1976).[49]

Another way in which sentence (4) above can be rephrased is by means of nominalization. Generally, this process involves changing parts of speech into nouns. If, for instance, they are formed from lexical verbs or adjectives, they may denote actions, states or different arguments (Comrie and Thompson 1985: 358). One of the 'products' of nominalization, which appears in the examined corpus, is the action nominal. It is a noun formed from a verb accompanied by one or more elements of the predicate or proposition. For instance, the expression:

(6) *the enemy's destruction of the city*

is understood as the action of destroying the city (object) performed by the enemy (subject) (Comrie and Thompson 1985: 358). Analogically, sentences (4) and (5) could be rephrased as:

(7) *the surgeon's operation of the patient*

(8) *the patient's operation by the doctor*

respectively, depending on Voice. In the second case, however, genitive is used (Comrie and Thompson 1985: 365). According to Kress and Hodge (1981) who discuss this process, English verbs are associated with actions and processes, whereas English nouns with objects, abstract notions and concepts. Consequently, Gunther Kress and Robert Hodge (1981) view the change from a verb to a noun as eradicating the sense of action from a sentence (1981: 21) where activities are referred to as entities (cf. Fairclough 2001: 43; O'Halloran 2003: 115). This effect of nominalization will be discussed further in the empirical part of the present work.

Apart from syntactic and semantic points of view, yet another perspective from which the relations of the constituent parts of a sentence can be defined is the cognitive perspective and it will be dealt with in the following subsection.

---

49 The interface of the perspective, grammatical subject and Agent is discussed by Anna Duszak (1989). Cf. also Duszak (1987).

5.2. The figure and ground distinction

According to Ronald Langacker (1987), "[m]eaning is a mental phenomenon that must eventually be described with reference to cognitive processing" (1987: 97). In other words, comprehension takes place in the human mind and the patterns of its functioning are supposed to shed light on the understanding, for instance, of a given text. Consequently, the analytical part of the present work draws on one of the concepts from cognitive linguistics. In this field of study, it is assumed that the elements of language are indicative of more general cognitive processes (Langacker 1987: 99; Evans and Green 2006).

One of the basic cognitive abilities is the figure/ground distinction (or segregation, as in Evans and Green 2006: 69), i.e., the ability to differentiate between a focal point and its scene (Langacker 1987). As Langacker (1987) explains, it is based upon the premise that if a person is shown a black board with a white dot on it, he/she will probably focus on the white dot (1987: 120). Following this line of reasoning, "[w]hile one entity is typically privileged and represents the figure, the second entity is given less prominence and is referred to as the ground or reference object" (Evans and Green 2006: 69).

According to Leonard Talmy (2001), this distinction is omnipresent also in language. Here it is Figure that "needs anchoring" whereas Ground "does the anchoring".[50] These two may refer to each other in various configurations, for instance those of time, cause/result, etc., yet what lies at the heart of this distinction is the different allocation of prominence to the two (2001: 311).

Talmy (2001) terms Figure and Ground cognitive-semantic categories and investigates their distribution both at the level of single and complex clauses. As regards the former, in the sentence:

(9) *The pen lay on the table.*

according to the distinction at hand, *the pen* acts as the Figure which is presented against *the table*, the Ground. Consequently, the Figure is defined in terms of its orientation to the Ground (Talmy 2001: 312). Yet, while in (9), the alignment is spatial in nature, it can also position two elements towards each other on a temporal axis. Such cases are often realized at the level of a complex sentence. In the example:

(10) *He exploded after he touched the button.*

50 Talmy (2001) uses upper case to indicate their manifestation in language.

the action of exploding receives the function of the Figure which takes place after touching the button, i.e., the Ground, which constitutes the temporal background.

Moreover, it is possible to isolate a set of characteristics of elements that function as Figures and Grounds:

Table 4. Figure-ground segregation, as encoded in language (adapted from Talmy 2001: 315–316)

Figure	Ground
has unknown spatial (or temporal) properties, to be determined more moveable	acts as reference entity, having known properties that can characterize the Figure's unknowns more permanently located
smaller	larger
geometrically simple (often pointlike) in its treatment	geometrically more complex in its treatment
more recently on the scene/in awareness	earlier on the scene/in awareness
of greater concern/relevance	of lesser concern/relevance
less immediately perceivable	more immediately perceivable
more salient, once perceived	more backgrounded, once the Figure is perceived
more dependent	more independent

The analysis of medical case reports in Chapter Five will demonstrate how some of these features are manifested linguistically.

Furthermore, according to Talmy (2001), this mode of cognitive processing is in line with the determination of syntactic elements (2001: 313; cf. Evans and Green 2006: 69). If applied at a sentence level, it is possible to isolate the most prominent information from its setting. From this perspective, according to Langacker (2000), subjects and objects may act as Figures and Grounds respectively thanks to their potential for drawing respective amounts of attention (2000: 31). In the following sentence:

(11) *Smoke slowly filled the room.*

the Figure and Ground alignment tallies with the subject and object assignment, which underscores the prominence of the former element in relation to the latter (Talmy 2001: 336). Semantically, this is so because the meaning of the verb allocates the focus[51] (Langacker 2000: 34), which has been demonstrated on the basis of thematic roles and their hierarchy (cf. Givón 1984, 1990 in subsection 5.1.). In this context, Figure is associated with a "resulting event" (Talmy 2001: 337). Functionally, the two positions of subject and object are primary and secondary topics of a clause respectively (Langacker 2000: 31) thanks to the type of information they carry.

This way, the subject and object slots, associated with the most prominent arguments in terms of semantics, and particular functions, additionally find their rationale in a more general cognitive process. The notions of subject and object run through Langacker's (2000) explication of the figure and ground distinction and of other concepts as well. Both pairs serve the function of vantage points with different foci on subject/figure and object/ground respectively. What is more, this correlation lies at the heart of cognitive grammar which assumes the union of syntax and semantics (Langacker 1987: 1; cf. Table 3 above). These interrelations will be demonstrated in the examined medical case reports.

Yet another observation Langacker (2002) makes is that "[g]rammatical structures do not constitute an autonomous formal system or level of representation: they are claimed instead to be inherently symbolic, providing for the structuring and conventional symbolization of conceptual content" (2002: 11). In other words, grammar can be treated as scaffolding for a message created by a language user. What is more, similarly to Halliday (1979), Langacker (2002) holds that grammatical structures do not presuppose any specific interpretation. What they do is simply offer a multitude of versions of the same message at the speaker's/writer's disposal (Langacker 2002: 12). Therefore, in Chapter Six, the conclusions from the textual study will be confronted with some other readers of the said medical case reports.

In subsection 1.4. in Chapter One a brief discussion of Sapir-Whorf hypothesis has been offered. It needs to be added that cognitive linguistics supports the weak version of the hypothesis in that, from the cognitive perspective, language both mirrors and engenders certain ways of thinking (Evans and Green 2006: 101). This aspect will also be addressed in Chapter Six.

After the discussion of the theoretical aspects and analytical tools for the textual analysis of the corpus, the description of the data and methods used therein will be given. Next, the quantitative and qualitative results of the study will be presented and discussed.

---

51 *Focus* in the sense of prominence and not rheme, i.e., new information; the word *focus* in the latter sense will not be used in the present work.

Chapter Five: The analysis of medical case reports

In Chapter Five, first, the examined data as well as the methods of analysis will be described and next, the results of the quantitative and qualitative analyses of the case reports will be presented and discussed. This will allow to test the following hypotheses:

(1) The abstraction from the patient results partly from the type of information conveyed in sections of case reports, but also partly from specific lexical and grammatical choices on the part of an author.
(2) Patient imaging as demonstrated in the studied case reports is in line with the premises of the biomedical model.
(3) Patient's reactions, symptoms, biological processes and treatment he/she undergoes tend to be rendered separate from him/her.

The first hypothesis illustrates the approach adopted in the present work to studying patient imaging in the corpus as informed by John Swales's (1990) genre analysis (cf. section 3. in Chapter One). The second hypothesis concerns medical discourse as contextualized in the biomedical model and has been formulated on the basis of the account of the evolution of the case report genre against the background of the history of medicine, which demonstrated how the changing modes of reasoning and methodologies in medicine affected the way patients were described (cf. Chapter Two). Finally, the third hypothesis was made on the basis of the literature on patient's representation in medical discourse (cf. section 6. in Chapter Three). To test these hypotheses, the results from both quantitative and qualitative parts of the textual analysis will be used. In the first part, the frequencies of occurrence of different types and positions of direct reference to patients in particular sections and between them will be counted which will help to examine the first hypothesis. A closer look at particular sections of the case reports and how they image patients and their experience of illness, which will be the aim of the second part of the textual analysis, will allow to tests the remaining two hypotheses.

1. Data

1.1. General information

In the first stage of the empirical part of the present work, a corpus of 56 medical case reports has been compiled taken from four international medical journals targeted at health professionals. The rationale behind the choice of the genre of case report was the fact that this text-type does not present general medical knowledge or detailed results of clinical research, but it discusses particular patients suffering from particular diseases. In other words, case reports give the account of diagnosis and treatment but always in the real context referring to a given person.[52] What is more, it is the genre which brings together all the elements of the medical management of a patient – recounting his/her history, performing physical examination/tests, as well as therapy and the results of treatment which are described in respective sections of the genre. This way, all the past and present aspects of the patient's health are composed into a report of a case. Moreover, the choice of the genre to be studied influenced the way in which patient imaging in the present work has been approached. As the case report genre combines all the elements of the patient's history of illness, the attempt will be made to investigate different modes of patient imaging as used and, possibly, dictated by the type of information appearing in particular sections of the texts. The choice of this approach has been informed by Swales's (1990) genre analysis.

The reference will also be made to the context of the biomedical model and medical culture in general as factors influencing the production and reception of professional medical discourse. In other words, the aim of the textual analysis of the case reports is not to foreground patient-objectifying techniques, but to present a complete linguistic picture of the variety of ways in which the authors write about patients. What is more, apart from contextualizing those ways in the current model of medicine, it will be determined whether there are any correlations between the imaging modes and the focus of particular sections. Such an approach ensures that the texts under study will not be examined for selected linguistic features, as it has been the case in the literature on the topic, but will draw on those works in which the context of the production of the texts is taken into consideration (cf. section 6. in Chapter Three). In doing so, patient imaging will be investigated from the proximal perspective of the sections of the case report genre and from the distal perspective of the biomedical model and medical culture (cf. proximate and distal perspectives on the case report genre in Chapter One).

52 I am indebted to Joanna Nowak for drawing my attention to this particular genre.

The choice of the journals to be analyzed was guided primarily by the Journal Impact Factor[53] which should guarantee not only high quality of research but also linguistic excellence.[54] The decision was also made not to opt for journals which are devoted to any specific medical disciplines. Consequently, *The Lancet*, *The Journal of American Medical Association*, *The New England Journal of Medicine*, and *The British Medical Journal* have been selected.[55] They scored as 18th, 23rd, 2nd and 127th on the list in the year 2006 respectively.[56] The publications of these journals are all available online and in this way they were obtained.

The articles were selected via the web pages dedicated to the journals through typing the phrase "case report" to be found either in a title or in the body of a text. If the returned article was a full-length publication, whose structure followed Elizabeth Rowley-Jolivet's (2007) division (cf. section 8. in Chapter One) and was affiliated to the institution in an English-speaking country, the text was included in the corpus. This selectional restriction was motivated by the fact that it is the medical culture of the English-speaking countries that is referred to throughout the present work as the context of the production and reception of the examined texts (cf. Chapter Three). There were no specifications as for the time frame or topics of the texts in the corpus. Therefore, the selected articles cover the period between 1995 and 2008 and are devoted to a variety of medical fields such as: dermatology, nephrology, viral diseases, neurology, microbial diseases, venereal diseases, urology, orthopedics, infectious diseases, endocrinology, otolaryngology, rheumatology, obstetrics and gynecology, primary care, neurophysiology, anesthesiology, neuropsychology, pharmacology, toxicology and ophthalmology. This way, a corpus of 56 medical case-reports with the total number of 73,773 words has been compiled, with 15 articles from *The Lancet* (LA), 13 from *The Journal of American Medical Association* (JA), 16 from *The*

53 "[T]he Journal Impact Factor [is] the ratio of the number of citations to the previous two years of the journal divided by the number of articles in those years – this is essentially the average number of recent citations per article" (http://en.wikipedia.org/-wiki/Journal_Citation_Reports). The list of journals which rank highest can be found in *The Journal Citation Report* published by the International Science Index. It includes journals of various disciplines.

54 All the selected journals are also peer-reviewed.

55 *The Journal of American Medical Association* and *The New England Journal of Medicine* are American journals whereas *The British Medical Journal* is British. As regards *The Lancet*, its editorial offices are in London and New York.

56 The Impact Factor for 2006 was the latest list available at the time when the decisions concerning the corpus were made.

New England Journal of Medicine (NEJM) and 12 from *The British Medical Journal* (B).[57] Abbreviations LA, JA, NEJM and B will be used as codes to refer to particular journals throughout this work, especially when quoting fragments of the case reports from the corpus in the qualitative analysis (cf. section 4.).

1.2. Structure of the articles

The account of the qualitative and partly quantitative analysis of patient imaging in the texts (cf. sections 2. and 4.) will follow the order of their sections with particular emphasis on the aim of each section. Such an approach to the texts and arrangement of the data presented is motivated by the fact that, as will be demonstrated further, in many cases the specific mode in which patients are described and referred to is partly dictated by what a given section aims to mediate, following the requirements of the genre.

Generally, a case report is composed of three sections, namely a brief Introduction, a more elaborated Case Report body and a final section that concludes the presented material – Comment/Discussion (Rowley-Jolivet 2007). It has also been mentioned that a case report resembles a narrative in that it describes the patient's course of a disease and treatment, with respective sections overlapping with the parts of a story (cf. section 8. in Chapter One). At the same time, medical journals have their own guidelines concerning the composition of case reports. As a result, they may differ in length and sections. In some cases, journals may even have their own case report designs. The examined texts are not an exception. The following table presents the structures of the case reports from the four journals and the numbers of each type in the corpus:

Table 5. The structures of the case reports in the corpus

Journal	Structure
LA	1st type: Abstract, Introduction, Methods, Results, Discussion; (1)
	2nd type: introduction, case report body, comment/discussion; (14)
JA	1st type: Abstract, Introduction, case report, methods, results, comment; (1)
	2nd type: abstract, introduction, Case Report, comment; (2)

57 There exists a separate journal which publishes only case reports (*The Journal of Case Reports*), which, admittedly, could have made the processes of data collection and subsequent analysis easier and quicker. Yet, it has been decided to compile a corpus of texts from four source journals rather than only one as the differences in structures of the texts were within the scope of genre requirements. What is more, four source journals instead of one ensured the diversity of the corpus.

Journal	Structure
JA	3rd type: introduction, case report body, comment/discussion; (9)
	4th type: letter which is at the same time a case report and follows the introduction – case report body – comment/discussion structure; (1)
NEJM	1st type: Abstract, Presentation of Case, Differential Diagnosis, Clinical Diagnosis, Pathological Discussion, Discussion of Management, Anatomical Discussion; (1)
	2nd type: Presentation of Case, Differential Diagnosis, Clinical Diagnosis, Pathological Discussion, Anatomical Diagnosis; (3)
	3rd type: Abstract (Summary), introduction, Case Report, Methods, Results, Discussion; (1)
	4th type: introduction, Case Report, Methods, Results, Discussion; (4)
	5th type: introduction, Case Report, Methods, Discussion; (1)
	6th type: introduction, Case Report, Discussion; (6)
B	1st type: introduction, Case Report, Comment/Discussion; (6)
	2nd type: introduction, case report body, comment/discussion; (1)
	3rd type: Introduction, Case Report, additional sections depending on the topic; (1)
	4th type: case report body, additional sections depending on the topic; (1)
	5th type: Case Report, additional sections; (3)

As Table 5 shows, although they belong to the same genre, the case reports in the corpus differ in their structures, depending on a journal in which they are published. With one exception, all case reports from *The Lancet* are unified one-page texts, which reflects the journal's guidelines for the authors requiring a 600-word manuscript (cf. 2nd type in Table 5). The texts do not have marked sections, yet they follow the structure of Introduction, Case Report body and Comment/Discussion (Rowley-Jolivet 2007; cf. section 8. in Chapter One).[58] Only one case report from *The Lancet* is significantly longer (6 pages) and consists of specific sections which are all marked (cf. 1st type in Table 5).

The case reports from *The Journal of American Medical Association* are more varied and belong to two different groups. The first group contains texts which

58 In Table 5 capital letters are used in the names of sections only if the texts have these sections marked. Furthermore, the name *case report body* refers to the main body of the case report, which contains all information except for the one typically assigned to Introduction and Comment/Discussion. The *case report*, on the other hand, refers to a brief description of a patient, which is only the part of a case report body. In the body of the present work, however, if not stated otherwise, capital letters are used in the names of sections following Rowley-Jolivet's (2007) practice and division.

are longer and structured, the former feature complying with the publisher's requirement (from 1000 to 1500 words; cf. 1st and 2nd types in Table 5). The texts from the other group come from the *Morbidity and Mortality Weekly Report* section and consist of Introduction, Case Report body and Comment/Discussion, all of which are partly or not marked (cf. 3rd type in Table 5). The case report in the form of a letter (cf. 4th type in Table 5) also follows the typical structure of case report (cf. Rowley-Jolivet 2007), yet it is very short (259 words).

The case reports published in *The New England Journal of Medicine* seem most varied and extensive. The first group includes several-page texts with only two clearly marked sections (cf. 6th type in Table 5). The second group contains long (2000 words – the publisher's requirement) publications with marked sections (cf. 3rd, 4th and 5th types in Table 5). The third group belongs to the series of *The case records of the Massachusetts general hospital* (cf. 1st type and 2nd type in Table 5). These case reports are substantially longer (between 3000 and 5000 words) and very complex, with marked sections whose names differ from the rest of the case reports in the corpus. What is more, this group of texts has a very detailed discussion section in which a few specialists jointly arrive at a diagnosis.

All *British Medical Journal* case reports include some form of the Case Report body but they differ in the presence of Introduction, Comment/Discussion and/or other topic-necessitated parts. The publisher expects these texts to follow the sequence of: the patient, intervention, comparison, and outcome, yet these guidelines pertain to the content of the texts, not to the marking of specific sections. As regards the length, case reports in this journal should not exceed 1200 words.

All in all, the structures of the case reports differ in the presence, names and length of particular sections as well as their content. In some journals a number of aspects may come under one section while in others these aspects are treated separately. Yet, the structure as presented by Rowley-Jolivet (2007) is uniform for all the examined case reports and the observed differences concern basically the nomenclature, the assignment of material to particular sections or are topic-specific.

Additionally, the editors of the four journals were inquired about any guidelines or recommendations for the authors regarding patient reference in the texts. Of interest was whether there is any mode of patient reference that would not be accepted and would require correction before publication, which, in turn, would have the consequences for the authors' modes of writing. Only the editors of *The British Medical Journal* and *The New England Journal of Medicine* replied and said they do not impose any restrictions as regards patient reference except for the need of preserving patients' anonymity.

2. Quantitative analysis: methods

2.1. Selection, classification and distribution of patient references

The analysis of the corpus of the case reports consisted of two stages, which can be classified as quantitative and qualitative. The quantitative analysis was preceded by a three-step data handling. First, each article was carefully read in search of any words that directly referred to the patients described there, following Elinor Ochs's (1992) notion of indexicality (cf. Fløttum et al. 2006; Howald 2008). These were not only the words *patient*, but also personal and possessive pronouns and other nouns, e.g., denoting sex (*woman, man*), occupation (*worker, soldier*), kinship terms (*mother*), etc. (cf. Table 6 below). After the compilation of the list of all the words that referred to the patients described in the examined texts, the tokens were isolated and classified with the help of *WordSmith Tools 5* and its tools *Concord* and *WordList.*

When counting patient references a number of selection procedures were adopted. Firstly, as regards the very texts, examined were only the bodies of texts, excluding tables, graphs, photograph captions, etc. If a given text was preceded by an abstract, it was also omitted, as the focus of the analysis fell specifically on the ways of presenting information in particular sections and not in the techniques of its condensation. What is more, only those fragments which referred to the generally understood patient's condition and treatment were taken into consideration. Therefore, the sentences describing, for instance, patient's occupational background, descriptions of the circumstances in which the patient fell ill as well as post-mortem examinations were excluded from the analysis. By exclusion is meant that these fragments were not included in the corpus and the patient reference contained therein was not counted in. Secondly, as regards the very reference, most case reports in the corpus describe one patient suffering from a particular disease. Yet, if other people were referred to in the context of their health-related issues (for example the subjects of cited studies), they were also counted as patients although they were not the main characters of the texts. Thirdly, singular and plural forms of the same word were counted as tokens of the same word.

It also needs to be emphasized that in the present quantitative analysis of patient references in the corpus only direct references to the patients were taken into consideration. By direct reference are meant such indexical examples as *patient, he, his,* etc., but not, for example, *the head.* The last type was excluded from the quantitative analysis due to considerable difficulties in its isolation and classification (cf. Table 6 below) and analyzed only in the qualitative part (cf. section 4.).

The second step in the process of data handling was to classify the words referring to patients according to their reference (i.e., the whole/part relation) and their sentential position, i.e., Subject, Object, Location and Other. As far as the former classification is concerned, patient references were divided into those which referred to the whole person (personal pronouns and nouns, for instance *she* and *woman* respectively) and those which referred to his/her body-part or the aspect of health/treatment (possessive pronouns and nouns in the possessive, for example *her* and *woman's* respectively).[59] Moreover, examples such as *maternal* in *maternal genes* or *patient* in *patient management* were treated as possessives, i.e., denoting a patient's body-part or the aspect of his/her treatment respectively.

However, there were also sentences which considered generally understood patient management, but the tokens indexing the patient therein did not refer to patient's body or the aspects of health/treatment. These tokens were not counted in while the very sentence was still added to the corpus. Consequently, examples like (12) and (13) were counted in while the ones of type (14) were not included.

(12) *patient's ankle*
(13) *her operation*
(14) *his doctor*

There was no such problem with references to the patient as a whole, as in this case, a particular sentence either contained a patient reference or not.

Table 6 presents the words directly indexing the patients that were isolated from the texts at hand in the selection procedure and classified according to their reference. The total number of words indexing patients that were isolated following the selection procedures is 2001, and the numbers of tokens of individual words are given in brackets. The words were grouped into eight categories, namely: pronouns, generic or gender-specific references, medical references, references denoting age, references denoting professions, names, kinship references and other references.

As can be seen in Table 6, although all the texts concern patients, they can be referred to in many other ways. Apart from the whole/part relation and nouns/pronouns differentiation, patient references can also be divided into the indefinite/explicit and definite/inexplicit ones.

59 Throughout this work, the references to patients as whole persons and references to their body-parts/aspects of health/treatment will also be referred to as whole- and part-references respectively.

Table 6. Direct references to the patients as testified in the examined corpus

Group		Example
Pronouns	Whole	I (1), she (198), her (13), he (198), him (5), they (17);
	Part	her (143), his (72), their (18);
Generic or gender-specific references	Whole	man (36), woman (91), female (1), male (1), girl (8), boy (1), person (32), individual (16), couple (4), people (13), one/other (6), those (7), humans (21), human being (1);
	Part	man's (1), human (38);
Medical references	Whole	patient (524), subject (3), contact (8), recipient (39), donor (27), antidonor (4), vaccinee (9), volunteer (1), participant (1), host (1), population (7), group (8), case (20);
	Part	patient's (86), patient (5), donor's (7), donor (8), donor-specific (6), recipient's (3), recipient (1);
References denoting age	Whole	fetus (1), infant (34), baby (3), child (16), adolescent (8), adult (12), elderly and debilitated (1);
	Part	fetal (5), infant (2), infant's (8);
References denoting professions	Whole	student (3), worker (22), coworker (2), employee (1), staff (1), personnel (2), physician (1), nurse (1) chemist (1), microbiologist (1), researcher (1), professor (1), assistant (1), soldier (1), recruit (4);
Names	Whole	Ms A (5), Mrs B (4), Mrs Bariatrico (5), Ms D (2), Ms H (2), Ruth (6);
	Part	Ms A's (1), Mrs B's (2), Mrs Bariatrico's (1);
Kinshipreferences	Whole	mother (14), daughter (4), sister (10), aunt (1), grandmother (3), father (1), brother (2), grandfather (1), twin (11), sibling (1), family (2), offspring (1), partner (2), spouse (3), husband (3), wife (3), parent (1);
	Part	mother's (4), maternal (11), paternal (1);
Other references	Whole	minority (2), member (5), resident (9), civilian (1), citizen (2), neighbor (1), traveler (5), refugee (2), survivor (1), smoker (1), drug user (1), consumer (1), whites (2), nonwhites (1), numbers (16), most (1);

As Deborah Schiffrin (1994) explicates, the difference between the two types depends on whether a speaker and/or reader is able to identify who/what is referred to, which, in turn, is closely related to the reference position in discourse. When mentioning someone/something for the first time, indefinite/explicit reference is used to signal that new information is given, e.g., *a patient*, whereas references that have already been mentioned will be marked by definite/inexplicit references, e.g., *he* (1994: 198–199; cf. Ariel 1988: 68). This distinction allows to identify referential progression in discourse, with nominals and names coming first and followed by pronouns which can refer back (cf. Howald 2008).

As regards the second classification, i.e., Subject, Object, Location and Other labels, these are syntactic/semantic categories which combine the sentential position of a reference and its meaning (cf. "the syntax-semantics interface" in Van Valin and Lapolla 1997: 139 in subsection 5.1. in Chapter Four). Consequently, under Subject subsumed are words referring to the patient as a whole person, occupying the subject position of the sentence, i.e., preceding the finite verb, regardless of the Voice (cf. 13 below). This means that, semantically, these can be Agents, Patients, Experiencers, Benefactive, or Themes.

The Object category includes the words that follow the finite verb and are direct or indirect objects, being Patients, Benefactive or Themes affected by the action denoted by the verb (cf. 16 below; Table 3 in subsection 5.1. in Chapter Four and Table 13 in section 4. for the detailed classification of the roles in the examined texts). As regards the very classification, the corpus included both examples obvious to classify (cf. 15 below) and less obvious ones, e.g., with nominalization (cf. 18 and 19 below).

(15) *The patient was given a course of antibiotics.*
(16) *We gave her three doses of the drug.*
(17a) *The onset of illness in our patient was not typical.*
(17b) *The method was not successful in this patient*
(17c) *In our patient, this method was successful.*
(17d) *The transplantation from the donor to the recipient was successful.*
(18) *patient's use of aspirin*
(19) *screening patients*

In such cases, every occurrence of patient reference was carefully examined with relation to the meaning of the verb and examples similar to (18) were treated as part-references, i.e., the aspect of his/her treatment, while examples of type (19) as belonging to the Other group, as their sentential positions in such cases could not be classified as belonging to the three main categories.

Location is the position of a word referring to the patient found in a prepositional phrase, functioning as an adverbial complement or adjunct with a locative/directional meaning. This category has a few varieties as the prepositional phrase may modify a noun phrase (17a) or occur sentence-finally/initially (17b and 17c respectively). In these three examples, the patients assume the thematic role of Locative. However, they may also be portrayed as Sources or Goals in medical procedures (17d and Table 13 in section 4.). Despite the very identification of those varieties in terms of positions and roles, they were subsumed under the category of Location, as they shared the mode of imaging the patient as an area of medical activity, which differs significantly from describing patients as active participants or those to whom medical procedures are applied. In other words, there is a difference between patients acting/undergoing states/treatment, acting upon patients in medical procedures and being imaged as areas of medical activity.

Furthermore, only those words that referred to patients as "wholes" were classified according to the position they occupied in sentences, whereas the words denoting patients' body-parts/health-related issues, i.e., in the possessive, were not considered in the analysis of their sentential positions.

The choice of the categorization of patient references according to the combination of their sentential positions and thematic roles in preference to either of the factors individually was motivated by the character of the data. On the one hand, close reading of the texts revealed numerous cases in which thematic roles of the patients described were difficult to establish. In some other cases, patient references seemed to have more than one thematic role. These aspects would make the classification problematic. On the other hand, as has been already discussed in subsection 5.1. in Chapter Four, apart from thematic roles also syntactic position determines prominence in texts.

Consequently, combining the syntactic configurations and semantic features of patient references seems to offer suitable analytical categories. This way, under the category of Subject subsumed are both the initial position in a sentence and the status of the patient who acts or undergoes states/medical treatment, with particular attention to him/her. In the category of Object, on the other hand, the attention is shifted from the patient to the doer/affecting element/performed procedure.

Although the underlying meaning of *patients undergoing medical procedures* and *procedures being performed on them* is the same, the perspective of the sentential position offers an opportunity to study actual authors' selections who, regardless of whether, for example, a patient is the Agent or the Patient in a sentence, can decide to place the reference in the Subject position, i.e., foreground him/her sententially.

While thematic roles seem to be, to a large extent, a matter of the content of the text under examination, the choice of the sentential positions and, thus, the sentential prominence, rests upon the author. In the case of Location, however, the very choice of imaging the patient as an area of medical activity determines his/her sentential prominence which will be lesser than in the case of patients who act or are acted upon, i.e., the categories of Subject and Object respectively. In this light, the patient reference in (17c) cannot be classified as Subject because of the status of the described patient as the background for the discussed medical fact. All in all, while in the case of the Subject category the initial position can be occupied by references having two distinct thematic roles (Agent or Patient/Experiencer/Benefactive/Theme, etc.), in Location, the references have the roles connected with spatial configuration (Locative, Source and Goal) and can be distributed in different sentential positions (cf. Table 3 in subsection 5.1. in Chapter Four, Table 13 in section 4. and examples 15–19). Such a state of affairs requires an appropriate approach to the studied tokens and the above developed categorization seems suitable for the present analysis.

As regards the third step in the data handling process, the frequency of occurrence of patient references was analyzed within and between the sections of the case reports (cf. subsection 5.3.). Although the texts in question vary in their structure depending on a journal (cf. subsection 1.2.), it can be assumed that, generally, they consist of Introduction, Case Report body and Comment/Discussion. In other words, regardless of the marking of sections or their presence/absence, most of the case reports contain a brief introduction of a patient, the account of his/her history, results of physical examination and/or laboratory tests, the course of treatment and discussion. Therefore, in the analysis, the tokens of interest were assigned to three main parts (and their subsections, i.e., History, Examination and Treatment in the Case Report body; cf. Rowley-Jolivet 2007) associated with particular types of information included there (cf. Atkinson 1995).[60] This decision was made in attempt to overcome the problem, firstly, of the lack of overlap between the structures of the case reports and, secondly, that certain types of information appear in many sections, not only in the ones with which they are associated.

Regarding the varied structure, the general division into Introduction, Case Report body and Comment/Discussion was adopted, and any other sections, marked or unmarked, e.g., Methods or Results, were classified as containing the information linked to these three main sections. As regards the association of information with particular sections, it was often the case in the texts that, for

60 Although History, Examination and Treatment are subsections of the Case Report body, patient imaging will be analyzed in each of them separately, both in the quantitative and qualitative study. Throughout this work they will be referred to either as History, Examination and Treatment or the History section, Examination section and Treatment section. Moreover, in the qualitative part, the Examination section will be discussed as divided into physical examination and medical tests to underlie these two different medical events. However, this will be done only for the purpose of the qualitative analysis.

instance, the patient's history, which usually comes in the Case Report body, was referred to in other sections, where applicable.

Following the adopted procedure, if sentences describing the patient's history appeared in the Comment/Discussion section, though the history had already been described, these sentences were treated as belonging to the Comment/ Discussion part. If, however, the patient's history purposefully appeared in a different section and it was the history proper and not the reference to the already mentioned account, it was classified as the History section. Any other treatment of such cases would mean intervention into the original composition of the texts, as, very often some parts are blended fluidly into another parts and their separation would change the structure and the arrangement of ideas. This, in turn, would result in analyzing and grouping sentences (as opposed to sections) on the basis of their content.

All in all, each article was coded, assigned the sentence and word counts, as well as the counts of particular patient references in sections of the case reports. Due to space restriction, the description of only one case report from the corpus is given here.

2.2. Statistical analysis: tests and methods

Firstly, the problem of different lengths of the articles had to be solved. The shortest article in the corpus has 400 words whereas the longest 4690 words, which gives a range of 4290 words. This means that if the occurrence of a particular word was to be examined in these articles, it is likely that the word could appear more frequently in longer texts. To overcome this problem, the method of normalization was adopted in which occurrences of the words of interest in a single article are divided by the total number of words in this article and then multiplied by one thousand (cf. Biber et al. 1998: 263). Consequently, the observed frequencies of patient references were recalculated to the frequencies appearing per one thousand words of the articles. This way, all the articles could be compared with each other because they are examined, as if their lengths were the same (cf. studies by Fløttum et al. 2006; Rundblad 2007).

Secondly, in order to choose appropriate statistical tests, the data at hand were checked for their distribution. To this end, the Lillefors test was carried out which revealed that the majority of the examined references were not normally distributed, in this case they were distributed asymmetrically. Consequently, if the distribution of the tokens was other than normal, non-parametric tests had to be used. Moreover, asymmetrical distribution also means that the median rather than the mean is a better measure of location (cf. subsection 2.3.).

The quantitative analysis of the corpus consisted of two stages. In the first stage, the frequencies of occurrences of patient references were compared against each other within particular sections in the whole corpus. In the second stage, the frequencies of the same groups of words were compared between different sections of the case reports in the whole corpus. In other words, in the first stage, it was checked whether, for example, the frequency of whole-references was significantly different from part-references in the Introduction section. In the second stage, in contrast, it was compared whether the frequencies of one group of words, for instance in the Object position, were significantly different between two sections, for example between History and Treatment, and which section exactly was characterized by the greater frequency of the selected word group.

Consequently, as regards the first stage, in order to tabulate the frequencies of the words referring to patients as whole persons with the words referring to their body-parts/aspects of their health, i.e., whole- and part-references (cf. Table 6), the one-sided Wilcoxon test was applied which allows to determine which type of patient reference occurs more frequently and whether this difference is statistically significant.

In the case of tabulating the frequencies of patient references in four sentential positions, two tests were required. First, the Friedman test was used, as it allows to compare more than two groups of data and to determine whether they are significantly different from one another or not. Yet, the test shows only this and it cannot ascertain which pairs of groups exactly are different. Therefore, multiple pairwise tests needed to be performed with the aim of: (1) isolating those pairs of groups of words in particular sentential positions where the difference between their frequencies was statistically significant; and (2) determining word groups which occurred more frequently. However, while the objective of this test was the same as in the comparison of frequencies of part- and whole-references, in this case the one-sided Wilcoxon test with the Bonferroni correction was used. The very Bonferroni correction is the summary error rate that should not be exceeded divided by the number of comparisons. The significance level for the Wilcoxon test and the Friedman test is $p<0{,}05$.

As regards the Wilcoxon test with the Bonferroni correction, the level of significance is the same as in the two previous tests but because of the fact that there were six combinations of the compared pairs (groups of words in different sentential positions), the test was composed of six sub-tests and each result was likely to have occurred by chance. That is why the level of significance for the whole test ($p<0{,}05$) was divided by the number of the sub-tests ($0{,}05/6=0{,}0083$). If the significance level for each test was assumed to be $p<0{,}05$, then the summary probability of the results of all six sub-tests occurring by chance would be greater than 0,05.

Therefore, the level of significance for multiple comparisons had to be lowered so that the summary error of these comparisons would not be greater than 0,05.

In the second stage of the statistical analysis, the frequencies of whole/part references and references in four defined sentential positions were compared between particular sections in the whole corpus. In this case, the procedure of determining whether the frequencies of the same groups of words were significantly different in different sections was nearly the same as comparing the frequencies of different groups of words within one section of the article. First, the Friedman test was applied which compared the frequencies of one group of words in different sections and showed whether these differences are statistically significant. If there was at least one case in which the occurrence of one given patient reference type in one section was significantly different than in another section, the result of the Friedman test was also statistically significant. Then, in order to say in which pairs of sections exactly a given group of words appeared significantly more frequent, the one-sided Wilcoxon test with the Bonferroni correction was used. In this case, different sections were compared in pairs with respect to the occurrence of a given group of references.

When tabulating the frequencies of different groups of words within one section, the number of sub-tests performed was six (for each compared pair of reference groups). This also meant that the significance level for the applied tests ($p<0,05$) was divided by the number of six sub-tests (cf. above). In the case of the comparison of one reference type in different sections, the number of pairs of sections between which one group of references was compared was ten. Therefore, the significance level for the applied tests ($p<0,05$) was divided by ten sub-tests which gave the value of 0,005 as the significance level for each sub-test.

Consequently, because of the fact that the aim of the second stage of the statistical analysis was to contrast the frequencies of one reference type in different case-report sections, there was no differentiation into the whole/part comparison and the comparison of the sentential positions as it was the case in the first stage. In the second stage, only pairs of particular sections were compared with regard to the occurrence of a given reference type. This meant that the use of the Wilcoxon test in the whole/part comparison was eliminated and only the Wilcoxon test with the Bonferroni correction was applied to compare frequencies of one group of references between particular sections. What is more, patient references in ten pairs of sections were compared as opposed to six pairs of reference groups in the first stage. In the case when the result of the Wilcoxon test with the Bonferroni correction for a particular pair of reference groups is statistically significant, but the values of medians for these two groups are 0,0, the value of mean and Q3 can also be consulted.

As regards the tools for the analysis, all the tests were carried out with the help of Statistica 8.0 PL, by StatSoft.

2.3. Illustration of the method

The following example explicates how the results presented in section 3. have been obtained. Table 7 presents the distribution of the examined variables in all Comment/Discussion sections in the entire corpus. Subject, Object, Location, Other, Whole and Possessive are the groups of interest. N is the number of all the Comment/Discussion sections in the corpus. It may be different from the total number of articles, as not every journal contains all the sections typical of the genre of case report. The Mean is the average value of the variable under investigation. The median, on the other hand, is the value that is in the very middle of all the values arranged in ascending order. As has already been mentioned, due to the asymmetrical distribution of the references under investigation (cf. subsection 2.2.), the median is a better measure of location than the mean. Q1 and Q3 designate the first (lower) quartile and the third (upper) quartile respectively, which together with the second quartile (the median) divide the data into four equal parts.

Table 7. Distribution of the examined variables in the Comment/Discussion section in the whole corpus

Comment/ Discussion	N	Mean	Standard deviation	Minimum	Q1	Median	Q3	Maximum
Subject	55	3,1	2,9	0,0	0,5	2,7	4,7	15,2
Object	55	0,6	1,1	0,0	0,0	0,0	1,0	4,6
Location	55	3,1	2,9	0,0	1,3	2,1	4,3	11,6
Other	55	1,0	1,3	0,0	0,0	0,0	1,8	4,9
Whole	55	7,8	5,8	0,0	3,7	6,8	11,0	27,3
Possessive	55	2,3	2,3	0,0	0,0	1,7	3,7	9,4

What is more, the values of a given data set that are located between Q1 and Q3 are most typical, whereas those below Q1 and above Q3 those which are most extreme. Minimum and Maximum stand for the minimal and maximal values. Finally, Standard deviation is the measure of statistical dispersion which shows the average dispersion of the tokens that are close to the mean value. In sum, all these values serve to describe more accurately the distribution of the examined variables in the texts.

Table 8. Comparison of the frequencies of whole- and part-references within sections in the whole corpus

Section	Intro	Hist	Exam	Treat	Disc
Wilcoxon test	0,000	0,000	0,020	0,000	0,000

Knowing the distribution of the examined variables (cf. Table 7), it is possible to determine which type of reference, i.e., whole- or part-references, occurs more frequently, for example in the Comment/Discussion section in the whole corpus. To this aim, the values of medians of Whole and Pos from Table 7 need to be compared. Table 7 shows that the value of median for Whole is 6,8 and the value of median for Pos is 1,7.

The result of the Wilcoxon test for the Comment/Discussion section is statistically significant (p<0,05, cf. Table 8 – the results which are statistically significant are given in bold; and subsection 2.2.) which allows to say that the frequency of occurrence of whole-references in this section is significantly higher than the frequency of occurrence of part-references.

Table 9. Comparison of the frequencies of sentential positions of patient references within sections in the whole corpus

Section		Intro	Hist	Exam	Treat	Disc
Friedman test		0,000	0,000	0,000	0,000	0,000
post hocWilcoxon tests with Bonferroni correction (p=0,05/6=0,0083)	Obj – Sub	0,000	0,000	0,000	0,000	0,000
	Loc – Sub	0,000	0,000	0,000	0,000	0,370
	Oth – Sub	0,000	0,000	0,000	0,000	0,000
	Loc – Obj	0,000	0,242	0,002	0,040	0,000
	Oth – Obj	0,432	0,173	0,088	0,001	0,010
	Oth – Loc	0,001	0,040	0,017	0,037	0,000

The frequencies of patient references in particular sentential positions can be compared in a similar way. For instance, the value of medians for Subject and Object in the Comment/Discussion section are 2,7 and 0,0 respectively (cf. Table 7). However, the result of the Friedman test determines only whether all the frequencies of the compared groups (in this case only whole-references in four specified sentential positions) are similar to each other or not. If no (p<0,05, cf. subsection 5.2.2.), then it can be said that not all the groups occur comparably frequent. Yet, in order to specify which reference groups are significantly different from one another, the result of the Wilcoxon test with the Bonferroni correction needs to be consulted. In the case of the Subject and Object pair in the Comment/Discussion section, the difference is statistically significant (p<0,0083, cf. Table 9), which validates the claim that the frequency of patient references in the Subject position is significantly higher than the frequency of these references in the Object position in this section.

The measuring of statistical significance of the differences in the frequencies of the same groups of words between sections in the second stage of the statistical analysis proceeded similarly.

Table 10. Comparison of the frequencies of whole- and part-references and sentential positions between sections in the whole corpus

Reference type		**Sub**	**Obj**	**Loc**	**Oth**	**Whole**	**Pos**
Friedman test		**0,000**	**0,010**	**0,000**	**0,000**	**0,000**	**0,000**
post hocWilcoxon tests with Bonferroni correction (p=0,05/10=0,005)	Hist – Intro	0,135	0,164	0,008	0,014	0,488	0,206
	Exam – Intro	0,419	0,037	0,131	0,155	0,196	0,000
	Treat – Intro	0,000	0,004	0,007	0,297	0,000	0,000
	Disc – Intro	0,120	0,002	0,000	0,000	0,000	0,000
	Exam – Hist	0,038	0,199	0,164	0,155	0,164	0,002
	Treat – Hist	0,002	0,002	0,213	0,124	0,000	0,000
	Disc – Hist	0,467	0,001	0,000	0,000	0,000	0,000
	Treat – Exam	0,000	0,001	0,198	0,476	0,000	0,102
	Disc – Exam	0,022	0,001	0,000	0,000	0,000	0,093
	Disc – Treat	0,001	0,283	0,000	0,000	0,044	0,476

Table 11. Distribution of the examined variables in the Introduction section in the whole corpus

Introduction	**N**	**Mean**	**Standard Deviation**	**Minimum**	**Q1**	**Median**	**Q3**	**Maximum**
Subject	55	2,5	2,5	0,0	0,9	1,7	3,5	11,3
Object	55	0,2	0,4	0,0	0,0	0,0	0,0	1,8
Location	55	0,8	1,4	0,0	0,0	0,0	1,1	7,7
Other	55	0,2	0,4	0,0	0,0	0,0	0,0	1,9
Whole	55	3,6	3,2	0,0	1,6	2,3	5,4	14,6
Possessive	55	0,5	0,9	0,0	0,0	0,0	0,9	3,7

Using the information concerning the distribution of variables in general (cf. the samples in Table 7 and Table 11), it is also possible to determine whether a particular group of patient references is statistically more frequent in one section in comparison with another, for instance the Location position between Introduction and Comment/Discussion sections in the whole corpus. Table 7 shows that the value of median for Location in the Comment/Discussion section is 2,1, whereas for the Introduction section is 0,0 (cf. Table 11). The result of the Friedman test for the Location position is statistically significant ($p<0,005$, cf. Table 10 and subsection 2.2.) which allows to say that the frequency of occurrence of the words in the Location position is significantly greater in the Comment/Discussion section than in the Introduction section in the whole corpus.

In the following section, the results of statistical analysis of the examined variables will be presented, yet without referring to specific values obtained in the test.

3. Quantitative analysis: results

In the current section, the results of the quantitative study of the corpus of case reports will be presented. Following the modes of analysis explained in subsection 2.3., firstly, the presentation will include the statistical analyses of: (1) the difference between frequencies of the words indexing the whole patients vs. their body-parts/aspects of their health/treatment; (2) the differences between the frequencies of patient references in four defined sentential positions. These differences will be compared within particular sections in the corpus (cf. subsection 3.1.). Secondly, the frequencies of whole- and part-references and of references in four defined sentential positions will be compared between particular sections, also in the whole corpus (cf. subsection 3.2.). In other words, in the first stage, it will be compared, for instance, whether patient references appear significantly more frequently in the Subject position than in the Object position in the Introduction section in the whole corpus. In the other stage, on the other hand, the comparison will be made between the frequencies of, for example, patient references in the Location position in Examination and Treatment (cf. subsection 3.2.). The rationale behind these comparisons is that each section of the text has its aim, i.e., the type of information to be mediated, which requires particular linguistic means of expression. It follows that if the aim of, for example, Examination is to record the results of physical examination and medical tests, it can be assumed that the textual prominence will be given to body-parts/aspects of patient's health, which are checked/examined. Such a type of information would be reflected, for instance, in the greater use of possessive pronouns or nouns in the possessive, i.e., part-references, rather than the references to a patient as a whole person. Consequently, the following two comparisons will allow to test the first hypothesis (cf. p. 115).

The following presentation of results of the analysis of the frequencies of patient references within and between sections (cf. subsection 2.3.) will follow the order in which these sections are arranged in the case report genre, while the following descriptions will provide the information concerning the statistical significance of particular comparisons.

3.1. Whole vs. part and sentential positions within sections in the whole corpus

In Introduction, the frequency of occurrence of whole-references is significantly higher than of part-references. As regards the four defined sentential positions, patient references in the Subject position occur more frequently than in other positions. The references in the Location position are more frequent than in the Object and Other positions. The difference in the frequencies between Object and Other positions lacks statistical significance.

The Case Report body includes History, Examination, and Treatment (cf. Atkinson 1995; Rowley-Jolivet 2007). As regards History, similarly to Introduction, the references to patients as wholes are significantly more frequent than the references to the patient's body-parts/aspects of health/treatment. Also the frequency of patient references in the Subject position is significantly higher than in any other position. Differences between other positions lack statistical significance.

The Case Report body includes History, Examination, and Treatment (cf. Atkinson 1995; Rowley-Jolivet 2007). As regards History, similarly to Introduction, the references to patients as wholes are significantly more frequent than the references to the patient's body-parts/aspects of health/treatment. Also the frequency of patient references in the Subject position is significantly higher than in any other position. Differences between other positions lack statistical significance.

In Examination, it is whole-references that are significantly more frequent than part-references. As regards sentential positions, the Subject position of patient references is more frequent than the rest of positions. The Locative position occurs significantly more frequently than the Object position. Differences between references in other positions are, similarly to the previous section, not statistically significant.

The Treatment section is similar to Introduction, History, and Examination in that whole-references occur here significantly more frequently than part-references. Also the occurrence of patient references in the Subject position is significantly more frequent than in any other position. As regards the examined words in the Object position, they occur more frequently than in the Other position.

In Comment/Discussion, the frequency of occurrence of whole-references is significantly higher than of part-references. Regarding the sentential positions, the Subject position of patient references is statistically more frequent than Object and Other positions. Patient references in Location are more frequent than in Object and Other. Differences between patient references in Object and Other positions are not statistically significant.

3.2. Whole and part and sentential positions between sections in the whole corpus

No groups of patient reference appeared significantly more frequently in Introduction and History in comparison with other sections. Part-references have a significantly greater frequency of occurrence in Examination than in Introduction and History. The Treatment section is characterized by: (1) greater frequency of the Subject position of patient reference than any other position; (2) greater frequency of the Object position of patient reference than Introduction, History, and Examination; (3) greater frequency of whole-references than Introduction, History, and Examination; and (4) greater frequency of part-references than Introduction and History. The Comment/Discussion section includes greater frequencies of: (1) the Object position of patient reference than Introduction, History, and Examination; (2) whole references than Introduction, History, and Examination; and (3) part references than Introduction and History. The frequency of references in Location and Other positions is greater in Comment/Discussion than in any other position.

3.3. Discussion of the results of the quantitative analysis

The aim of the quantitative part of the analysis of case reports has been to determine whether there is any relationship between the frequencies of different types and positions of direct references to patients and the type of information conveyed in particular sections of case reports (cf. the first hypothesis, p. 115).

In the first stage of the quantitative analysis, the frequencies of pairs of particular patient references within one section have been compared statistically. As regards the two types of patient references, the results reveal that whole-references appear significantly more frequently than part-references in all sections of the case reports. This finding means that in all sections patient reference more frequently takes the form of (21) rather than (20).

(20) *His CD4 count was 621 (range: 775–1385) with a normal CD8 count.* LA3

(21) *She had complained of worsening holocephalic headache 3 days earlier and seemed "groggy".* LA14

(22) *He was prescribed oral amoxicillin for a possible upper respire tory tract infection but returned the following day complaining of unsteadiness and upper limb weakness.* LA12

(23) *The patient underwent a right lower lobectomy.* NEJM10

(24) *We gave her intravenous heparin, then warfarin, and stopped the oral contraceptives.* LA15

(25) *In March 2000, tender, left axillary adenopathy and fever (temperature, 38.6°C) developed in a 33-year-old microbiologist at the U.S. Army Medical Research Institute for Infectious Diseases who had type 1 diabetes mellitus.* NEJM8

(26) *An 84-year-old woman presented with a bruise on her face from a fall the previous day. She had impaired mobility, and a history of bronchial asthma, ischaemic heart disease, non-insulin de- pendent diabetes mellitus, hypertension, and ovari4 mman cysts. On examination, she had a large, firm, tender mass in the left lower abdomen which she said she had first noticed a year and a half previously.* LA10

As regards the frequencies of patient references in four defined positions, references in the Subject position are more frequent than in the three remaining positions in Introduction, History, Examination, and Treatment sections. The results of frequencies of the references to the whole patient and the references in the Subject position in Introduction and History agree with the aims of these sections which are rather patient-oriented, introducing him/her and describing his/her past history of illness respectively. On the other hand, significantly greater frequencies of the same groups of references in Examination, Treatment and, partly, Comment/Discussion sections run counter to their focus.

Yet, it needs to be clarified at this point that into the category of Subject fall not only examples such as (21) but also (22) and (23). On the one hand, sentences (21) and (23) differ from (22) in Voice, with (21) and (23) being active while (22) passive. On the other hand, (21) is different from (22) and (23) in that in (21) the patient is the Agent of the sentence whereas in the latter two the patients are assigned the role of Benefactive and Patient respectively. Yet, in all three examples the patients occupy the topical positions regardless of the information imparted. In other words, the patients are themes, i.e., the known information, in the progression of the texts (cf. 26 and section 4. for the elaboration of these issues).

As regards patient references in Location (25), their frequency of occurrence is greater than in the remaining two positions – Object and Other – in Introduction and Comment/Discussion. Location also occurs statistically more frequently than Object in the Examination section. The finding of Location as a significantly frequent position of patient references is particularly of interest. The broader context of this result and its interpretation will be given in the qualitative part of the analysis of the corpus in subsection 4.3.

Patient references in Object (24) are statistically more frequent than in the Other position only in the Treatment section. It needs to be stressed that in (24) the treatment, which is new information, i.e., rheme, is described from the perspective of the doctor. In (25), it is the condition which is the topical element.

The aim of the second stage of the quantitative analysis has been to determine whether the occurrence of the same reference group is statistically different in different sections. The tests yielded statistically significant results for all the groups under examination.

The results of the comparison of frequencies of particular reference groups between sections reveal that, as regards Possessive, generally, its frequency increases as the texts progress. It appears significantly more frequently in Examination and Treatment than in Introduction and History. Content wise, Examination and Treatment on the one hand and Introduction and History on the other represent two different types of sections of the case report genre, with different aims and foci. While the former two concentrate on different aspects of the patient's body in the process of examination and therapy, the latter two center around the very patient, introducing him/her and giving details of his/her medical history respectively. In the light of this fact, the significantly more frequent use of the Possessive reference in Examination and Treatment, which means concentrating on particular aspects of the patient's body as in (20) above, seems to be in line with the type of information mediated there.

What is more, the finding of the Object position of patient references appearing more frequently in Treatment than in Introduction, History, and Examination, relegating patients to the objects to which medical procedures apply, seems to agree with the mode patient imaging in Treatment too. In these examples, the position of patient reference does not grant him/her the status of point of reference but rather of an aspect mentioned in the description of treatment (cf. 24 above). At the same time, the Treatment section is also characterized by the significantly greater use of references in the Subject position than the rest of sections and the significantly greater use of whole-references than Introduction, History, and Examination.

As regards Comment/Discussion, the Location position of patient reference occurs here significantly more frequently than in any other section. Part-references are significantly more frequent in Comment/Discussion than in Introduction and History. Also the Object position of patient references is significantly more frequent in the final section of the case report genre than in Introduction, History, and Examination. These findings accord with the particular ways of patient imaging used in Comment/Discussion which reflect the aim of this section, i.e., focus on the aspects of the patient's condition/treatment which is the topic of a text (cf. section 8. in Chapter One as well as subsection 4.3.). However, Comment/Discussion is also characterized by the significant frequency of the Whole category (whole-references) in comparison with all the parts except for Treatment. This finding, on the other hand, does not accord with the type of information associated with the final section of the case report genre and can be interpreted, as in the case of Treatment and its significantly greater frequencies of the Subject position and whole-references, rather as a choice on the part of the authors.

Consequently, the results of quantitative analysis confirm the relationship between the frequencies of particular patient references and the type of information conveyed in sections of the case reports. At the same time, the analysis shows statistically significant frequencies of patient references which do not match the aims of some sections. In these cases, the authors seem to have chosen the patient's perspective, regardless of the focus of the sections. This aspect will be discussed further in the qualitative analysis.

Finally, the very results of the tests merit some attention. As has been demonstrated, more statistically significant results have been obtained for Examination, Treatment, and Comment/Discussion, which are relatively longer than Introduction and History. Generally, the longer the text, the greater power and precision of statistical tests. In other words, longer texts make it easier to determine statistically significant differences in the frequencies of occurrence of particular words than shorter texts where the material is too little to reveal these differences even if they indeed occur.

3.4. Further remarks

It needs to be underlined that the sentences referring to patients are not only those which refer to patients directly. There are other sentences which consider patients but they contain other manifestation forms of the patient, e.g.,

(27) *On the 13th hospital day, a diagnostic procedure was performed.* NEJM13
(28) *Magnetic resonanceimaging of the head revealed cortical atrophy.* NEJM5

In (28), the *head* appears without its owner and only the definite article denotes whose part of the body is dealt with. In (27), the procedure, though performed on the patient, is presented in abstraction from him/her. The decision to exclude the above-demonstrated examples (as part-references) from the quantitative analysis was motivated by two difficulties (cf. subsection 2.1.). The first one concerns the actual words that could possibly be counted as tokens of patient reference. Potential instances would be the already mentioned body-parts, bodily fluids, etc., but medical procedures or symptoms would be more problematic, as their inclusion would require determining in each case whether they are mentioned with relation to the patient at hand or in general. Therefore, it has been decided to analyze such examples only in the qualitative part (cf. subsection 4.2.).

4. Qualitative analysis: Results

While in the quantitative part, the patient references of interest have been studied from the perspective of their frequencies within and between sections of the case reports, in the qualitative part, particular examples of sentences from the texts will be provided, which will allow to examine the references in their co-texts. In detail, patient's prominence in the texts will be determined by looking at syntactic structures of the sentences containing the words referring to the patients and the words used to describe them. Furthermore, particular attention will be given to the words/expressions which pertain to the patient's experience of illness, e.g., verbs, adjectives, etc., denoting mental/bodily reactions. Additionally, analyzed will also be sentences in which patients are either referred to indirectly, e.g., through their body-parts, as in (27) above, or are textually absent, as in (28) above, but in which medical procedures performed on the patients are described. These particular examples of patient imaging will be discussed with reference, on the one hand, to the information presented in particular sections, and, on the other hand, to two modes of disease presentation, hierarchical levels of medical description and a broader context of the biomedical model, with a view to explaining varieties of patient reference. This analysis will allow to examine the second and third hypotheses concerning the objectifying character of the modes of writing about patients in the texts and their contextualization in the biomedical model respectively (cf. p. 115). As a starting point for the qualitative part, the isolated patient references were assigned their thematic roles on the basis of Bas Aarts's (1997) list, which was complemented for the needs of the analyzed material (cf. Table 3 in subsection 5.1. in Chapter Four). To this end, the meanings of the verbs taking the words referring to patients as their arguments were studied.

Table 12. Thematic roles of patients in the corpus

Role	Description	Examples
Agent	patients' volitional actions	*On September 18, he presented to the medical clinic with severe dyspnea, weakness, and a petechial rash on the legs.* JA2
Patient	patients undergoing treatment or changes of their condition	*The donor underwent laparoscopic removal of her left ovary under general anesthesia.* NEJM4 *The patient deteriorated rapidly with swinging pyrexia of 41oC and died 2 weeks later, in September, 2003.* LA3
Experiencer	patients experiencing states	*After eight months he realized he was misusing the drug and stopped taking it suddenly.* BA2
Recipient	patients as recipients of drugs, organs, etc.	*Our patient received six months of directly observed antituberculosis therapy, the regimen recommended by the American Thoracic Society and the Centers for Disease Control and Prevention (CDC).* NEJM3 *Of the 5 patients who received multiple transfusions from this donor, 2 experienced 2 reactions each: 1 had 2 mild/moderate reactions, and the other had both a mild/moderate and a severe reaction.* JA8
Benefactive	patients who benefit from treatment	*It is extremely unlikely that the restoration of ovarian function in this patient after transplantation was due to residual follicles in the streak ovary of the recipient ....* NEJM4
Maleficiary	adverse effects of treatment to patients	*We are unable to determine if plasma transfusions from the implicated donor had a negative impact on the clinical course of the patients who were excluded from the analysis because of the complexity of their underlying illness.* JA8
Possessor	examined here are not patients but their body-parts or characteristics of their state of health	*We also found that because of the location of the infant's lesions, it was difficult to keep them covered to prevent autoinoculation.* JA5 *The results of the patient's laboratory tests on hospital admission are shown in Table 1.* NEJM9
Locative	diseases or their manifestations as localized in defined groups of patients or in their specific body-parts; where treatment is administered or diagnoses are made	*Whipple's disease was first described in 1907 in a patient with migratory polyarthritis, cough, diarrhea with malabsorption, weight loss, and mesenteric lymphadenopathy.* NEJM5

Role	Description	Examples
Target	specific groups of patients aimed at for treatment or targets of infection	*These findings do not provide definitive evidence of the route of exposure for the patient reported here, but they are consistent with the hypothesis that the exposure to B anthracis may have resulted from receipt of mail that was cross-contaminated with spores.* JA3
Source	patients as sources of diseases, organs or specimens	*NP specimens were obtained from exposed persons if they reported having a cough illness 20 days after their last exposure to the patient.* JA11
Goal	patients are goals when a disease is transmitted from one patient to another	*The mechanism of transfer from the vaccinee to the spouse is uncertain.* JA5
Theme	sentences where patients act as themes provide details of their condition (these are revealed by various diagnostic procedures) or when they are relocated to another medical facility	*When the woman was evaluated for splenomegaly in our clinic in February 1996, she denied all symptoms of illness.* NEJM2

The aim of this thematic role analysis was to look more carefully at patient references in their co-texts and to determine some tendencies in their occurrence, both in terms of semantics and syntax. In the following subsections giving account of patient imaging in the case report sections, the above-summarized patients' theta-roles will be developed.

4.1. Introduction section

The examined case reports commence with the introduction of a patient, as the aim of this subsection is to briefly explain the reason of his/her presentation or referral and, if applicable, to give some demographic facts about the patient, such as sex, age, sometimes occupation or ethnic origin.

(29) *A nine-year-old* girl *presented to the National Institutes of Health Clinical Center with weight gain, growth arrest, hypertension, abdominal striae, acne, hirsutism, proximal muscle weakness, mood swings, and increasing skin pigmentation.* NEJM10

(30) *64-year-old* woman *presented to the emergency department with a stiff painful jaw.* LA14

(31) She *had complained of worsening holocephalic headache 3 days earlier and seemed "groggy".* LA15
(32) *The* woman *felt healthy ....* NEJM2
(33) *A* man *of 27 presented with low back pain of acute onset that was complicated by pain radiating down his right leg.* B10
(34) *Last week (p 588) we presented the case of* Ruth, *a 66 year old housewife who presented to her general practitioner with a two to three month history of feeling "out of sorts" and an erythematous papular rash affecting the fingers, dorsum of the hands, knees, elbows, and neck.* B9
(35) *In 1994, splenomegaly was documented in a 72-year-old* woman *from the Greek island of Karpathos during a routine examination (her first in many years).* NEJM2

The ailments described in this section are usually restricted to (0) and (1) levels of medical hierarchy (cf. Table 1 in subsection 4.1. in Chapter Four), which consider conditions of the whole body or its parts. These conditions tend to be directly felt by patients, which allows to present them as experiencers of particular symptoms. This can be observed in examples from (30) to (34) in which verbs and adjectives referring to certain bodily/mental reactions are used, for instance: *acute pain*, or *painful jaw*. As these are the words denoting subjective perception, what is narrated here is the account of an illness, i.e., as experienced by an individual, as opposed to a disease objectively observed by a physician. This subjectivity can be seen especially in (31) and in (34) in which the lay terms *groggy* and *out of sorts* are used respectively to describe patient's general condition. Therefore, in this part, it is the patient who is granted the agency of complaining and reporting what he/she feels. Yet, it is achieved only symbolically through the authorial persona, as the patient's account is given in the third person (cf. section 6. in Chapter Three) and such colloquial expressions as in (31) and in (34) are rarely used. (31) is an interesting example also because it mixes the lay term *groggy* with medical lingo – *holocephalic headache*. Also the already mentioned (34) combines both an everyday expression, i.e., *out of sorts*, with specialized vocabulary, namely *erythematous papular rash*. As a result, with words pertaining to mental or somatic experience, the mode of disease description that is used here is *psychological* (cf. section 2. in Chapter Four). On the other hand, examples like (29) and (35) represent the *nominalist* mode, as they do not refer to how the patients feel. Additionally, in (35), the patient is imaged as a container in which a given disease, an "isolatable entity" (Blois 1984: 92), is *documented*.

Language wise, the quantitative analysis in section 3. has revealed two important findings concerning Introduction. In the comparison of frequencies of occurrence of types of patient reference within this section, it is personal pronouns or nouns (i.e., whole-references) that are significantly more frequent. When the frequencies of patient references are compared with respect to their sentential positions, it is the Subject position that appears most frequently (cf. comparison between whole/part references and of four defined sentential positions in Introduction in subsection 3.1.). However, the comparison of frequencies of groups of patient references between particular parts yielded different results. Firstly, the Subject position is significantly more frequent in Treatment than in any other section of the case report genre. Secondly, the comparison of reference types between sections showed that the Whole category appears significantly more frequently in: Treatment and Comment/Discussion than in Introduction, History, and Examination, which is at odds with the aims of these two sections (cf. subsections 4.2. and 4.3.).

Nevertheless, there seems to be some evidence to claim that, in the Introduction section, the patients are imaged as whole persons (as discussed by Wade-Halligan 2004: 10) who are the primary topics and content of the clauses (cf. Givón 1990: 137–138; Halliday 1994: 75). Only in the sentence where the disease is found *in* the patient is she demoted from the Subject position and moved to the predicate group. This operation makes it possible to function as rheme, i.e., new information, which comes to be treated as the background for the point of reference – the pathology (cf. 35 above and section 5. in Chapter Four). What is more, this occurrence of patient reference in Location as in (35) is of a different nature from those which appear in Comment/Discussion (cf. subsection 4.3.). Yet, within Introduction, patient references in this position are significantly more frequent only than in Object and Other. Therefore, all in all, it can be said the patient is the center of attention of Introduction.[61]

4.2. Case Report body section

While Introduction is relatively brief, the Case Report body is rather complex and includes three subsections, namely History (the past history of illness), Examination (physical examination/tests as well as diagnosis) and Treatment (subsequent treatment). History is optional, depending on the subject of a text, whereas the latter two appear in almost all examined case reports. It is so, because,

61 As has already been said, sometimes the type of information associated with a particular part may be found in other sections due to specificity of a particular topic. Therefore, the structure of case reports presented here should be treated as an organizing principle rather than an absolute division dictating the material included there.

according to Paul Atkinson (1995), the Case Report body (in his treatment – Complication) is "developed through concatenations of outcomes such as laboratory tests values and the findings of physical examinations" (1995: 104).

The first type of information included in the Case Report body is the patient's history of illness and it can be presented in the following ways:

(36) *A 48-year-old chemistry* professor *was admitted to Dartmouth–Hitchcock Medical Center, in Lebanon, New Hampshire, on January 20, 1997, with a five-day history of progressive deterioration in balance, gait, and speech.* NEJM1
(37) *She was in average health for someone of 82 and had a medical history that included hypertension, a myocardial infarction (three years previously), and a fractured wrist (eight years before).* B3
(38) *His medical history was negative for underlying illnesses.* JA2
(39) *There was no recent history of headache, chills, sweats, sore throat, rhinorrhea, hemoptysis, chest pain, abdominal pain, nausea, vomiting, or diarrhea.* JA3
(40) *During the preceding 2 months, following the death of a close friend,* she *had experienced depressive symptoms, including decreased appetite and increased general fatigue.* JA3
(41) *He had developed the ulcer in January, 2003, and had been receiving podiatry care in the community.* LA9
(42) *He took regular methadone but no other prescription drugs.* LA12
(43) *Her only medication was oral contraception.* LA15
(44) *Medications included zoledronic acid (4 mg) given intravenously each month, dexamethasone (40 mg weekly), furosemide, potassium supplements, and conjugated estrogen cream.* NEJM14

The patient's history can be presented either in a compact form of one sentence or a few which give a detailed account of his/her previous health problems. If the compact version is chosen, possibly due to space restrictions, ailments tend to be treated as entities that are enumerated (cf. 37 and 39 above). In detail, in sentences (36) and (37), the words referring to the patients occupy the Subject positions, as opposed to (38) and (39). Here the history is underscored, yet, while in (38) it is still presented as belonging to the patient, in (39) there is no mention of him/her. As a result, patient's textual prominence decreases from (36) and (37) to (38) and (39), with (39) being entirely abstracted from the patient. A similar case is in (42), (43) and (44), which give the facts from the history of illness. Here, it is possible to convey the image of a patient as an active participant in the process of treatment (42), underscore the therapy (43) or focus only on the therapy (44).

It needs to be emphasized that in the first stage of the quantitative analysis of patient references in this section of the case reports, similarly to the

Introduction section, whole-references were found to occur more frequently than part-references and the Subject position was found to be significantly more frequent than any other position (cf. subsection 3.1.). However, the analysis of the types of patient reference and their sentential positions between sections did not produce evidence for the claim that whole-references and the Subject position are significantly more frequent in this section than in any other sections (cf. subsection 3.2.).

Furthermore, although the information mediated in History varies from level (0) to (4) of medical description (cf. subsection 4.1. in Chapter Four), the mode of disease presentation is *nominalist*, i.e., based on the enumeration of symptoms, conditions, reactions, etc. What is more, this process of listing contributes to the imaging of a disease as an entity, i.e., "it" (as discussed by Blois 1984: 97; Hunter 1991: 135; Lupton 1994: 19; Fleischman 1999: 8–9 and Woods 2006: 129, cf. section 2. in Chapter Four). This might be explained by the very nature of this section of the case report genre which serves the purpose only of imparting information about diseases that a patient underwent without concentrating on their character or course. However, if the history takes the form of a longer description, it may portray a patient as undergoing particular states (40) or developing some pathological changes (41), which is closer to the *psychological* mode (cf. section 2. in Chapter Four).

Clearly then, the mode of history presentation is varied. It may partly depend on the amount of space it is given and, to some extent, on the specificity of the presented material. While examples (36–37) and (40–41), with the patients as the subjects, bear resemblance to Introduction, examples (38–39) and (42–44) present his/her history, medications or conditions, either with reference to the diseased – (38) and (42–43) – or without it – (39) and (44). As a result, a gradual shift in the perspective from a patient to disease announces a more disease-oriented text which is to follow.

The next section of the Case Report body addresses the assessment of the patient's condition. It usually takes place at two levels. The first part of the diagnostic procedure delivers the external evidence based on the doctor's observation of the patient's body, its reactions and signs of diseases which are interpreted accordingly.

(45) *On examination* she *was feverish (38°C), with exudate on her tonsils and tender cervical lymph nodes.* B8
(46) *She was afebrile and growth was on the 50th centile.* LA5
(47) *Physical examination showed that* he *had reduced forward flex-ion of the lumbar spine; straight leg raising was limited to 45° on the right hand side.* B10

(48) *Examination of the ear, nose, and throat detected no discharge or signs of inflammation.* NEJM9

(49) *On examination, we found large venous ulcers on both legs, and bilateral ankle oedema (figure).* LA12

(50) *On examination of the mouth, there was red, raised soft tissue in the right mandible bicuspid and cuspid region, with mucosal ulceration and exposed bone underlying it.* NEJM14

(51) *Cough was weak; ....* LA12

In this section of the Case Report body, the observation of the external signs of a disease is given. In other words, the material dealt with here is restricted only to the sensorially perceivable phenomena, hence the medical description reaches only as far as the second level, i.e., the whole body, body-parts and systems (cf. section 1. in Chapter Four).

As regards disease presentation, except for specific conditions in (45) and (46) where the patients are referred to as whole persons, changes in the patient's body are separated as entities, so they are not part of the patient's experience of illness (cf. 48–51). Kathryn Staiano (1986) contrasts examples such as (45) and (46) with (47). Presenting patients as being in particular conditions, as in (45) and (46), contributes to viewing the states as experienced by the patients. "Having" diseases, as in (47), on the other hand, refers to them as "objects" abstracted from the patient's experience. Yet, in (47), although the condition is described as an entity, here the patient is textually present, in contrast to sentences (48–51) where there is no direct reference to the patients. The mode of imaging in examples (48–50) is possible thanks to the process of nominalization, which, by transforming an action performed on the patient to a thing, allows to delete the one to whom it applies and refer solely to the medical procedure (cf. subsection 5.1. in Chapter Four). Furthermore, due to the observable character of pathological changes described here, their features are conveyed by means of the adjectives pertaining to the senses of feeling, sight, and hearing, as in (45), (49), and (51) respectively (see Staiano 1986: 31).

Physical examination is usually followed by a series of medical tests. The modes of their presentation are the following:

(52) *He had regular sinus rhythm with a postural drop in blood pressure of over 30 mm Hg without concomitant tachycardia; a sign of autonomic dysfunction.* LA12

(53) *The patient's arterial-blood gas values while breathing oxygen were as follows: pH, 7.27; partial pressure of carbon dioxide, 43 mm Hg; and partial pressure of oxygen, 133 mm Hg.* NEJM7

(54) *Chest radiographs revealed a right-sided pleural effusion and pneumonia in the right lung.* NEJM16

(55) *Cystoscopy showed an inflamed bladder that bled on distension, and we sent biopsy samples for analysis; …* LA6

(56) *We took skin biopsies which showed dense non-caseating granulomata in the lower dermis with no clonal proliferation.* LA3

(57) *A sciatic stretch test on his right leg had positive results, and responses to light touch and pin prick were reduced on the lateral side and over the dorsum of the right foot.* B10

(58) *Peripheral hormones measured in the infertile twin one day before the transplantation remained at menopausal levels: 75 mIU of FSH per milliliter, 32 mIU of luteinizing hormone (LH) per milliliter, and 4 pg of estradiol per milliliter.* NEJM4

(59) *The bladder appeared to be decompressed and contained an indwelling catheter.* NEJM13

This section of the Case Report body is dominated by the quantitative and qualitative results of medical tests. The prevalence of such material reflects the widespread application of modern diagnostic equipment which allows to measure and observe every function or element of the human body respectively. According to Richard Ashcroft (2000), this focus on technology constitutes another textual reflection of the development of medicine, i.e., the introduction of technological innovations which started in the nineteenth century. Apart from crossing the barrier of the human body, new diagnostic means supplied physicians with more accurate information which was earlier limited to patients' accounts. Therefore, what this section conveys is the objective account of a disease rendered by devices or machines, which appears to be free from human involvement. This, in turn, dictates a certain mode of data presentation, namely "technology as the agent" (Anspach 1988) as demonstrated by (54) and (55), where diagnostic procedures *show* or *reveal* the results (cf. section 6. in Chapter Three). Such a type of reference implies the presence only of the machines, as if without doctors or patients.

As regards patient presentation, examples (52), (53), (54) and (56) show the already familiar gradation of patient's prominence in the texts, i.e., from the Subject position in (52) to his/her textual absence in (54) and (56). Although it may seem that the dominant mode of presenting the results of tests for the examined corpus is (53), the statistical analysis of the frequencies of whole- and part-references within this section reveals that it is whole-references that appear more frequently than part-references (cf. subsection 3.1.). However, if particular types and sentential positions of patient references are examined between sections, the Possessive group appears significantly more frequently in Examination than in Introduction and History sections. It follows that in comparison to these two sections, in Examination the reference is made more frequently to the aspects of patient's body-parts/condition/treatment. This finding accords with the aims of this particular section, i.e., recounting the results of medical examination and giving details of medical tests. Nevertheless, it needs to emphasized that statistical significance was obtained only for two sections of the case report genre (cf. subsection 3.2.).[62]

As a result, it may be said that in this section patient‘s presence tends to be marked by the values which stand for his/her state of health. Tests results are, according to Atkinson (1995), "the litany of medical facts" which render the patient's body fragmented into various numbers or representations, reflecting his/her condition. Atkinson (1995) claims that this is an example of "the biomedical disaggregation or distribution of the body" (1995: 107). Moreover, as this section contains information revealed by laboratory tests, medical description goes to the bottom levels of the hierarchical scale (cf. subsection 4.1. in Chapter Four), usually considering biological processes which are cellular or molecular in nature. Changes at these levels are not directly perceivable by patients, therefore, as Oliver Sacks (1983) observes, the description becomes "the cold facts – the patient's biodata ... [and] there is ... no residue of the living experience" (1983: 207).

The last feature of the part dealing with medical tests is focus on body-parts/organs as demonstrated in example (59) above. The history of medicine might be helpful in explaining this particular linguistic phenomenon. According to Rudolf Virchow (1880, as referred to by Nowell-Smith 1995: 52), whose work in autopsy and pathological anatomy underlies the biomedical model, all diseases stem from the dysfunction of tissues. Following this medical premise, Nowell-Smith (1995: 52) concludes that physicians' gaze was directed to pathological lesions which began to be associated with specific organs or systems. As a result, organs and tissues claimed centrality in medical case writing (cf. section 2. in Chapter Two), as they came to be perceived as the location of diseases. In (59), the organ is the primary topic of the sentence. What is more, it is presented

62 While in the qualitative analysis, the discussion of the Examination section is divided into two parts to emphasize the different nature of these two medical events, in the quantitative analysis, the section was not so divided due to the possible difficulties in its separation. Therefore, the results of the statistical analysis of Examination given here refer to the section as a whole.

separately, standing metonymically for the patient, as there are no other direct references to him/her. This type of imaging utilizes the functional type of the whole-part relation (*functional parts*, cf. section 4. in Chapter Four) in which the part is presented as the constituent of a larger mechanism. From this perspective, the aim of this linguistic means is to draw attention to the condition of this part and its potential pathology.

In (54), (55) and (56), the patient is also textually absent despite the fact that certain procedures performed on him/her are described. Even when the reference is made to his sensation, only his body-part is mentioned (cf. 57). Lastly, (58) is an example of the already mentioned mode of presenting patients as containers, this time as a location in which a given test is performed. In this section, the Location position of patient reference occurred significantly more frequently than the Object position.

All in all, what takes the center stage in this section is the type of test and the information it provides, whereas a patient, if textually present, is the background for the imparted medical facts (cf. section 7. in Chapter Four). Such a mode of writing is in line with the biomedical model, i.e., concentrating on biological changes which are clearly abstracted from a patient.

The last section of the Case Report body deals with the course of treatment which has been chosen in accordance with the preceding diagnosis. The aim of Treatment is to give the account of medical procedures performed on patients with a view to restoring their health. As in the case of Introduction, History and Examination, there are many ways in which these procedures are described with relation to the patient:

(60) *Approximately 45 minutes after initiation of the FFP transfusion, the patient experienced respiratory arrest.* JA7

(61) *The patient was treated with ketoconazole alone and then in combination with the glucocorticoid antagonist mifepristone, but the drugs did not control the hypercortisolism.* NEJM10

(62) (*She responded to Lugol's iodine solution (KI 10%), one drop perfeed, given from day 20 to 46.* LA5

(63) *… the infant's right ear passed the screening test but the left ear required further evaluation by an audiologist.* JA9

(64) *His muscle soreness subsided quickly.* NEJM7

(65) *The ulcer was initially managed with regular debridement, antibiotics, and pressure relieving footwear.* LA9

(66) *We started co-trimoxazole, rifampicin, ketoconazole and azithromycin (500 mg daily) as well as dexamethasone (4 mg qds) for cerebral oedema.* LA3

(67) *Amniotomy was performed and an infusion of oxytocin was start ed.* B7

(68) *After seven days, rigors, headache, and fever (temperature of up to 39°C) developed that recurred in a quartan pattern for five cycles and that resolved after the methotrexate was stopped.* NEJM2

(69) *Two months later — one year after the initial diagnosis of tuberculosis — fever, a productive cough, and severe dyspnea developed.* NEJM3

(70) *We gave her intravenous heparin, then warfarin, and stopped the oral contraceptives.* LA15

As can be observed in the above-given examples, patient imaging varies across sentences. Generally, all the instances consider treatment that patients undergo, so there is no question of their agency. What differs is whether or not the given patient is referred to, and if so, how it is done. In other words, the sentences vary in their perspective or the very presence or absence of the patients. Firstly, in (60), the patient is imaged as experiencing a particular state. In (61) and (62), although the patients are not active participants but rather those to whom medical procedures apply, they are textually prominent thanks to the Subject position of the word *patient* and the personal pronoun respectively, and it is their perspective from which this treatment is described. The examples can be contrasted, on the one hand, with (70), where the patient, though present, is demoted to the Object position, whereas the medical treatment, discussed in this section, is presented from the perspective of the doctor. In (66) and (67), on the other hand, there is no mention of the patients who undergo these procedures. In the latter case, even doctors who perform them are not textually present. Here, rather than to patients themselves, the readers' attention is drawn to the performed treatment and its specific execution, i.e., to the so called "medical techniques and therapeutics" (Ashcroft 2000: 288). It is another textual reflection of developing medical practice and the importance attached to the choice of the appropriate management.

In her study of medical records produced in hospitals, Margaret Van Naerssen (1985) observed that in her corpus forms such as (70) were dispreferred in favor of the Passive Voice with patients in the Subject position (1985: 56). Also the first stage of the quantitative analysis of patient references in four sentential positions within Treatment showed that they occur significantly more frequently in the Subject position than in any other of the defined positions (cf. subsection 5.3.1.). Different results were obtained when the Object category was examined between sections of the case reports. Statistical significance was obtained for the greater occurrence of patient references in the Object position in Treatment than in Introduction, History, and Examination (cf. subsection 3.2.). As it has been already mentioned, in examples such as (70), the point of reference is particular treatment.

Example (69) describes a condition, which, though developing in the examined patient, is presented in abstraction from the undergoer. In (68) *headache* is mentioned but not as an experienced condition (cf. Grice and Kramer-Dahl 1992: 75) and without reference to its context, developing as if on its own. Moreover, the intermediate versions between (60–62) on the one hand, and (66–67) on the other hand, are (63) and (64) which focus attention on the patient's body-part, as in (63), and condition, as in (64) (cf. focus on body-parts above). However, in the two latter examples, the patients are textually indexed by means of a noun in the possessive and a possessive pronoun respectively. This type of patient reference was found to occur significantly more frequently in the Treatment section than Introduction and History. This contrasts with the already mentioned study of medical records by Van Naerssen (1985: 63), where possessive pronouns were absent when referring to patients. At the same time, in the comparison of patient references between sections, the frequency of occurrence of the Whole reference is significantly greater in Treatment than in Introduction, History, and Examination sections, which, bearing in mind the finding concerning also part-reference, points to a variety of modes of patient reference in this section.

Lastly, in (65), the treated pathological change is underscored, again without reference to the patient. The case in which a pathological lesion is in the center of attention tallies with the biomedical focus on a disease. In this framework, it is a pathological change that should be treated as opposed to an ill person who remains outside the scope of the biomedical interest.

Consequently, however varied, patient imaging in Treatment includes many examples which tend to abstract from the patients, while giving the account of treatment. It may be argued that the aim of this section is to present technical details of the chosen therapy and patients are merely those who undergo it. Nevertheless, the descriptions tend to omit the very subject of medical procedures and relegate him/her to the object to which they apply. Yet, statistical analysis of the type and sentential position of patient reference both within sections and between them did not give evidence for the claim that it is only part-references that are used here to index patient's textual presence. It is rather a mixed picture with the greater occurrence of whole-references than in sections where such references would be expected to appear more frequently, due to the aims of those sections (for example than in Introduction and History). Whole-references were also found to occur significantly more frequently with respect to part-references within this section. Yet, part-references appeared here significantly more frequently than in Introduction and History. Furthermore, the greater frequency of patient references occurring in the Subject position in Treatment than in any other section in the whole corpus points to a great variety of means of expression used here by authors and does not allow to classify it solely as a patient-objectifying section. This finding suggests that although the Treatment section is clearly treatment-oriented, it contains sentences conveying information from the patient's perspective (cf. 61 and 62).

However, the sentences with patient references in the Subject position from this section need to be distinguished from those appearing in Introduction. In the latter, patients are imaged rather as Agents presenting to hospital and reporting their problems, which is typical of Introduction. Such information is not found in Treatment and even if patients appear here in the Subject position, what is usually described is their condition or the procedures they undergo. As a result, the multitude of ways in which the patient can be both textually foregrounded (cf. 60–62 above) and abstracted from his/her body in the description of treatment (cf. 65–69 above) is nowhere else to be seen in the case report genre.

4.3. Comment/Discussion section

The purpose of the final section of case report is to discuss the examined case of a disease with reference to the already available research and to draw general conclusions. In this section, a patient may be referred to in terms of the aspect of his/her body and treatment with a view to comparing or contrasting the case with other cases and considering implications for medical practice.

(71) *Having sustained two fractures from simple falls, my patient was understandably worried about further fractures.* B3

(72) *Since our patient did not have normal levels of luteinizing hormone, we speculate that tumoral luteinizing hormone secretion was continuous, that abnormal glycosylation of the molecule de creased its clearance, or that both of these processes occurred.* NEJM11

(73) *This patient's seizure, probably caused by essential oil of worm wood, apparently led to rhabdomyolysis and subsequent acute renal failure.* NEJM7

(74) *0.1–0.2% of pregnant women have Graves' disease, which affects 1–1·5% of their offspring.* LA5

(75) *The onset of illness in this patient is consistent with the hypothesis that infection may have resulted from exposure to small numbers of B anthracis spores.* JA3

(76) *We report the first documented case of inadvertent contact vaccinia transmission from mother to infant through direct skin-to- skin and skin–to–mucous membrane contact while breastfeeding.* JA5

(77) *Many of the reported cases are children and only two cases have survived.* LA3

(78) *In considering the management of this patient's condition, it is reassuring that none of the primary tracheal glomus tumors that have been reported have been associated with metastases.* NEJM15

Similarly to other sections, the author's reference to the examined patient is made here with the help of deixis. It may index a particular aspect of his/her condition, as in (73), the whole person, as in (72), or the patient's mental state, as in (71). Statistical analysis of patient references in subsection 5.3. revealed that the described patients are referred to more frequently by means of whole- than part-references in Comment/Discussion. The Whole group also occurs significantly more frequently in Comment/Discussion than in Introduction, History, and Examination. As regards refocusing attention to some aspects of patient's body/treatment, while in (73) it is achieved by using a noun in the possessive, in (75) and (76) the metaphor of a patient as a container is employed, which draws readers' attention to a disease that develops in a patient or is transmitted from one patient to another patient respectively. The frequency of occurrence of this linguistic means with respect to the other three sentential positions within this section of the case report genre is not statistically significant (cf. Location in subsection 3.1.). However, the analysis of frequencies of Location between sections revealed that Location occurs significantly more often in Comment/Discussion than in Introduction, History, Examination, and Treatment. These findings allow to claim that Location is characteristic of this section (cf. subsection 3.2.).

Referring to the patient as to the closed area of medical treatment allows to abstract from the particulars of the case and discuss it from a broader perspective of the already existing literature, which is the aim of this section. However, as has been already alluded in subsection 3.3., the occurrences of patient references in Location from the Comment/Discussion section differ from those in Introduction. The example from Introduction included patient reference in Location in the predicate group (cf. 35 above).

In contrast, in (75), the prepositional phrase with the referent modifies the noun phrase located in the Subject position, which is the focus of the sentence. Yet, the very reference to the patient as an area of medical activity seems to direct attention to what happens *in* the patient. Also locating patient references in the Object position enables the authors to concentrate on other aspects of interest, as in (74) (cf. *offspring*). This operation, in turn, makes it possible to center on a particular medical fact, which becomes the point of reference, with the patient being one the aspects that are mentioned. As the results of statistical analysis in subsection 3.2. show, it is the Comment/Discussion section where this position of patient reference appears more frequently in comparison to Introduction, History, and Examination.

Yet another way of centering around a particular medical aspect is the word *case*. In medical texts, it may point not only to the occurrence of a particular disease but also to a patient, as in (77). Therefore, patient imaging in the final section of the case reports refers not to a patient as the "whole self" (Wade-Halligan 2004: 1400) but to a disease manifestation in his/her body that has been subject to treatment (cf. subsection 4.1.). This conclusion can be illustrated with sentence (78), which explicitly states that what is managed is the patient's condition and not the patient being in this condition.

Concluding, the qualitative analysis of the compiled corpus of medical case reports clearly shows that patient imaging in the texts in question is varied and ranges from a *patient-centered discourse* to an *objectifying discourse*. While the first one presents patients as experiencing individuals and, therefore, as participants in the process of diagnosis and treatment, the other describes decontextualized bodies as locations of diseases or treatment. This dichotomy tallies with the underlying premises of the biomedical model and is conditioned, firstly, by linguistic choices made on the part of the author and, partly, by the type of information given in particular sections of the case report genre. In the following two subsections the two discourses will be discussed in detail.

4.4. Patient-centered discourse

As there is a mode of practicing medicine which encourages patient's active participation in the process of diagnosis and treatment and takes into consideration his/her experience of illness (cf. subsection 3.4. in Chapter Three), so there is a *patient-centered discourse* which reflects the model linguistically. The acknowledgement of the patient's presence in medical texts is achieved in two ways, namely by foregrounding them as well as recognizing them as experiencing individuals.

Firstly, the qualitative analysis has shown that patients come to the fore when they are presented as active participants in the process of diagnosis and treatment. Such a mode of writing is possible when their volitional actions are described:

(79) *At that time, the patient reported difficulty in concentrating, memory loss, and occasional loose stools.* NEJM5

(80) *A 64-year-old woman presented to the emergency department with a stiff painful jaw.* LA14

Sentences (80) and (79) portray patients as visiting the health unit and reporting their health problems respectively. The patients function here as the Agents of the sentences, i.e., the instigators of the actions denoted by the verbs. As has already been mentioned, participants in a given sentence can be compared to actors in a little drama (cf. Aarts 1997: 80 and subsection 4.1. in Chapter Four). The roles they play are hierarchically ranked and the Agent is the most prominent participant. What is more, being the Agents of the sentences, patient references hold the most prominent sentential position, namely the Subject position, which makes them the referents of the rest of sentence (cf. subsection 5.1. in Chapter Four). As a result, their significance in terms of semantics and syntax foregrounds them in the texts.

Such examples can be found in the first section of the case reports, i.e., Introduction, where the account of the patient's presenting condition is given, though from the physician's perspective. Therefore, such a mode of imaging patients is conditioned primarily by the aim of the section of a case report. Yet, as case reports overwhelmingly describe medical procedures as performed on patients and not their experience of illness, the type of information as presented above is limited. Nevertheless, even if a patient is described as undergoing treatment, which means that he/she is not the Agent, it is still possible to foreground him/her in a sentence. This can be done by keeping him/her in the Subject position (cf. 79 and 80 above) or using the Passive Voice (cf. 83 below).

(81) *He underwent tracheostomy and was ventilated mechanically for the next few days.* B5
(82) *The patient deteriorated rapidly with swinging pyrexia of 41°C and died 2 weeks later, in September, 2003.* LA3
(83) *He was treated with broadspectrum antibacterial agents (i.e., vancomycin, ceftriaxone, and metronidazole) and antivirals (i.e., acyclovir and foscarnet).* JA2

As a result of the meaning of the verbs in (81), (82) and (83), the patients take the thematic role of Patient. Nevertheless, their position is still central, as they are those to whom the sentences refer in the context of particular treatment (81 and 83) and condition (82). This effect is possible thanks to the location of patient references in the Subject positions, as in (81) and (82). In the case of (83), where the patient, due to the meaning of the verb, cannot be the Agent and is not in the Subject position in the Active Voice, the Passive Voice can be used. This option enables Patients to be the sentential topics while Agents, in this case physicians who perform the described procedures, are textually absent. Consequently, although patients' status in examples (81), (82) and (83) is different from, for example (79) or (80) above, the readers' attention is still drawn to the patients as being managed or experiencing changes of their conditions and not exclusively to treatment or diseases.

It follows that even if a given section of the case report does not deal with patients' volitional actions, linguistic means make it possible to concentrate on the patients. This means as well that the mode of patient imaging depends only partially on the type of information presented. The foregrounding of patients in sentences seems also a matter of the author's choice of linguistic resources and how he/she wishes to phrase specific information.

This mode of reasoning can be supported by the results from the second stage of the quantitative analysis where the frequency of patient references in the Subject position in the Treatment section is significantly greater than in any other section of the genre under examination in the whole corpus. Also the Subject position of patient references occurs significantly more frequently when compared to the other sentential positions within the Treatment section in the whole corpus.

As has already been stated, content wise, Treatment is not typically associated with the *patient-centered discourse*. Yet, it needs to be emphasized that in the above-given examples, although patients are sententially prominent, they are presented as Patients, i.e., experiencing conditions or undergoing treatment, which is not the mode of patient imaging characteristic of the Introduction section.

By contrast, the second element of the *patient-centered discourse*, i.e., the presentation of the patient's experience of illness, is a categorical choice. Such information is either present, i.e., thought as relevant, or not. Table 13 below lists selected textual references to the patient's mental or bodily experience of illness, divided according to the parts of speech, whereas the subsequent examples demonstrate these references in their particular sentential co-texts.

Table 13. References to the patient's experience of illness

Part of speech	Examples
Nouns	*anxiety, pain, complaint, problem, fatigue, ache(s), difficulty, disorientation, confusion, discomfort, malaise, weakness, soreness, distress, satisfaction;*
Verbs	*complain, suffer from, feel, experience;*
Adjectives/phrases	*confused, disoriented, painful, painless, worried, depressive, surprised, determined, searing, out of sorts, groggy, sore;*

(84) *Although the man complained of a headache for the next 24 hours, he recovered completely.* JA6

(85) *She developed pain and massive inflammation at the injection site, was told she was allergic to the toxoid and should not have further tetanus immunizations.* LA14

(86) *Having sustained two fractures from simple falls, my patient was understandably worried about further fractures.* B3

(87) *He had incapacitating leg pains and increasing difficulty walking.* LA7

(88) *He immediately felt rectal pain; four hours later he developed dysuria, frequency, and frank hematuria.* B12

(89) *He developed acute pelvic discomfort at the time of injection, followed by urgency, dysuria, fever, and aching in the left testis.* B12

As the examples in Table 14 above demonstrate, the authors of medical case reports under study acknowledge the way patients react to illness in a two-fold manner. It can be presented either as an "isolatable entity" associated and, therefore, mentioned with a particular condition (cf. 85, 87 and 89) or described as a state that can be experienced (cf. 84, 86 and 88). In the former case, the means of expression are nouns, which allow to list symptoms, while in the latter case, the verbs which denote particular experience, and adjectives which describe the state in which the patient finds himself/herself. Additionally, there is one adjective and a phrase that seem to belong to lay lexicon – *groggy* and *out of sorts* – rendering information closer to the patient's account.

The sentences below Table 13 describe patient's discomfort. The verbs: *complain, feel, ache* and the adjectives: *worried* on the one hand, and nouns: *pain, discomfort, difficulty* on the other denote the experience of particular reactions and states or refer to them as abstracted elements of a disease respectively (cf. Table 13 above). Yet, regardless of whether listed or described as an experience, all these manifestations of how patients feel are mentioned in the co-texts where patients are referred to as whole persons (in contrast to their body-parts only) and where they are the subjects of the sentences, i.e., the point of reference of the sentence. Such instances can be found primarily in the Introduction section where the patient's account of his/her health is presented. Occasionally, similar examples may also appear in the Case Report body, where some references can be made to how a patient feels during, for example, surgery, and in Comment/Discussion, where the outcome of treatment is evaluated and patient's feelings about his/her condition may be included.

All in all, such a mode of writing as the one described above is clearly in line with the broadly understood patient-centeredness in medicine. Firstly, the focus falls on the whole person of a patient, which is achieved by the use of personal pronouns or nouns referring to people and not to the parts of their bodies/aspects of condition/treatment, and by placing the words indexing the patients in the Subject position. The latter is possible both in active and passive sentences, depending on the semantic features of verbs. As a result, regardless of the patient's thematic status as Agents or Patients, they are the topics of the sentences.

Secondly, the patient's experience of illness is presented, which, though filtered through the author's/physician's lenses, clearly acknowledges the psychological (patient's feelings) and social (patient's inability to perform certain activities) aspects of illness. Consequently, rather than presenting them as entities separated from an experiencer, conditions, symptoms, or reactions are literally *felt* by the patient, therefore, incorporated into the patient's experience.

It follows that the *patient-centered discourse* focuses on the whole person and recognizes other than biological aspects of ailment. The result is a narrated story of illness, which is contextualized in an experiencing individual, something that is not possible in the biomedical model. Furthermore, it has been pointed out that the presence or absence of the examples of the *patient-centered discourse* is not always conditioned by the aims of a particular section, but may also be the author's choice. However, as the counterexamples below demonstrate, in some cases the authors may choose to convey given information in a different way.

(90) *There was a history of hypertension, glaucoma, hypercholesterolemia, obesity, osteoarthritis, and an episode of sciatic pain caused by a synovial cyst at the L4–L5 level.* NEJM14

(91) *Although* her *weight loss, anorexia, and brief intermittent episodes of loose stools were consistent with gastrointestinal involvement, three upper endoscopies with small-bowel biopsies performed over a four-year period failed to reveal gross or microscopical evidence of Whipple's disease.* NEJM5

As can observed in (90), it is not only a disease but also a somatic sensation that can be presented as a separate entity. In this case, although in (90) the *pain* is mentioned, it is done in the *nominalist* manner. Other diseases included in this list (cf. 90) are enumerated without the reference of the undergoer as well. Therefore, although sentence (90) contains the word denoting a bodily sensation, it is not described as experienced by the patient. As regards example (91), it informs about a test performed on the patient, but she is not acknowledged as the one undergoing this procedure. The reference is made also to her in the context of certain symptoms, but it is done only in the form of a possessive pronoun, so the perspective is directed from the patient to the symptoms and the procedure. Such sentences, though seemingly patient-oriented, are examples of the *objectifying discourse* which will be discussed in the next subsection.

4.5. Objectifying discourse

A few important features of medical discourse have already been discussed. Firstly, medical discourse does not deal with patients experiencing illness but with them being the objects of treatment. Secondly, the fact that medical practice has drawn on developing technology and the possibilities it offers has been reflected in medical texts where the role of diagnostic and treating devices has been linguistically foregrounded. Also the dominant biomedical model which focuses on diseases and their pathological manifestations exclusively has contributed to the centrality of the body-parts in texts which tend to be described separately from a patient (cf. sections 6. and 7. in Chapter Three). The three above-given characteristics are also the defining features of the *objectifying discourse* in the examined case reports. They have been found to objectify patients in three respects. Firstly, patients' mental/somatic experience is given without the reference to the experiencers. Secondly, the texts separate patients from their bodies, either writing solely about the affected/treated body-parts or abstracting from their owners. Thirdly, also medical procedures are either foregrounded or dealt with without mentioning those who undergo them.

For one thing, as has already been stated in subsection 4.4., the textual presence of the patient's experience of illness is one of the characteristic features of the *patient-centered discourse*. Examples (84–89) above clearly portray this experience as contextualized in particular patients who are referred to as whole persons. In contrast, mentioning pain or any other sensations without reference to an experiencer may not be treated as the *objectifying discourse*.

(92) *We started a magnesium infusion to maintain ionized magnesium levels of 1·5–2·0 mmol/L, as* muscle spasms *were consistently worse once the serum magnesium fell below 1·5 mmol/L.* LA14

(93) *The development of* pelvic pain *at the time of injection and urinary symptoms within a few hours was highly suggestive of a misplaced injection into the prostatic or periprostatic tissue.* B12

The above-given sentences enumerate two bodily reactions – *muscle spasms* and *pelvic pain* – and abstract them from their experiencers. Instead, the focus falls here on the treatment procedure while patients' bodily responses are described as accompanying biological conditions. Such instances treat the patients themselves and their reactions or symptoms separately and, consequently, do not acknowledge patients' suffering or any other discomfort stemming from the abnormal condition. As a result, the reactions and symptoms seem to have value in themselves without the need of contextualizing them in patients.

The second group of examples includes sentences in which it is the patient's body-parts that take center stage:

(94) *One month later* the spleen *was no longer palpable; at six months, the size of the spleen was normal (13 cm) on ultrasonography.* NEJM2

(95) *We were concerned about the viability of* the kidney, *because of the persistent oliguria and elevated lactate dehydrogenase level, and about the development of a catastrophic vascular event, possibly related to the acute humoral rejection that had been diagnosed a few days earlier, at the time of the first biopsy.* NEJM13
(96) *The left side of* the chest *was not explored.* NEJM10

What these sentences concern is the condition of the body-part (organ, etc.) itself (94 and 95) or its treatment (96) and not the patient whom this surgery concerns. These examples, i.e., where parts stand for wholes – patients (cf. section 4. in Chapter Four), represent a metonymic type of reference. Here body-parts which are treated or whose condition is assessed seem to exist individually in the text. Their separation is an assumed feature, firstly, by virtue of the specificity of the genre that describes diseases in particular patients, and, secondly, of the local character of treatment. It follows that even if the patient is not mentioned, every time patient-related issues are dealt with, readers know who they are reading about.

What is more, admittedly, when a disease is described, reference will be made more frequently to the treated body-parts than to the whole persons. Consequently, a patient becomes objectified as he/she is reduced to his/her body on which medical procedures are performed. It needs to be added, however, that if the body-part is accompanied by a possessive pronoun, then a link between the body and its owner is established. This aspect will also be discussed further in the section devoted to other patient imaging techniques.

Thirdly, there are also sentences which, again, abstract from a patient but this time while describing various medical procedures – from tests to surgery. Regardless of whether they concern the whole patient or his/her body-part, patients may be textually absent.

(97) *Pituitary MRI was normal; inferior petrosal sinus sampling excluded pituitary-dependent Cushing's disease; and octreotide and CT scans of chest, abdomen, and pelvis* showed *no abnormality other than bulky adrenal glands consistent with adrenal hyperplasia.* LA11
(98) *Physical examination confirmed the previous findings and did not* show *any warning signs or indications of progressive involvement.* B10
(99) *On the evening of admission, transplantation of a cadaveric kidney into the left iliac fossa was performed without incident, except that endarterectomy of the left common iliac artery was necessary before creation of the anastomosis;* ... NEJM13

Admittedly, the sentences describe medical procedures and tests by means of which information concerning the patient's health is obtained. Therefore, specific diagnostic devices are presented as *showing* (97 and 98) whereas the operation is the primary topic of sentence (99). Yet, the textual absence of patient references contributes to the instructive character of these examples, which seem to be telling how to perform a given procedure rather than describing patient management.

As regards any features of the *objectifying discourse* that were revealed by the quantitative analysis, the results of its second stage showed that the Possessive group appears significantly more often in Examination and Treatment than Introduction and History. Also patient references in the Object position are more frequent in Treatment than in Introduction, History, and Examination. These results go in line with particular ways of imaging patients in Examination and Treatment sections, i.e., referring to the examined/treated parts of the patients' bodies.

All in all, the *objectifying discourse* derives its name from the fact that this mode of imaging renders patients invisible while giving the account of their somatic/mental reactions and medical procedures. In other words, the discourse does not provide a textual link that would connect patients to their bodies and would index patients as experiencing individuals.

A final comment regarding the analysis of two discourses in the examined case reports should address the very classification of patient imaging therein either as *patient-centered* or *objectifying.* It was based upon the premise that each section of the text has its aim, i.e., the type of information to be mediated, which requires particular linguistic means of expression.

It follows that if the aim of, for example, Treatment is to give the account of the patient's therapy, it can be assumed that the textual prominence will be given to medical techniques and body-parts which are subject to treatment. Following this line of reasoning, this section should be characterized by more frequent references to various aspects of his/her body or treatment which would be reflected, for instance, in the greater use of possessive pronouns or nouns in the possessive rather than to a patient as a whole person, by means of pronouns and nouns. However, the results of the quantitative analysis of patient references in section 3. support this initial prediction only partially.

Admittedly, there are findings showing that the type of information conveyed in a given section affects the language of the author, for example the greater frequency of whole-references than part-references and the dominating Subject position in the Introduction section, and significantly more frequent part-references in Treatment than in Introduction and History. On the other hand, such findings as the greater frequency of patient references in the Subject position in the Treatment section than in any other section and significantly more whole-references in Treatment than in Introduction seem to suggest that, notwithstanding some tendencies, the authors of the examined texts appear to be relatively free in their writing choices, utilizing a variety means of expression, including those which introduce the patient's perspective.

As a result, regardless of the demonstrated tendencies, which accord with the aims of the sections and allow the classification of patient imaging therein either as *patient-centered* or *objectifying discourse*, it is not possible to state that each section uses either of them exclusively. Consequently, it seems appropriate to see the discourses of the genre of case report as a continuum of various modes of patient imaging which appear in every section.[63] Also the very fact that each section of the case report genre includes various ways of referring to patients, ranging from *patient-centered* to *objectifying* ones, seems to support the idea of a case report as a continuum (cf. subsection 4.7.).

The following subsection where other patient imaging techniques will be presented will give further evidence to the continuous nature of the discourses in the studied case reports.

4.6. Other patient-imaging techniques

The examples presented in this subsection will not be discussed from the perspective of the types of information conveyed in particular sections of the case report genre, but how the readers' attention is drawn to different aspects of information given. Firstly, the presentation of patients as grounds will be discussed which, together with the container metaphor, exemplify two spatial configurations in patient imaging in the examined texts.

In subsection 5.1. of Chapter Four, the figure and ground distinction has been introduced. It has been hinted at that also texts and sentences may display such an alignment, depending on their syntactic and lexical configurations. The below-given sentences exemplify this distinction:

(100) *A purple mass developed at the same site months later, followed by similar nodules on the trunk.* LA3

(101) *On physical examination, the rash was most prominent on visible parts of the body, including the face and anterior neck.* JA7

(102) *The 2 lesions noted on her philtrum and left cheek had eschar formation, with the beginnings of ulceration with mild surrounding erythema.* JA5

(103) *An 84-year-old woman presented with a bruise on her face from a fall the previous day.* LA10

63 I would like to thank Professor Karol Janicki for his suggestion to approach the studied aspects in the case reports under examination as a continuum.

In (103), the patient stands in the Subject position which makes her the primary topic and content of the clause (Givón 1984: 137–138; Halliday 1994: 76). Consequently, although the figure – the pathological lesion – has its ground – the face – the whole patient can be treated as another ground, due to her whole-reference and prominent sentential position. In (100), the pathological change – the figure – is imaged as the Agent appearing in a particular location – the ground. As opposed to (103), in (100) and (102) the changes occupy the Subject positions while the grounds – the bodies – metonymically represent the patients.

What is more, in contrast to (103), in (100) and (101), the body-parts appear in abstraction from their owners due to the absence of direct patient references and only the definite articles denote whose parts of the body are dealt with. Such a mode of patient imaging as the one in (100) and (101) tallies with the assumptions of the biomedical model and with the reign of technology in medical practice. In this mode, as in the dominating biomedical model, the emphasis is on the treated pathological changes and the affected body-parts.

Besides, the textual separation of the body from a patient resembles the way bodies are examined and assessed with the use of modern diagnostic means (cf. section 2. in Chapter Three and subsection 4.5. in this chapter). Furthermore, (102) is similar to (100) and (101) in that the skin condition occupies the same position as figures from the two latter examples. Yet, in (102), the patient is referred to by means of the possessive pronoun, which indexes his/her presence and does not separate him/her from the affected body-part.

The figures and grounds from examples (100–103) comply with the defining features of this alignment proposed by Talmy (2001: 315–316; cf. Table 4 in subsection 5.2. in Chapter Four). As opposed to their grounds, the pathological changes from the examples are "smaller", "pointlike" but "of greater relevance" due to the fact that they are targeted by diagnostic and therapeutic procedures. The figures are also "dependent" on the grounds in that the grounds define pathological changes through their location. The grounds, on the other hand, are "larger" as these are either patients or their body-parts. Moreover, they are "more permanently located" in comparison to figures whose nature is incidental and temporary. The grounds are also "less relevant" because there are viewed as the scene against which the figures are noted (cf. Talmy 2001: 315–316).

The other spatial configuration in patient imaging in the corpus is portraying patients as containers (cf. section 4. in Chapter Four). This mode is used in the contexts of both diagnostic and therapeutic procedures. Although patients are textually present, they do not hold sententially prominent positions. Their references are located in the position of complements of prepositional phrases functioning as adverbial complements or adjuncts, i.e., denoting the place of the facts or procedures under examination.

What is more, these examples can also be viewed as the extension of the figure and ground distinction where the patients as locations are the grounds for the matters that are primary topics of the sentences, i.e., disease and treatment. As Grice and Kramer-Dahl (1992) observe, the "patient … is presented less as a person than as an experimental resource" (1992: 64).

(104) *Illness in the two Louisiana residents was attributed to shellfish that was not prepared or handled properly, perhaps because of difficult living conditions after the hurricanes.* LA5

(105) *In March 2000, tender, left axillary adenopathy and fever (temperature, 38.6°C) developed in a 33-year-old microbiologist at the U.S. Army Medical Research Institute for Infectious Diseases who had type 1 diabetes mellitus.* NEJM8

(106) *Once osteonecrosis of the jaw develops, bisphosphonates are generally discontinued, as they were in this patient, although there are no data to suggest that this practice is helpful.* NEJM14

(107) *Fifteen months after the patient's injury, staff members reported possible leg flexion and eye closure on two separate occasions in-response to command, but the responses were rare and inconsistent during the next two months.* NEJM6

(108) *In our patient, two-site immunoassays for luteinizing hormone demonstrated elevated levels.* NEJM11

Due to the syntactic configuration of the words referring to patients, they are presented as containers which serve as the backgrounds for the described bodily states/changes (105 and 108), illness (104) or medical procedures (106). As a result, the readers' attention is focused on these aspects as opposed to the examples of the *patient-centered discourse* in which patient references were foregrounded (cf. 84–89 in subsection 4.4.). Moreover, the sentences in which the patients take the role of Sources of diseases, organs or specimens are also examples in which the container metaphor is utilized (cf. Table 12 in section 4.). It is interesting to note that the container metaphor seems to be at odds with the viewing of diseases as entities. In the former imaging technique, a disease is found and treated in the interior of the patient's body, while in the latter, diseases (also symptoms, reactions, etc.) are entities enumerated in textual abstraction from the body (cf. 107).

As regards the results of the quantitative analysis in section for the Location position, in the first stage, Location was not found to be the dominant position with regard to the other three positions in any of the sections of the case report genre. However, in the second stage, where the frequencies of one type of patient reference were compared between sections, Location was found to occur significantly more frequently in Comment/Discussion than in any other section.

The above-given sentences illustrate the many ways in which authors may choose to write about patients and their diseases and that it is up to the authors what mode they will select and where they decide to lay stress. Admittedly, the authors of medical texts write about patients' conditions and treatment, but, as example (99) above demonstrates, it is possible to write about treatment and its methods without underscoring the fact that it considers human beings and their individual experience.

Thirdly, in many descriptions, the *nominalist* account of a disease is utilized, where diseases are described as isolatable. As regards patients, in this account, they are referred to as cases, which means that they come to be equated with the realizations of specific conditions (cf. section 6. in Chapter Three).

(109) *Complications during the course of her illness included hypertension, heterotrophic ossification, recurrent sinusitis, a femoral fracture, and deep venous thrombosis.* NEJM6

(110) *The patient's clinical course was characterized by a prolonged prodromal illness with fluctuating fatigue and clouded thinking, preceding progressive neurological deficit by 2 years.* LA7

(111) *The cohort of identified recipients of blood transfusion from donors who subsequently developed vCJD totals 66 individuals, of whom 42 have died (including both cases described above and the patient reported here) and 24 are alive.* JA7

(112) *For the remaining 29 (45%) cases, infection was acquired in the United States.* JA1

(113) *The small number of other cases of tuberculosis caused by this strain in the community at the time of the relapse makes it highly unlikely that the patient was reinfected with either a drug-susceptible or a drug-resistant M. tuberculosis variant of the same clone.* NEJM3

In examples (109) and (110) specific symptoms are enumerated like entities. A slightly different version of this concept appeared also in the *patient-centered discourse*, where patients were imaged as 'having' symptoms or diseases (cf. example 47 in subsection 4.2. and example 87 in subsection 4.4.). Yet, in those cases, the patients were referred to as whole persons and they occupied the Subject positions, whereas here their textual presence is marked by means of the noun in the possessive and the possessive pronoun respectively. In (111) and (112), the words *case* refer to the patients who are taken as examples of diseases, as opposed to (113) where the word case denotes an individual occurrence of a disease. Consequently, both diseases and patients are objectified, the former through the *nominalist* account, the latter through referring to them as cases (cf. Grice and Kramer-Dahl 1992: 73).

Lastly, there are also longer fragments of texts where body-parts, symptoms, biological processes or particular treatment are presented in abstraction from a patient. Patients are either textually absent or are not described as undergoers or experiencers of the procedures and reactions respectively. It seems that it may be understandable not to mention patients when writing about certain detailed analyses of specimens, tests at the cellular level, etc. Yet, it appears that describing patient's reactions and symptoms should entail mentioning the very patient as well, as it is him/her whom this experience concerns.

Additionally, it should be stressed that it is not the possible difficulty in identifying who undergoes the treatment dealt with in the case reports, as, by definition, case reports tend to present one particular patient who suffers from a previously unknown disease or a disease which manifests itself in an unusual way. The issue is whether patients' presence should be given more prominence in those parts of texts which refer to the matters directly affecting patients and their experience of illness.

(114) *Chest examination revealed bibasilar rhonchi without rales. No murmurs, rubs, or gallops were heard on cardiac auscultation. The abdomen was soft, without rebound tenderness or organomegaly. Examination of the joints, legs, and arms was essentially normal. No lesions or rashes were noted on the skin. No focal deficits were noted on neurologic examination; there were no cranial-nerve palsies.* NEJM9

(115) *Necrotic bone was removed, and at the end of the procedure, we could see healthy bleeding bone at the base of the wound. Penicillin was given for 14 days, and the mouth rinses with chlorhexidine gluconate were continued. The new extraction site healed well, but during the next 3 months, the mandibular defect with exposed bone persisted, despite aggressive oral hygiene with chlorhexidine gluconate mouth rinse and antibiotics.* NEJM14

(116) *Three years earlier, the patient had been referred to the oral and maxillofacial surgery clinic for evaluation and extraction of three teeth: the mandibular right cuspid and first bicuspid and the mandibular left second bicuspid. Dental extractions were per-formed on an outpatient basis with local anesthesia. The right mandibular teeth were extracted nonsurgically; the mandibular left second bicuspid required a surgical extraction with flap elevation and bone removal.* NEJM14

Example (114) contains the course of physical examination of the patient with a detailed description of symptoms which can be seen, felt and heard, but the reference is made only to particular body-parts. Examples (115) and (116) address medical procedures as performed on particular patients, but again they are textually absent when specific activities are enumerated. In example (116), the patient appears only at the beginning of the fragment, yet he/she is not referred to when his/her body is treated.

Additionally, if the authorial persona is considered, the three above-given fragments exemplify impersonal medical accounts in which both the treated patients and those who perform this treatment are not textually acknowledged. In consequence, the fragments become purely scientific texts which instruct how to treat particular cases of diseases.

4.7. Discussion

Concluding, depending on the type of patient reference and its sentential position, the following scale of modes of patient imaging in the examined corpus can be proposed:

Patient's perspective

(117) *The patient underwent thymectomy, which did not lower her plasma corticotropin concentration.* NEJM10

Patient as the object of medical procedure

(118) We gave her intravenous heparin, then warfarin, and stopped the oral contraceptives. LA15

Patient as a location

(119) *Whipple's disease was first described in 1907 in a patient with migratory polyarthritis, cough, diarrhea with malabsorption, weight loss, and mesenteric lymphadenopathy.* NEJM5

Patient's body-part/aspect of condition/treatment

(120) *To treat her nonfunctional kidney and scarred bladder, we then did a left nephrectomy and caecocystoplasty.* LA6

(121) *I needed to establish the extent to which her management could be evidence based and, where possible, to determine the optimum management using evidence based medicine.* B3

(122) *His urinary symptoms settled after a two week course of ciprof-loxacin and diclofenac.* B12

Indirect reference – body-part

(123) Imaging studies of the neck, chest, abdomen, and pelvis were normal. NEJM10

Patient as a case

(124) *Two of the 18 US cases of inhalational anthrax reported prior to the recent bioterrorism-related outbreak had underlying lung disease; one had beryllium exposure and chronic pulmonary fibrosiss and the other had underlying pulmonary sarcoidosis.* JA3

Abstraction from the patient

(125) *Repeated vitreous examinations revealed lymphocytes, neutronphils, and foamy macrophages and slender rod-shaped structures suggestive of bacteria that were positive on periodic acid–Schiff (PAS) staining, but no malignant cells.* NEJM5

The above-given scale begins with three sentences referring to whole persons (117–119) which occupy three different positions: the subject, the object and the complement of a prepositional phrase respectively. In the case of (119), the patient functions as a location (container) where a disease is found. Moving down the scale, more impersonal are sentences which refer only to various aspects of patient's health and treatment (121 and 122) or to body-parts (120). In (123) only the definite article points to whose body-parts are mentioned. Lastly, various diagnostic or treating procedures can be described without those to whom they apply (125).

Consequently, language wise, the scale starts with the nouns and a personal pronoun referring to the whole person with varying degrees of sentential prominence (cf. 117–119), then moves to possessive pronouns (or nouns in the possessive) referring only to patients' bodies, symptoms or the aspects of treatment (cf. 120–122), and ends with sentences in which individual body-parts (123) and the treatment (125) are described in abstraction from the person. The patient may also be referred to as a *case* (124). As has already been described in previous subsections, these varying forms of reference can be classified as various modes of patient imaging, ranging from *patient-centered* to *objectifying* ones.

Table 14 summarizes the results of the quantitative and qualitative analyses of patient imaging in sections of the case reports (corresponding parts of a narrative are given in brackets) with reference to the hierarchical levels of medical description and modes of disease presentation (cf. sections 1. and 2. in Chapter Four). This is the most common arrangement of information in the examined texts. However, as has already been discussed, very often a particular type of information is given earlier or later in the texts than the structure dictates. What is more, sometimes additional sections are included while others omitted, depending on the specificity of the topic. As regards the results of the quantitative analysis, it confirmed only partially the influence of the aim of a section on the ways in which patients are written about. The findings of the statistical tests also pointed to a significant diversity of modes of patient imaging within sections, which appears to be the decision on the part of the authors, who may choose to foreground the patient irrespective of the topic of a particular section.

Table 14. Patient imaging in sections of the case report genre with respect to hierarchical levels of medical description (Blois 1984)

Case report section	Hierarchical level of medical description	Patient imaging
Introduction (Orientation)	Levels 0–1	Subjective experience of illness
Case Report body (Complication)	History: levels 0–4 Physical examination: levels 0–1 and tests: levels 1–9 Treatment: levels 3–9	Disease as "it" Focus on body-parts/biological processes and symptoms/changes; objective account of a disease Focus on medical procedures and body-parts; objective account of a disease
Comment/ Discussion(Evaluation/ Result)	Levels 3–9	Patients as locations

Also the qualitative analysis demonstrated that, although two types of discourses about patients can be identified, patient imaging in particular sections in the examined corpus should be treated as a continuum of modes of patient reference. Therefore, Table 14 above lists the types of information that typically appear in case report sections and the corresponding modes of writing. In other words, the above-given division is meant only to point to specific content appearing in sections of case reports and their consequences for the form as testified in the examined corpus.

To summarize, the aim of Chapter Five has been to present and discuss the results of the quantitative and qualitative analyses of patient imaging in the corpus of case reports under examination. Firstly, the findings of statistical analysis of the distribution of patient references were presented. Of interest was the comparison of frequencies of particular patient references within case reports sections and between them. The first hypothesis formulated before the analysis was that the aims of particular sections would affect the linguistic means used therein and, therefore, particular differences in the frequencies of patient references were anticipated. Such an approach was meant as an alternative to concentrating only on patient-objectifying techniques and their impressionistic interpretation (cf. section 6. in Chapter Three).

The results obtained confirmed the prediction only partially, pointing to more varied means used in particular sections than it had been expected. In the qualitative part, each section of the case report genre was discussed in detail, concentrating on particular modes of patient imaging and their co-textual environment. The many modes of patient presentation were interpreted with reference to the aims of particular sections and selected distinctions and conceptualizations offered by the sociology of medicine and the semiotics of disease and illness (cf. Chapter Four). Additionally, some elements of the current context of the production of the texts as well as of the history of medicine were addressed where relevant. Reference was also made to the findings of the quantitative study of the texts, which significantly informed the qualitative analysis.

The results of the statistical analysis supported the qualitative description while the qualitative part contextualized the quantitative results. In detail, whereas the quantitative part provided the evidence for the substantial diversity of the modes of patient imaging within the sections, the qualitative part allowed to look at specific examples of patient references in the texts and revealed that in each section, regardless of its aim, it was possible to draw up a list of alternative ways of writing about patients, creating a continuum of modes with visible tendencies. This observation allowed to construct a scale of modes of patient imaging in the studied corpus (cf. subsection 4.7.). Additionally, the qualitative part made it possible to analyze also those sentences/text fragments which refer to the patients but do not contain direct patient references.

With regard to the third hypothesis (p. 115), the identified *objectifying discourse* confirms that the patient's reactions, symptoms, biological processes and the treatment he/she undergoes tend to be rendered separate from him/her in the examined texts. This results from the failure to present patients as experiencers as well as from the textual separation of patients from their bodies, diseases and treatment (cf. subsection 4.5.). What is more, the features of the *objectifying discourse*, illustrated with numerous examples cited from the case reports, were found to be in line with the premises of the biomedical model, which confirms the second hypothesis (p. 115).

In the following chapter, the results of the study of reception of patient objectification will be presented and discussed, whose design was based primarily on the findings of the investigation of different modes of patient imaging as testified in the examined case reports.

Chapter Six: Readers' reception of patient imaging in medical case reports

After the examination of patient imaging in the corpus of medical case reports, the other step of the empirical part was to complement the results of the textual analysis. This decision was guided by the conviction that the outcomes of the linguistic investigation and their interpretation reveal only selected aspects of the examined matter and that they should be confronted with the lay people's perspective on the issue under study. This assumption is in line with the second definition of the term discourse, i.e., the comprehension of a text (O'Halloran 2003, cf. subsection 1.1. in Chapter One), which was adopted for the purpose of the present work. Such a step, however, is not often taken in discourse studies. As a consequence, while the analyses of language samples in various frameworks proliferate, it is more difficult to find research that would offer more than the linguist's analysis and interpretation of language usage.

It needs to be stressed at this point that the perspectives other than the linguist's should not be considered merely in terms of validating or refuting the results of his/her studies. Admittedly, these perspectives may happen to do so, but, more importantly, they may also shed light on the outcomes and add another dimension to the studied matter. In other words, other angles do not leave the results closed in the hermetic box of the linguistic analysis and interpretation, but provide alternative and/or non-specialist viewpoints. It is the present author's belief that these viewpoints may prove to be a valuable addition to the textual analysis. In detail, while in Chapter Five the construction of the patient persona in the case reports has been investigated, in this chapter the reception of this construction will be presented.

The two studies in the empirical part of this work not only draw on two different perspectives but also on two different research traditions. The study of medical case reports from the linguist's point of view (consisting of the quantitative and qualitative parts) complemented by a questionnaire administered to a wider audience means combining both qualitative and quantitative methods which is believed, following Zoltán Dörnyei, to "overcome the weaknesses" (2007: 45) of either of them used individually. While the qualitative approach does not represent larger populations and depends heavily on the context, the quantitative approach is limited to numbers and is abstracted from the context. Yet, when the two are mixed, the results of the first add to the outcomes of the other "putting flesh on the bones" (Dörnyei 2007: 45). In his treatment of the mixed method research, Dörnyei (2007) discusses a quantitative analysis combined with a qualitative one. However, in the present work, the quantitative and qualitative analyses of the corpus are accompanied by a quantitatively oriented questionnaire.

The choice of medical texts as the data to be studied with regard to text reception also requires some elaboration. In Chapter Three, the alternative models of medicine have been discussed. It has been observed that patient-centeredness is an umbrella term for recent trends in medical practice that attempt to redefine the patient-doctor relationship. Yet, although spoken discourse in medical settings has been extensively researched with a view to improving the quality of physicians' encounters with patients, the role of written medical discourse in the context of patient-centered medicine has been grossly underrated.

A possible cause of this state of affairs may be that, generally, medical texts are not associated with the process of the formation of values and attitudes towards patients. The lack of such studies may suggest that interaction in the doctor-patient dyad is the only medical practice in which ways of talking and thinking about patients are produced and reproduced. The research in written medical discourse, on the other hand, appears to aim solely at revealing how researchers construct their professional identities and promote their findings. However, it is the present author's belief that writing and reading medical texts may also be an important factor affecting doctors' perception of patients.

In addition, the role of medical literature in the context of medical students and novices in medical culture should be stressed. For many of them, medical publications are not only obligatory reading and/or a source of knowledge but also the examples to follow when it comes to the appropriate register and style of communication. Medical students may treat such publications as the mode of writing which is widely used and accepted, and consequently, the one to be copied. Therefore, if these texts objectify patients in any way, such findings require linguistic scrutiny.

1. Subjects and methods

As has already been stated in the beginning, the idea behind the questionnaire administration has been to determine whether the linguist's interpretation of the examined matter may be shared by other, non-specialist readers. Consequently, the language patterns that had been examined in the analysis of the corpus were given to a group of selected subjects to see whether their reception of the texts would coincide with or contradict the outcomes yielded in Chapter Five. The following section will briefly describe the target group for the study as well as the methods of questionnaire administration.

What had to be taken into account in the sampling procedure was the fact that an applied questionnaire required reading of professional medical texts. Case reports that comprise the corpus were written by researchers working in clinics or other medical professionals, not infrequently contributing to joint projects published in medical journals. These authors are already established members of the medical profession for whom the mode of writing under study is part and parcel of their practice. It is the mode of writing they have to comply with in order to have their papers published as well as the mode they know from other specialist publications. Yet, although these researchers have the necessary expertise to read the texts, they were not chosen as subjects for the study. It was assumed that because of the fact that they have already internalized the discourse under examination, they would probably be unable to approach the form of texts in a critical manner.

As the prospective subjects were expected to answer questions regarding the form and content of specialist medical texts, also the lay audience had to be excluded due to their lack of medical knowledge. Therefore, a compromise between the two extremes was the choice of medical students. On the one hand, selecting students at a certain stage of medical education was to ensure that they have the basic knowledge to understand the texts under study. They were not expected to be specialists in the issues dealt there, yet they were supposed to know what they were reading about in general. On the other hand, students of medicine are not established in the medical field yet and, consequently, have not internalized certain modes of writing. Far from claiming that students do not know the modes, it was assumed that if students do not publish or produce medical documentation on an everyday basis, they might be more critical of how patients are written about. In other words, it was believed that their medical knowledge sufficed to make some conclusions about the studied texts but, at the same time, their lack of medical practice ensured their unbiased approach to the studied discourse. What is more, the questionnaire did not aim at checking students' comprehension of medical issues described or terminology used in the texts. It was particular formulations with the author/patient references that were under examination.

The questionnaire was administered at Karol Marcinkowski University of Medical Sciences in Poznan in Poland between January and April 2009. The very process of data collection was consulted with the head of the School of Foreign Languages at University of Medical Sciences. The total number of people to which the questionnaire was administered was 202 and they were divided into two groups. The first group were third year Polish students (174) and the other were second year international students (28). As regards the sampling procedure, first, only students of general medical faculty were taken into consideration, excluding any other specializations, e.g., pharmacy or dentistry. Next, the sample was limited only to those who have completed the first year of their studies. The rationale behind this decision was that these students have partially mastered laboratory sciences (Becker et al. 1977; Flexner 1990), which ensures their ability to cope with the texts under study.[64] Further selection procedures regarded the level of English of the two groups. Due to the fact that foreign students attend courses where the language of instruction is English, their language proficiency is expected to be relatively higher than that of Polish students who learn English only as their second language. Consequently, as regards Polish students, only third year students were chosen, as the third year is the last year of foreign language course, and, therefore, their level of language skills is supposed to be the highest. This decision was also consulted with and approved by the head of the School of Foreign Languages. Moreover, the very procedure of administration was preceded by a pilot study in which the questionnaire was tested on two groups of students – international and Polish ones. As the groups did not find either the tasks or the language difficult, I proceeded further with the administration.

The questionnaire was administered during English classes on the school premises. Each time a given English teacher was contacted in advance to request the permission. The teachers were told that the questionnaire concerned the students' interpretation of the medical texts for professionals. The same information was given to the students before the administration of the questionnaire. They were told that the questionnaire was not about giving correct/incorrect answers but about how they understood and perceived the selected fragments of the texts. The students were also asked not to provide any answer if they did not know how to answer a question. The questionnaire was administered to eight out of nine groups of third year Polish students and to all three groups of second year international students of general medical faculty. The very procedure lasted from twenty to thirty-five minutes.[65]

---

64 Although this assumption about the knowledge of medical students was based solely on the materials concerning medical education in the US, the UK and Canada (cf. subsection 3.3. in Chapter Three), it also agrees with the curriculum of Karol Marcinkowski University of Medical Sciences in Poznan.

65 As regards the very sample, originally, it was supposed to consist of students who study medicine in the United Kingdom. In order to get access to those students,

2. Questionnaire design

The questionnaire consisted in the reading of two texts (Text 1 and Text 2) differing in their modes of writing. The difference lay in the presence or absence of both author and patient references. Text 1 was a fragment of one of the case reports from the corpus in its original version. Text 2 was the same fragment but in an altered form. The changes involved removing author and patient references or exchanging them for the Passive Voice or some other impersonal construction, for example, *his full blood count / full blood count* or *we started itraconazole / itraconazole was started* respectively. Yet, the modifications were made only in the sentences which dealt with medical procedures presented either as performed by physicians or applied to patients.

It also needs to be stressed that Text 2, i.e., Text 1 after the present author's modifications had been introduced, was the same as the majority of the texts included in the corpus with regard to the use of the Passive Voice and the references to the patients and authors of the text. In other words, the use of patient/author references as attested in Text 1 was very rare in the corpus whereas its altered form represented the form of the majority of the texts. This also dictated the decision to include the text with patient/author references in the original and the version without patient/author references as modified by the present author and not the other way round. The rationale behind this choice was that since the majority of the reports in the corpus was in the form without the references at hand, the task of modifying the text with references was more straightforward. On the other hand, since the reports with the references to patients and authors were scarce, the material to copy a certain writing style was insufficient to make generalizations about the frequency of the possible use of references. There were no other changes in the text.

---

medical schools in the UK were contacted via email in order to request for permission to administer the questionnaire. Each time the type and aims of the study were briefly outlined. Out of eight schools to which the emails were sent only two replied. In the first case, after a lengthy exchange of emails in which several people from the institution were consulted (including the ethical committee), I was refused the permission to administer the questionnaire on the grounds that the study would be of no benefit to the school. In the other case, a member of the school authorities suggested that the questionnaire could be administered via email and referred me to the president of the Student Medical Education Committee who was supposed to handle the distribution. In the end, the questionnaire was successfully distributed among students, yet I received no replies. It was also impossible to determine whether the lack of response from other institutions was due to the fact that the present study did not generate any interest, or maybe because the emails were treated as spam.

The students were to read both versions and answer three questions, which were given below the texts. The respondents were asked which text was more interesting, easier to read, and, finally, which one they preferred. In two questions, the students were also asked to give reasons for their answers. The aim of this task has been to determine students' preferences for and subjective opinions on the two modes used in the fragments.

The following sections will be devoted to the presentation and discussion of the results of the questionnaire. This time, however, the exact numbers of answers given by the students have been calculated only to percentages and have not been checked for their statistical significance, as in this case no comparisons were made.

3. Results and analysis of the questionnaire

As has been already stated, the aim of questionnaire has been to elicit students' reactions to two medical texts, which differed in the presence/absence of patient and author references. The task consisted in the reading of two texts and answering of three questions. While the first question was meant to be an introductory one asking only to choose the text which seemed more interesting, the purpose of the other two was to elicit which text was easier to read and which one the subjects preferred respectively as well as the reasons for both choices. The aim of each question was not, however, to check the comprehension of the texts but only to elicit subjective and impressionistic opinions on the two modes of writing as exemplified in the texts.

Below the task in the questionnaire is given as well as Table 15 which presents the results. If the answer was given in Polish, the text was translated. Only answers including the number of the text (both with and without the explanation) were counted in as a vote for a particular text. The answer "both" was counted as a separate answer.

Text 1

> *32-year-old man presented in March, 2003, with a purple nodule on his right elbow (figure). He had had a motorcycle accident in Bolivia the previous year, sustaining minor abrasions to the elbow. A purple mass developed at the same site months later, followed by similar nodules on the trunk. He was otherwise asymptomatic and had no history of drug use. We found no palpable lymphadenopathy or hepatosplenomegaly. We considered the diagnoses of cutaneous lymphoma, lupus vulgaris or deep fungal infection. His full blood count, urea and electrolytes, erythrocyte sedimentation rate, immunoglobulins, syphilis, yeast*

and HIV 1 and 2 serology, mycobacterial and fungal culture, and chest radiograph were all unremarkable. His CD4 count was 621 (range: 775–1385) with a normal CD8 count. We took skin biopsies which showed dense non-caseating granulomata in the lower dermis with no clonal proliferation. We started itraconazole while awaiting cultures, but the patient stopped treatment after 14 days. 8 weeks later, he was admitted in an acute confusional state. Cerebral CT showed multiple space-occupying lesions in the right cerebral hemisphere with oedema, hydrocephalus and a midline shift. This was consistent with cerebral lymphoma, although infection could not be excluded. We did another skin biopsy which showed amoebic trophozoites within granulomata. Balamuthia serology was strongly positive at a titre of 1:10 000 confirming disseminated Balamuthia mandrillaris infection. We started co-trimoxazole, rifampicin, ketoconazole and azithromycin (500 mg daily) as well as dexamethasone (4 mg qds) for cerebral oedema. The patient deteriorated rapidly with swinging pyrexia of 41oC and died 2 weeks later, in September, 2003. Postmortem examination showed herniation induced by raised intra-cranial pressure. Smear of brain tissue showed B mandrillaris, which was isolated in culture at Birkbeck College, using human brain microvascular endothelial cells. LA3

Text 2

32-year-old man presented in March, 2003, with a purple nodule on his right elbow (figure). He had had a motorcycle accident in Bolivia the previous year, sustaining minor abrasions to the elbow. A purple mass developed at the same site months later, followed by similar nodules on the trunk. There were no other symptoms or history of drug use. No palpable lymphadenopathy or hepatosplenomegaly were found. The diagnoses of cutaneous lymphoma, lupus vulgaris or deep fungal infection were considered. Full blood count, urea and electrolytes, erythrocyte sedimentation rate, immunoglobulins, syphilis, yeast and HIV 1 and 2 serology, mycobacterial and fungal culture, and chest radiograph were all unremarkable. CD4 count was 621 (range: 775–1385) with a normal CD8 count. Skin biopsies were taken which showed dense non-caseating granulomata in the lower dermis with no clonal proliferation. Itraconazole was started while awaiting cultures, but the patient stopped treatment after 14 days. 8 weeks later, he was admitted in an acute confusional state. Cerebral CT showed multiple space-occupying lesions in the right cerebral hemisphere with oedema, hydrocephalus and a midline shift. This was consistent with cerebral lymphoma, although infection could not be excluded. Another skin biopsy was done which showed amoebic trophozoites within granulomata. Balamuthia serology was strongly positive at a titre of 1:10 000 confirming disseminated Balamuthia mandrillaris infection. Co-trimoxazole, rifampicin, ketoconazole and azithromycin (500 mg daily) were started as well as dexamethasone (4 mg qds) for cerebral oedema. The patient deteriorated rapidly with swinging pyrexia of 41oC and died 2 weeks later, in September, 2003. Postmortem examination showed herniation induced by raised intra-cranial pressure. Smear of brain tissue showed B mandrillaris, which was isolated in culture at Birkbeck College, using human brain microvascular endothelial cells.

Which text was more interesting? _____
Which one was easier to read and why?

____

____

Which one do you prefer and why?

____

____

Table 15. The results in total in percentages

Question	Text 1	Text 2	The same	No answer
Which text was more interesting?	32%	54%	6%	8%
Which one was easier to read and why?	20%	68%	3%	9%
Which one do you prefer and why?	20%	66%	3% both: 1%	10%

As regards Text 1, 32% chose it as more interesting, 20% as easier to read and 20% as the preferred one (cf. Table 15 above). For those who chose Text 1, the fact that in this text the Active Voice was used contributed to the greater ease of reading. Some also called this text informal.

A few people wrote that Text 1 was easier because it was similar to a story, which made it simple to read, understand and to remember. One of them added that it seems as if it had been told by a doctor. One person associated it with a newspaper story, whereas another person contrasted the text with a text from a course book. Some saw Text 1 as more interesting or gripping, and one subject even added that he/she was curious how it would end.

Another group of subjects pointed to a more direct character of the text – classifying it as *personal* – which enabled the reader to identify with the described patient and the situation. As a result, the reader does not read "cold facts" but a story from the doctor's perspective. Yet another person claimed that the mode of writing of the text suggested doctors' involvement in the treatment. Therefore, the use of personal pronouns seems to have made the readers see not only the textual presence of the researcher but also of the patients (cf. Table 15 above).

For 54% of the students Text 2 was more interesting, for 68% it was easier to read and for 66% the preferred one. Informants who chose Text 2 claimed that it was easier to read and understand. However, a number of them admitted that it could have been the result of the second reading, i.e., the fact, that the differences between the texts were minor. Others explained that the ease with which they read the text could be attributed to the fact that Text 2 was precise and concise ("we do not get lost in the text") or that it pointed only to important facts. Others elaborated further claiming that it simply did not center on "unnecessary information concerning the history of this patient". Yet another person was more specific, writing that "bearing in mind masses of information a doctor faces, more compact forms are desired; phrases such as *we did* can be irritating and simply litter the text but, admittedly, they can make the text accessible to an average reader".

Another group made explicit comments on the language of Text 2 noting that it was more formal, professional ("a history is a document and it should be written in formal language" or "language associated with the function of such a text"), like medical language ("like a typical history of the patient's illness"), but also impersonal ("no wondering who is *we*") and without emotions. One of them added, however, that a more emotional approach should be executed in the patient's presence. This way of thinking also appeared in the comment of a subject who decided to make some additional notes on the other side of the questionnaire. They read: "The form of these texts is not an example of bad treatment of a patient; holistic thinking about the patient is always present, and, even if it is omitted in the analysis, it is present in the interaction with him/her".

A few pointed out that the form of Text 2 was more useful in medical practice, which followed the line of reasoning presented in one comment on Text 1, classifying it as more suitable to "an average reader". There were also people who observed that these two modes of writing might have two different aims. According to one subject, the choice of the mode depends on whether the doctor is familiar with the case or not. If the former is the case, Text 2 is enough to refresh the reader's memory. However, if the doctor does not know the patient, Text 1 is recommended. Yet another person wrote that Text 2 "is made to be read" whereas Text 1 "is like a document". Other subjects claimed Text 2 represented the mode of writing they got used to.

A separate group of comments were made by the people who in the last two questions selected one text and spoke unfavorably of the other. One person said that the form of Text 1 made it hard to concentrate on whereas another that it was too impersonal. Others maintained that it was Text 2 that was more difficult to focus on due to the use of the Passive Voice. What is more, it presented only "cold facts" or that "the sentences are thrown at the reader, creating informational chaos".

Although both texts were labeled by respective subjects as easy to read and understand, clear, succinct and interesting, there were also things that these texts differed in. Text 1 was perceived as personal and there were two reasons for this state of the affairs. While some claimed that this feature was the consequence of the way the patient was described, i.e., not as an "object" but more "humane", others attributed this personal character to the opportunity on the part of a reader to identify with the described case ("makes you part of the diagnosis team"). What is more, to a number of subjects Text 1 was similar to a story or a text from a newspaper, possibly because of the presence of personal pronouns contributing to a more direct character of the text.

Among the subjects in favor of Text 2, some stopped short of calling Text 2 impersonal and formal, others went further and described it as scientific and professional. Many of them explicitly pointed to the Passive Voice as contributing to this impression, whereas others explained that it meant that "important information is at the beginning of the sentences". One of the supporters of Text 2 said that "history is a document and it should be written in a formal language". This may suggest that, according to the informants, the Passive Voice is THE linguistic means favored in medical literature (in comparison to the text from a course book) and the only mode of writing ("I got used to such constructions in medical texts"). The informants also made mention of medical publications. Although they are not established researchers, they seem to know well what a scientific paper looks like when they say that, e.g., the mode of writing in Text 2 is "suitable for a scientific paper".

Another subject admitted that although he/she preferred Text 1, he/she "doubts whether personal pronouns are professionally used". This only proves how well-established this mode of writing is, even among those who are at this early stage of medical education. Consequently, for those subjects, impersonal and fact-oriented means professional, i.e., appropriate for scientific publication. This observation is especially interesting in the light of the fact that it is Text 1 that is the original one, while Text 2 is its modified version. It needs to be stressed, however, that examples similar to Text 1 seem rather rare and what served as the altered version in this task is actually common practice.

A comment saying that Text 2 is more useful in medical practice and that Text 1 is more appropriate for an average reader may also confirm this claim. Some other subjects who chose Text 2 added that the way it was written facilitated concentration on important facts, avoiding unnecessary details, which coincided with the biomedical mode of reasoning, i.e., the focus on a disease and not on a person.

Of note is that one of the subjects associated Text 2 with *House M.D.* series, whose main character is notorious for his unceremonious and abrupt behavior towards patients, treating them rather as interesting cases of diseases. In the case of Text 2, this comparison is very telling. However, there are also negative comments concerning Text 2. The fact that it is written in the Passive Voice makes it boring ("like listing"), hard to focus on and associated with "cold facts".[66]

It is also interesting to observe that although the two texts differed only in the presence/absence of references indexing researchers and patients, some readers claimed that the difference between the texts was a matter of more/less medical terminology, details or even length (both texts have the same number of words, i.e., 276). It may be possible that the presence/absence of the Passive in the texts might have somehow contributed to this effect.

There were also few contrasting instances of the respondents' evaluation of the texts. One person wrote that Text 1 was more "neutral" while another two claimed that it was more "impersonal". To one person it was Text 2 that seemed less formal. It is difficult, however, to determine whether the choice of these labels was the result of the evaluation while reading or misconception regarding the forms used therein.

In sum, 54% chose Text 2 as more interesting, while 32% Text 1. When it comes to which one was easier to read, 68% of the students said that it was Text 2, as opposed to 20% who chose Text 1. It was also Text 2 that was the preferred one for a greater number of respondents, i.e., 66%, as opposed to 20% who opted for Text 1.

Consequently, as regards the generated interest, the ease with which the texts were read and the preference, more than half of all the students chose Text 2, i.e., more impersonal text. In their comments regarding the reasons for their choices, the respondents mentioned not only linguistic features and their effect that made the reading interesting/easier but also the beliefs about the appropriateness of such texts. Some claimed that texts of this type should be impersonal and fact-oriented, these being the attributes of professionalism. Others maintained that less impersonality made the texts more interesting, patient-oriented and showed doctor's involvement. Still, Text 2 was overwhelmingly chosen as much easier to read and the preferred one.

---

66 In her study of the texts from the eighteenth, nineteenth and twentieth centuries, Britt-Louise Gunnarsson (2009) refers to the style of twentieth century's medical articles as "fact-listing" (2009: 66).

4. Discussion

The aim of the questionnaire has been to determine students' reception of patient imaging in medical case reports as examined in the analysis of the corpus in Chapter Five. The research question has been whether the present author's interpretation of the selected results from this study would be shared by other readers.

In the questionnaire, the focus has been on the students' reception of two modes of writing as exemplified in two medical texts differing in the presence/absence of patient/author references. The results show that the students vary in their subjective attitudes towards the texts. While some preferred the impersonal one praising its succinctness and conciseness, others opted for the more personal one, claiming that it was more compelling and exemplified a more humane approach to the patient. Of interest appears also the conviction shared by the proponents of the more impersonal text about the appropriateness of this mode of writing in medicine, which points not only to their apparent experience with such literature but also to the acceptance of the current state of affairs (cf. section 3.).

Consequently, from the perspective of the participating students, they do seem to see the patient in the text but they are also able to recognize the many diverse ways in which he/she is described. Moreover, they have their own idea what genre these texts represent, and what they are supposed to be. Yet, what cannot be overlooked about the results is that not all the students evaluated the texts in terms of their usefulness and appropriateness. Although the majority chose the more impersonal text, a number of the respondents acknowledged the second text as an alternative and were able to notice the effect that the presence of patient/author references made. While for some the case described was something they could identify with, for others it represented a more humane approach to the patient. As a result, for these subjects it was something more than an interesting case to analyze. It was a text about an ill person. However much these answers differ, they show great awareness of the matters under examination on the part of the respondents even at this early stage of their socialization into medical culture.

5. Methodological remarks

The outcomes of the conducted questionnaire have revealed one methodological shortcoming which merits some attention. It concerns the last question that the students were to answer after reading the two texts differing in the presence/absence of both patient and author references; the students were to decide which text they preferred. As opposed to two previous questions (*Which text was more interesting?* and *Which one was easier to read and why?*), the third question was not based on any criteria and addressed some indefinite students' preference. However, the results revealed that in some cases the students gave similar answers both to the question *Which text was easier to read and why?* and *Which one do you prefer and why?* This may point to some confusion on the part of the students caused by the lack of specifiable criteria for answering the question. It is possible that asking students about their preference in the first place and then to choose the text that was more interesting and easier to read, and to give reasons for their choice might have eradicated this confusion (cf. section 2.).

6. Implications for further studies

It has already been observed that communication in the doctor-patient dyad has received wide research interest, as it established a platform of cooperation between medical professionals and scholars working in other fields of study, such as linguists, sociologists, philosophers, ethicists, etc. The aim of this cooperation is to improve the quality of doctor-patient encounters contributing to the patient's greater satisfaction and better medical outcomes. At the same time the studies of written medical communication in the context of the patient-centered approach in medicine have attracted little attention. The possible reason of this state of affairs is that written communication, especially among medical professionals, is not conceived of as being of direct relevance to the patient. However, it is the present author's belief and, at the same time, the underlying idea of this work, that it does matter how patients are written about as the production and reception of such texts is one of medical practices and it reflects how patients are positioned therein. Therefore, in their socialization into medical culture, students ought to be made aware of the image of patients that emerges from professional medical texts. In this context, a longitudinal study should be carried out in which a sample of students could take courses in broadly understood medical humanities in order to learn how to deal with patients, respecting their dignity, experience of illness and the right to decide about their lives. Such courses should also be supplemented by a course of written medical discourse in which students would learn not only the appropriate style and mode of argumentation but also how to write about patients using the patient-centered approach. The students should then be followed in order to determine whether the courses shaping their attitudes to patients may have any effect on the students' modes of writing and, possibly, how the students evaluate the modes which are now in use. Furthermore, any studies of professional medical texts which concentrate on the patient persona have the potential to increase the scope for activity supporting the patient-centered medicine.

Conclusion: Summarizing the achievements of the work

The aim of the present work has been to examine critically patient imaging in the genre of medical case report, both with respect to the content as well as the form, i.e., the lexico-grammatical configurations of the texts. The rationale behind this research aim has been the apparent lack of studies of textual construction of the patient persona as opposed to the growing interest in doctor-patient interaction aiming at an improvement in this area. It is the present author's belief that medical texts for professionals are also worth linguistic attention as they project the image of the patient in Western medicine. Theory-wise, the present work is an example of a discourse analysis in which texts are studied with reference to the context of their production, both in terms of genre-specific functions they play and social practices in which they are used. The aim of drawing on and combining these two approaches has been to offer a complex view of patient imaging in case reports as contextualized in the biomedical model of medicine and written according to genre-specific requirements.

In order to study patient imaging in medical case reports, a corpus of 56 texts from British and American journals was examined for direct references to the patients described there. The references were then categorized and analyzed both from the quantitative and qualitative perspectives. The approach to patient imaging adopted in the present work was not intended to concentrate solely on the depersonalizing or objectifying examples but to see their use as influenced by two factors: what the genre is supposed to communicate and what methodological commitments and social practices accompany its production. This approach allowed to formulate three hypotheses concerning patient imaging in the corpus of case reports.

The first hypothesis was that in certain respects the texts tend to objectify patients and there are two contributing factors to be considered here: (1) the type of information included in specific sections of the case report genre; (2) the author's choice of linguistic means of expression. On the one hand, it was predicted that the types of information appearing in particular case report sections could affect the occurrences of certain words indexing patients therein. That is why the frequencies of the categorized types and positions of patient references were compared both within and between sections of case reports. In the quantitative part, the statistical analysis confirmed that in the section devoted to, for example the presentation of the methods of treatment, patients were indexed more frequently by references to patients' body-parts and aspects of their health/treatment than in other sections. Such patient imaging accords with the focus of the section, i.e., on the executed therapy.

While the type of information appearing in particular sections cannot be changed substantially, which linguistic resources are used seems to be less constrained. Therefore, whether the modes of patient imaging are objectifying or not may also depend on the author's choice of lexico-grammatical resources. The diversity of these choices can also be demonstrated on the basis of the Treatment section of case report, where patient references in the Subject position as well as the references to the whole person appear significantly more frequently than in other sections, for example in Introduction, which by default presents information from the patient's perspective. In this case, the authors seem to have chosen to foreground the patient regardless of the topic of the section.

Consequently, while some findings confirm the relation between the frequencies of occurrence of particular patient references and the aims of given case report sections, other results point to a greater variety of modes of writing about patients in the genre. The qualitative analysis where the examined patient references were inspected closely in their co-texts allowed to identify two modes of patient presentation, i.e., the *patient-centered discourse* and the *objectifying discourse*, depending on whether the texts acknowledged the patients' experience of illness and referred to them as whole persons or not. However, a closer examination of patient references in the qualitative study did not allow to classify patient imaging in particular sections of the case reports either as *patient-centered* or *objectifying*.

Similarly to the quantitative analysis, it was revealed that it is possible to find different modes of patient imaging, more or less impersonal, in each section. Therefore, notwithstanding statistically significant tendencies, the genre of case report can be seen as a continuum of discourses, referring to patients from various perspectives.

On the other hand, apart from the type of information conveyed in particular case report sections, it is also the current model of medicine, i.e., modes of reasoning, methodologies and objectives, that contribute to the way patients are imaged. This assumption has been formulated on the basis of the account of the development of the case report genre, which has been presented in the theoretical part of the present work.

It has been demonstrated how particular discoveries and inventions in diagnosis and treatment influenced conceptualizations of disease and the approach to the patient, namely how the patient was defined and positioned with respect to disease and medical management. Following this mode of reasoning, the second hypothesis was that patient imaging in the corpus under study would reflect the premises of the current biomedical model practiced in Western societies.

To this end, the necessary notions, distinctions and conceptualizations were drawn upon from the semiotics of disease and illness and the sociology of medicine, which have significantly informed the critical approach to the biomedical model and the analysis of its reflection in semantic, syntactic and, to a lesser degree, cognitive features of the studied texts. Consequently, the quantitative and qualitative analyses have also shown many instances where the type of information foregrounded in sentences complies with the premises and primary focus of the biomedical model. This confirms the second hypothesis.

Finally, numerous examples provided in the qualitative analysis have demonstrated that the examined case reports tend to present the patient's reactions, bodies and biological processes, etc., separately from him/her, which was assumed in the third hypothesis, formulated on the basis of the literature on patient imaging in medical texts.

Apart from the detailed description of the transformation of the mode of writing about patients in the genre of case report, the theoretical part included an account of the socialization of future doctors into medical culture. The relevant literature that has been cited points to the fact that what is taught in the course of medical education and how it is done contributes to the development of a detached and impersonal approach to the patient which is seen as professionally appropriate and helpful in dealing with patients. Therefore, the quantitative and qualitative analyses have been complemented by the questionnaire administered among the students of medicine.

The questionnaire was based on the selected results of the textual analysis and its aim was to elicit subjective reactions of the respondents to the modes of patient imaging in the presented fragments of the case reports, i.e., to determine whether the linguist's interpretation of the texts would coincide with the interpretation of other readers. In the task, the students were to read and evaluate two texts differing in the presence/absence of the references to the patient and the authors of the texts. The results showed that in spite of the fact that 65% of the students selected the text which textually abstracted from the patient/the authors of the text, claiming that lack of the references of interest contributed to the appropriateness of the style and its reader-friendliness, 25% of the people were in favor of the text referring to patients/authors of the text directly. In other words, there were students who observed that the patient's perspective in the text could be made more prominent thanks to the references under examination.

In the students' opinion, such a text is about a living person and not about an object. What is more, the answers given by the respondents show that already at this stage of their socialization into medical culture, the students seem to have clear views on what such texts should look like.

While discussing the premises of the biomedical model of medicine, it has been stated that its reductionist character contributed to the development of alternative models which seek to redefine the understanding of a diseased patient and the role of medicine in his/her treatment. This alternative approach, referred to as patient-centered medicine, resulted in various undertakings whose keynote was to sensitize both novices and practitioners to the patient's experience of illness and its appropriate management. One of the contributing disciplines which laid the foundations for these undertakings was linguistics, as it helped to linguistically describe doctor-and-patient interaction and pointed to areas for possible improvement. The present work is situated precisely in this body of research, but it aims to draw attention to professional medical texts.

Nowell-Smith (1995) concludes her article on case histories saying that "[m] edical cases are stories not of pain and fear but of medical intervention, and the leading characters are doctors, instruments, and organs" (1995: 64). Also the first experience with such texts makes the reader think that they are only about debrided lesions, resected tissues and diagnosed conditions. From the student's perspective, the text which does not directly refer to patients seems easier to read and focuses only on the important information. In their opinion, it is part and parcel of the way such texts are and should be written. Others, on the other hand, acknowledge the potential of the text which refers to patients directly. From the viewpoint of the present work, similarly to the students' perspective, the picture is not so grim as Nowell-Smith (1995) claims. However, unlike in the case of the student respondents, this conviction is not an opinion, but the conclusion drawn from the results of the textual analysis and interpretation of the corpus in which the studied texts run the gamut of all possible modes, including the varieties of the *patient-centered discourse*. What is more, the statistical analysis has revealed that the authors may adopt the patient's perspective also in sections which are examination/therapy-oriented.

At times, however, the patient as a main protagonist seems to be lost in the text, giving place to treatment. Therefore, it is the present author's belief that texts about new methods of treatment should still refer to patients as those who undergo this treatment, as opposed to their body-parts which are operated on.

In comparison with other sciences, the case reports examined here, as any other medical texts written for health professionals, are texts about human beings and in this way patients should be portrayed. Although the texts carry a message communicated only to fellow medical researchers, it should be a message concerning the patient as an experiencing individual whose suffering is to be alleviated and not a case of a disease treated in a particular way. Consequently, both medical students and doctors should be sensitized to the potential that language offers not only in communication with patients but also about patients.

Bibliography

Works cited and consulted

Aarts, Bas 1997: *English Syntax and Argumentation*. Houndmills: Macmillan Press.

Adams Smith, Diana E. 1984: Medical discourse: Aspects of author's comment. *English for Specific Purposes* 3, 25–36.

Albert, Tim 2004: Why are medical journals so badly written? *Medical Education* 38, 6–8.

Anaya-Prado, Roberto, Alexander H. Toledo, Luis H. Toledo-Pereyra 2006: The surgeon as a scientific writer. *Journal of Investigative Surgery* 19, 335–339.

Anspach, Renee R. 1988: Notes on the sociology of medical discourse: The language of case presentation. *Journal of Health and Social Behavior* 29, 357–375.

Ariel, Mira 1988: Referring and accessibility. *Journal of Linguistics* 24, 65–87.

Armstrong, David 1983: *Political Anatomy of the Body: Medical Knowledge in Britain in the Twentieth Century*. Cambridge: Cambridge University Press.

Armstrong, David 1984: The patient's view. *Social Science & Medicine* 24 (8), 651–657.

Armstrong, David 2002: *A New History of Identity. A Sociology of Medical Knowledge*. Basingstoke: Palgrave.

Arney, William Ray, Bernard J. Bergen 1983: The anomaly, the chronic patient and the play of medical power. *Sociology of Health & Illness* 5 (1), 1–25.

Ashcroft, Richard E. 2000: Teaching for patient-centered ethics. *Medicine, Health Care and Philosophy* 3, 287–295.

Atkinson, Dwight 1992: The evolution of medical research writing from 1735 to 1985: The case of the *Edinburgh Medical Journal*. *Applied Linguistics* 13, 337–374.

Atkinson, Dwight 2001: Scientific discourse across history: A combined multi-dimensional/rhetorical analysis of the Philosophical Transactions of the Royal Society of London. In: Douglas Biber, Susan Conrad, Randi Reppen (eds.) 2001: *Corpus Linguistics: Investigating Language Structure and Use*. Cambridge: Cambridge University Press, 45–65.

Atkinson, Paul 1988: Discourse, descriptions and diagnoses. In: Margaret Lock, Deborah Gordon (eds.) 1988: *Biomedicine Examined*. Dordrecht: Kluwer Academic Publishers, 179–204.

Atkinson, Paul 1995: *Medical Talk and Medical Work*. London: Sage Publications.

Atkinson, Paul 1997: *The Clinical Experience*. Aldershot: Ashgate.

Balint, Michael 1956: *The Doctor, His Patient and the Illness*. London: Pitman.

Balint, Michael, John Hunt, Dick Joyce, Marshall Marinker, Jasper Woodcock. 1984 [1970]: *Treatment or Diagnosis: A Study of Repeat Prescriptions in General Practice*. New York: Routledge.

Ball, Martin J. (ed.) 2005: *Clinical Sociolinguistics*. Malden, MA: Blackwell.

Barber, Charles L. 1962: Some measurable characteristics of modern scientific prose. In: John Swales (ed.) 1985: *Episodes in ESP*. Oxford: Pergamon Press, 3–14.

Baron, Richard J. 1985: An introduction to medical phenomenology: I can't hear you while I'm listening. *Annals of Internal Medicine* 103, 606–611.

Barton, David 1994: *Literacy: An Introduction to the Ecology of Written Language*. Oxford: Blackwell.

Barton, Ellen 2006: Trajectories of alignment and the situated ethics of end-of-life discussions in American medicine. In: Maurizio Gotti, Françoise Salager-Meyer (eds.) 2006: *Advances in Medical Discourse Analysis – Oral and Written Contexts*. Bern: Peter Lang, 23–42.

Bayle, Antoine-Laurent Jesse 1825: *Nouvelle Doctrine des Maladies Mentales*. Paris: Gabon.

Bazerman, Charles 1988: *Shaping Written Knowledge. The Genre and Activity of the Experimental Article in Science*. Madison: The University of Wisconsin Press.

Bazerman, Charles 1994: Systems of genres and the enactment of social intentions. In: Aviva Freedman, Peter Medway (eds.) 1994: *Genre and the New Rhetoric*. London: Taylor & Francis Publishers, 105–123.

Beagan, Brenda L. 2000: Neutralizing differences: Producing neutral doctors for (almost) neutral patients. *Social Science & Medicine* 51, 1253–1265.

Becker, Gay 1994: Metaphors in disrupted lives: Infertility and cultural constructions of continuity. *Medical Anthropology Quarterly* 8 (4), 383–410.

Becker, Howard Saul, Blanche Geer, Everett C. Hughes, Anselm Lo Strauss 1977: *Boys in White: Student Culture in Medical School*. London: Transaction Publishers.

Bensman, Joseph, Robert Lilenfeld 1973: *Craft and Consciousness: Occupational Technique and the Development of the World Images.* New York: Wiley.

Berge, Kjell Lars 2003: The scientific text genres as social actions: Text theoretical reflections on the relations between context and text in scientific writing. In: Kjersti Fløttum, Francois Rastier (eds.) 2003: *Academic Voices.* Oslo: Novus Press, 141–157.

Berger, Peter Ludwig, Thomas Luckmann. 1991 [1966]: *The Social Construction of Reality: A Treatise in the Sociology of Knowledge.* Longman: Penguin Books.

Bhatia, Vijay K. 1993: *Analyzing Genre: Language Use in Professional Settings.* London: Longman.

Biber, Douglas, Susan Conrad, Randi Reppen 1998: *Corpus Linguistics: Investigating Language Structure and Use.* Cambridge: Cambridge University Press.

Bichat, Françoois Xavier 1822: *General Anatomy, Applied to Physiology and Medicine.* Boston: Richardson and Lord.

Blois, Marsden S. 1984: *Information and Medicine.* Berkeley: University of California Press.

Bond, John, Senga Bond 1986: *Sociology and Health Care.* Edinburgh: Churchill Livingstone.

Boyd, Kenneth M. 2000: Disease, illness, sickness, health, healing and wholeness: Exploring some elusive concepts. *Medical Humanities* 26 (1), 9–17.

Brady, Donald W., Giselle Corbie-Smith, William T. Branch 2002: "What's important to you?": The use of narratives to promote self-reflection and to understand the experiences of medical residents. *Annals of Internal Medicine* 137 (3), 220–223.

Brennan, Susan E. 1995: Centring attention in discourse. *Language & Cognitive Processes* 10, 137–167.

Bub, Barry 2004: The patient's lament: Hidden key to effective communication: How to recognize and transform. *Journal of Medical Ethics* 30, 63–69.

Bühler, Karl 1990 [1934]: *Theory of Language: The Representational Function of Language.* Amsterdam: John Benjamins [*Sprachtheorie. Die Darstellungsfunktion der Sprache.* Jena: Gustav Fischer].

Burman, Erica, Amanda Kottler, Ann Levett, Ian Parker 1997: Power and discourse: Culture and change in South Africa. In: Ann Levett, Amanda Kottler, Erica Burman, Ian Parker (eds.) 1997: *Power and Discourse: Culture and Change in South Africa.* London: Zed Books, 1–14.

Calnan, James, Andras Barabas 1973: *Writing Medical Papers: A Practical Guide.* London: Heinemann.

Candlin, Sally 2006: Constructing knowledge, understanding and meaning between patients and nurses. In: Maurizio Gotti, Françoise Salager-Meyer (eds.) 2006: *Advances in Medical Discourse Analysis – Oral and Written Contexts.* Bern: Peter Lang, 65–86.

Capra, Fritjof 1985: *The Turning Point. Science, Society and the Rising Culture.* London: Flamingo.

Carroll, John Bissell 1956: Introduction. In: Benjamin Lee Whorf, *Language, Thought, and Reality*, Cambridge, MA: The M.I.T. Press, 1–34.

Cartwright, Frederick F. 1977: *A Social History of Medicine.* London: Longman.

Catenaccio, Paola 2006: The SARS crisis coverage in the *British Medical Journal* and *New Scientist.* In: Maurizio Gotti, Françoise Salager-Meyer (eds.) 2006: *Advances in Medical Discourse Analysis – Oral and Written Contexts.* Bern: Peter Lang, 279–301.

Chafe, Wallace 1976: Giveness, contrastiveness, definiteness, subject, topic and point of view. In: Charles N. Lee (ed.) 1976: *Subject and Topic.* New York: Academic Press, 25–55.

Charon, Rita 1992: To build a case: Medical histories as traditions in conflict. *Literature & Medicine* 11 (1), 115–132.

Charon, Rita, Joanne Trautmann Banks, Julia E. Conelly, Anne Hunsaker Hawkins, Kathryn Montgomery Hunter, Anne Hudson Jones, Martha Montello, Suzanne Poirier 1995: Literature and medicine: Contributions to clinical practice. *Annals of Internal Medicine* 122, 599–606.

Cohen, Henry 1961: The evolution of the concept of disease. In: Brandon Luch (ed.) 1961: *Concepts of Medicine.* New York: Pergamon Press, 159–169.

Coles, R. 1986: Literature and medicine. *Journal of American Medical Association* 256, 2125–2126.

Comrie, Bernard, Sandra A. Thompson 1985: Lexical nominalization. In: Timothy Shopen (ed.) 1985: *Language Typology and Syntactic Description.* Vol. 3: *Grammatical Categories and the Lexicon.* Cambridge: Cambridge University Press, 349–398.

Condrau, Flurin 2007: The patient's view meets the clinical gaze. *Social History of Medicine* 20 (3), 525–540.

Conrad, Peter 2005: *The Sociology of Health and Illness.* New York: Worth Publishers.

Coombs, Robert H. 1978: *Mastering Medicine*. New York: The Free Press.

Cooperrider, David L., Diana Whitney 2003: Appreciative inquiry. In: Kenneth J. Gergen, Mary M. Gergen (eds.) 2003: *Social Construction: A Reader*. London: Sage, 173–181.

Coulon, Alain 1995: *Ethnometodology*. Sage: London.

Crites, Stephen 1975: Angels we have heard. In: James B. Wiggins, Stephen Crites (eds.) 1975: *Religion as Story*. Oxford: Oxford University Press, 23–63.

Crombie, Alistair Cameron 1994: *Styles of Scientific Thinking in the European Tradition*. Vol. 1. London: Duckworth.

Daly, Jeanne 1989: Innocent murmurs: Echocardiography and the diagnosis of cardiac normality. *Sociology of Health & Illness* 11 (2), 99–116.

De Beaugrande, Robert-Alain, Wolfgang Ulrich Dressler 1981: *Introduction to Text Linguistics*. London, New York: Longman.

DeBakey, L., S. DeBakey 1983: The case report, I: Guidelines for preparation. *International Journal of Cardiology* 4, 357–364.

Descartes, René 2006 /1980/ [1637]: *A Discourse on the Method of Correctly Conducting One's Reason and Seeking Truth in the Sciences*. Translated with an Introduction and Notes by Ian MacLean. Oxford World's Classics. Oxford: Oxford University Press /Indianapolis: Hackett Publishing Company/ [*Le Discours de la méthode Pour bien conduire sa raison, et chercher la vérité dans les sciences Plus la Dioptrique, les Météores et la Géométrie Qui sont des essais de cette Méthode*. Leiden: Ian Maire (A Leyde De l'imprimerie de Ian Maire Avec Privilege)].

Donnelly, William J., Edward Hines 1997: The language of medical case histories. *Annals of Internal Medicine* 127, 1045–1048.

Donohoe, Martin, Susan Danielson 2004: A community-based approach to medical humanities. *Medical Education* 38, 204–217.

Dörnyei, Zoltán. 2007: *Research Methods in Applied Linguistics*. Oxford: Oxford University Press.

Dubertret, Louis 2006: Patient-based medicine. *Journal of European Academy of Dermatology and Venerology* 20, 73–76.

Dubois, B. L. 1986: From *New England Journal of Medicine* and *Journal of the American Medical Association* through The Associated Press to the local newspaper: Scientific translation for the laity. In: Theo Bungarten (ed.) 1986: *Wissenschaftssprachen and Gesellschaft: Aspekte der Kommunikation und des Wissenstransfers in der heutigen Zeit*. Hamburg: Akademion, 243–253.

Duszak, Anna 1987: *The Dynamics of Topics in English and Polish*. Warszawa: Wydawnictwa UW.

Duszak, Anna 1989: Egocentryzm dyskursu a struktura języka [Egocentrism of discourse and the structure of language]. In: Franciszek Grucza (ed.) 1989: *Bilingwizm, bikulturyzm, implikacje glottodydaktyczne: Materiały z XII sympozjum zorganizowanego przez Instytut Lingwistyki Stosowanej UW, Zaborów, 18-20 września 1986* [Bilinguism, biculturalism, glottodidactic implications: Materials from the 12th symposium organized by the Institute of Applied Linguistics of the University of Warsaw, Zaborów, September 18–20, 1986]. Warszawa: Wydawnictwa UW, 109–125.

Duszak, Anna (ed.) 1997: *Culture and Styles of Academic Discourse*. Berlin: Mouton de Gruyter.

Duszak, Anna 1998: *Tekst, dyskurs, komunikacja międzykulturowa* [Text, discourse, intercultural communication]. Warszawa: Wydawnictwa Naukowe PWN.

Edwards, Derek 1994: Whorf's empty gasoline drum and the Pope's missing wife. *Journal of Pragmatics* 22, 215–218.

Edwards, Derek 1997: *Discourse and Cognition*. London: Sage.

Eisenberg, Leon 1977: Disease and illness. *Culture, Medicine, and Society* 1, 9–23.

Emerson, Joan P. 2004: Behavior in private places. Sustaining definitions of reality in gynecological examinations. In: William D. Marelich, Jeff S. Erger (eds.) 2004: *The Social Psychology of Health: Essays and Readings*. Thousand Oaks, CA: Sage, 169–180.

Engel, George L. 1977: The need of a new medical model: A challenge for biomedicine. *Science* 196, 129–136.

Estroff, Sue E. 1993: Identity, disability and schizophrenia: The problem of chronicity. In: Shirley Lindenbaum, Margaret Lock (eds.) 1993: *Power, Knowledge and Practice: The Anthropology of Medicine and Everyday Life*. Berkeley: University of California Press, 247–286.

Evans, Vyvyan, Melanie Green 2006: *Cognitive Linguistics. An Introduction*. Edinburgh: Edinburgh University Press.

Fahnestock, Jeanne 1986: Accommodating science: The rhetorical life of scientific facts. *Written Communication* 3, 275–296.

Fairclough, Norman 1995: *Critical Discourse Analysis: The Critical Study of Language*. London: Longman.

Fairclough, Norman 2001: *Language and Power*. London: Longman.

Fairclough, Norman 2003: *Analyzing Discourse. Textual Analysis for Social Research*. London: Routledge.

Fairclough, Norman, Ruth Wodak 1997: Critical discourse analysis. In: Teun A. van Dijk (ed.) 1997: *Discourse as Social Interaction*. Vol. 1, London: Sage, 258–284.

Ferguson, Gibson 2001: If you pop over there: A corpus-based study of conditionals in medical discourse. *English for Specific Purposes* 20, 61–82.

Firbas, Jan 1974: Some aspects of the Czechoslovak approach to problems of functional sentence perspective. In: František Daneš (ed.) 1974: *Papers on Functional Sentence Perspective*. Prague: Academia, 11–37.

Firbas, Jan 1975: On the thematic and the non-thematic of the sentence. In: Nils Erik Enkvist (ed.) 1975: *Style and Text*. Stockholm: Sprakforlaget Skriptor AB, 317–334.

Fleck, Ludwik 1979 [1935]: *Genesis and Development of a Scientific Fact*. Chicago: University of Chicago Press [*Enstehung und Entwicklung einer wissenschaftlichen Tatsache: Einfuhrung in die Lehre vom Denkstil und Denkkollektiv*. Basel: Schabe & Co.].

Fleischman, Suzanne 1999: *I am..., I have..., I suffer from...*: A linguists reflects on the language of illness and disease. *Journal of Medical Humanities* 20 (1), 3–32.

Fleischman, Suzanne 2001: Language and medicine. In: Deborah Schiffrin, Deborah Tannen, Heidi E. Hamilton (eds.) 2001: *The Handbook of Discourse Analysis*. Oxford: Blackwell Publishers, 470–502.

Flexner, Abraham 1990: *Medical Education in the United States and Canada*. Boston: The Merrymount Press.

Fløttum, Kjersti (ed.) 2007: *Language and Discipline Perspectives on Academic Discourse*. Newcastle: Cambridge Scholars Publishing.

Fløttum, Kjersti, Trine Dahl, Torod Kinn. 2006: *Academic Voices – across Languages and Disciplines*. Amsterdam: John Benjamins.

Foucault, Michel 1994: What is enlightment? In: Paul Rainbow (ed.) 1994: *Michel Foucault: Essential Works*. Vol. 1: *Ethics*. Harmondsworth: Penguin, 303–319.

Foucault, Michel 2002 [1969]: *The Archeology of Knowledge*. London: Routledge [*Archéologie du savoir*. Paris: Editions Gallimard].

Foucault, Michel 2003 /1973/ [1963]: *The Birth of the Clinic. An Archaeology of Medical Perception*. 3rd ed. London: Routledge [*Naissance de la clinique - une archéologie du regard médical*. Paris: Presses Universitaires de France].

Fowler, Roger 1996: *Language in the News: Discourse and Ideology in the Press.* London: Routledge.

Fraser, Suzanne 2003: The agent within: Agency repertoires in medical discourse on plastic surgery. *Australian Feminists Studies* 18 (40), 27–44.

Fredriksen, Stale 2002: Diseases are invisible. *Medical Humanities* 28, 71–73.

Freidson, Eliot 1970: *Profession of Medicine. A Study of the Sociology of Applied Knowledge.* New York: Harper & Row.

French, Roger 2003: *Medicine before Science.* Cambridge: Cambridge University Press.

Fye, W. Bruce 1987: The literature of American internal medicine: A historical view. *Annals of Internal Medicine* 106, 451–460.

Garfinkel, Harold 1984: *Studies in Ethnomethodology.* Cambridge: Prentice-Hall.

Garfinkel, Harold, Harvey Sacks 1970: On formal structures of practical actions. In: John C. McKinney, Edward A. Tiryakian (eds.) 1970: *Theoretical Sociology.* New York: Appleton Century-Crofts, 337–366.

Gawande, Atul 2002: *Complications: A Surgeon's Notes on an Imperfect Science.* London: Profile Books.

Gee, James Paul 1999: *An Introduction to Discourse Analysis: Theory and Method.* New York: Routledge.

George, Daniel, Iahn Gosenhauser, Peter Whitehouse 2006: Medical professionalism: The nature of story and the story of nature. In: Delese Wear, Julie M. Aultman (eds.) 2006: *Professionalism in Medicine: Critical Perspectives.* New York: Springer, 63–87.

Gergen, Kenneth J., Mary M. Gergen 2003: Introduction. In: Kenneth J. Gergen, Mary M. Gergen (eds.) 2003: *Social Construction: A Reader.* London: Sage, 2–6.

Ghosh, Tista 2004: A case presentation. In: Kevin M. Takakuwa, Nick Rubashkin, Karen E. Herzig (eds.) 2004: *What I Learned in Medical School. Personal Stories of Young Doctors.* Berkeley: University of California Press, 154–160.

Gilbert, Nigel, Michael Mulkay 1984: *Opening Pandora's Box: A Sociological Analysis of Scientists' Discourse.* Cambridge: Cambridge University Press.

Givón, Talmy (Thomas Givon) 1984: *Syntax. A Functional-Typological Introduction.* Vol. 1. Amsterdam: John Benjamins Publishing Company.

Givón, Talmy (Thomas Givon) 1990: *Syntax. A Functional-Typological Introduction.* Vol. 2. Amsterdam: John Benjamins Publishing Company.

Good, Byron J. 1994: *Medicine, Rationality, and Experience: An Anthropological Perspective*. Cambridge, MA: Cambridge University Press.

Gordon, Deborah 1988: Tenacious assumptions in western medicine. In: Margaret Lock, Deborah Gordon (eds.) 1988: *Biomedicine Examined*. Dordrecht: Kluwer Academic Publishers, 19–56.

Gosden, Hugh 1992: Discourse functions of marked themes in scientific research papers. *English for Specific Purposes* 11 (3), 207–224.

Gosden, Hugh 1993: Discourse functions of subject in scientific research papers. *Applied Linguistics* 14 (1), 56–75.

Gotti, Maurizio, Françoise Salager-Meyer (eds.) 2006: *Advances in Medical Discourse analysis - Oral and Written Contexts*. Bern: Peter Lang.

Górska, Elżbieta 1999: *On Parts and Wholes. A Cognitive Study of English Schematic Part Terms*. Warsaw: University of Warsaw.

Grace, George William 1987: *The Linguistic Construction of Reality*. London: Croom Helm.

Greenbaum, Sidney, Randolph Quirk 1990: *A Student's Grammar of the English Language*. Harlow: Longman.

Greenhalgh, Trisha, Brian Hurwitz (eds.) 1998: *Narrative-based Medicine: Dialogue and Discourse in Clinical Practice*. London: BMJ Books.

Grice, Francis, Anneliese Kramer-Dahl 1992: Grammaticalizing the medical case history. In: Michael Toolan (ed.) 1992: *Language, Text and Context: Essays in Stylistics*. London: Routledge, 56–90.

Guido, Maria Grazia 2006: The discourse of post-traumatic stress disorder: Specialized genre conventions vs. West African refugees' narrative representations. In: Maurizio Gotti, Françoise Salager-Meyer (eds.) 2006: *Advances in Medical Discourse Analysis - Oral and Written Contexts*. Bern: Peter Lang, 87–109.

Gunnarsson, Britt-Louise 2001: Expressing criticism and evaluation during three centuries. *Journal of Historical Pragmatics* 2 (1), 115–139.

Gunnarsson, Britt-Louise 2009: *Professional Discourse*. London: Continuum.

Hafferty, Frederic W., Ronald Franks 1994: The hidden curriculum, ethics teaching, and the structure of medical education. *Academic Medicine* 69 (11), 861–871.

Hahn, Robert A. 1982: Treat the patient, not the lab: Internal medicine and the concept of 'person'. In: Atwood D. Gaines, Robert A. Hahn (eds.) 1982: Physicians of western medicine: Five cultural studies, Special Issue. *Culture, Medicine and Psychiatry* 6 (3), 219–236.

Hahn, Robert A., Atwood D. Gaines 1985: Among the physicians: Encounter, exchange and transformation. In: Robert A. Hahn, Atwood D. Gaines (eds.) 1985: *Physicians of Western Medicine*. Dordrecht: D. Reidel Publishing Company, 3–22.

Halkowski, Timothy 2006: Realizing the illness: Patients' narratives of symptom discovery. In: John Heritage, Douglas W. Maynard (eds.) 2006: *Communication in Medical Care. Interaction between Primary Care Physicians and Patients.* Cambridge: Cambridge University Press, 86–114.

Halliday, Michael Alexander Kirkwood 1970: Language structure and language function. In: John Lyons (ed.) 1970: *New Horizons in Linguistics.* Harmondsworth: Penguin Books, 140–165.

Halliday, Michael Alexander Kirkwood 1971: Linguistic function and literary style: An inquiry into language of William Golding's *The inheritors.* In: Seymour Chatman (ed.) 1971: *Literary Style: A Symposium.* New York: Oxford University Press, 332–333.

Halliday, Michael Alexander Kirkwood 1976: *Explorations in the Functions of Language.* London: Edward Arnold.

Halliday, Michael Alexander Kirkwood 1979: *Language as Social Semiotic. The Social Interpretation of Language and Meaning.* London: Edward Arnold.

Halliday, Michael Alexander Kirkwood 1994: *An Introduction to Functional Grammar.* London: Edward Arnold.

Halliday, Michael Alexander Kirkwood, Ruqaiya Hasan 1967: *Cohesion in English.* London: Longman.

Halliday, Michael Alexander Kirkwood, Christian M. I. M. Mathiessen 1999: *Construing Experience through Meaning.* London: Continuum.

Harden, Jane 2000: Language, discourse and the chronotope: Applying literary theory to the narratives in health care. *Journal of Advanced Nursing* 31 (3), 506–512.

Harwood, Nigel 2005: 'We do not seem to have a theory… The theory I present here attempts to fill this gap': Inclusive and exclusive pronouns in academic writing. *Applied Linguistics* 26, 343–375.

Hasan, Ruqaiya, Peter H. Fries 1995: Reflections on subject and theme: An introduction. In: Ruqaiya Hasan, Peter H. Fries (eds.) 1995: *On Subject and Theme.* Amsterdam: John Benjamins, xiii–xlv.

Helman, Cecil G. 1994: *Culture, Health and Illness.* Oxford: Butterworth Heinemann.

Heritage, John, Douglas W. Maynard. 2007. *Communication in Medical Care.* Cambridge: Cambridge University Press.

Herman, Joseph 2001: Medicine: The science and the art. *Journal of Medical Ethics* 21, 42–46.

Heslot, Jeanne 1982: Tense and other indexical indexical markers in the typology of scientific texts in English. In: Jorgen Hoedt, Lita Lundquist, Heribert Picht, Jacques Qvistgaard (eds.) 1982: *Pragmatics and LSP. Proceedings of 3rd European Symposium in LSP. Copenhagen 17-19 August 1981*. Copenhagen: Copenhagen School of Economics, 83–103.

Hodgkin, Paul 1985: Medicine is war: And other medical metaphors. *The British Medical Journal* 291, 1820–1821.

Hoekje, Barbara J. 2007: Medical discourse and ESP courses for international medical graduates (IMGs). *English for Special Purposes* 26, 327–343.

Hofmann, Bjørn 2001: The technological invention of disease. *Medical Humanities* 27 (1), 10–19.

Hojat, Mohammadreza, Michael J. Vergare, Kaye Maxwell, George Brainard, Steven K. Herrine, Gerald A. Isenberg, Jon Veloski, Joseph S. Gonnella 2009: The devil is in the third year: A longitudinal study of erosion of empathy in medical school. *Academic Medicine* 84 (9), 1182–1191.

Horowitz, Carol R., Anthony L. Suchman, William T. Branch, Richard M. Frankel 2002: What do doctors find meaningful about their work? *Annals of Internal Medicine* 138 (9), 772–776.

Howald, Blake Stephen. 2008: Variation of victim reference in the construction of serial murder identity. (Handout on the basis of the paper presented at New Ways of Analyzing Variation 37, 9 Nov. 2008.).

Howard, Jan, Fred Davis, Clyde Pope, Sheryl Ruzek 1977: Humanizing health care: The implications of technology, centralization, and self-care. *Medical Care* 15 (5), 11–26.

Huang, Yanling, Siouzih Lin 2010: A study of medical students' linguistic needs in Taiwan. *Asian ESP Journal* 60 (Spring), 35–58.

Hunter, Kathryn Montgomery 1991: *Doctors' Stories. The Narrative Structure of Medical Knowledge*. Princeton: Princeton University Press.

Hunter, Kathryn Montgomery, Rita Charon, John L. Coulehan 1995: The study of literature in medical education. *Academic Medicine* 70 (9), 787–794.

Hurwitz, Brian 2006: Form and representation in clinical case reports. *Literature & Medicine* 25 (2), 216–240.

Huth, Edward J. 1982: *How to Write and Publish Papers in the Medical Sciences*. Philadelphia: Institute for Scientific Information Press.

Hydén, Lars-Christer, Elliot G. Mishler 1999: Language and medicine. *Annual Review of Applied Linguistics* 19, 174–192.

Hyland, Ken 1996: Writing without conviction? Hedging in scientific research articles. *Applied Linguistics* 17 (4), 433–454.

Hyland, Ken 1998a: *Hedging in Scientific Research Articles.* Amsterdam: John Benjamins.

Hyland, Ken 1998b: Persuasion and context: The pragmatics of metadiscourse. *Journal of Pragmatics* 30: 437–455.

Hyland, Ken 2001: Humble servants of the discipline? Self-mention in research articles *English for Specific Purposes* 20, 207–226.

Iedema, Rick 2006: (Post-)bureaucratizing medicine: Health reform and the reconfiguration of contemporary clinical work. In: Maurizio Gotti, Françoise Salager-Meyer (eds.) 2006: *Advances in Medical Discourse Analysis – Oral and Written Contexts.* Bern: Peter Lang, 111–131.

Ingelfinger, Franz J. 1976: Specialty journals in philosophy and ethics. *The New England Journal of Medicine* 295 (23), 1317–1318.

Iris, Madelyn A., Bonnie E. Litowitz, Martha W. Evens 1988: "Problems of part-whole relations. In: Martha W. Evens (ed.) 1988: *Relational Models of the Lexicon.* Cambridge: Cambridge University Press, 261–288.

Jakobson, Roman Osipovič 1960: Closing statement: Linguistics and poetics. In: Thomas A. Sebeok (ed.) 1960: *Style and Language.* New York: The Technology Press of Massachusetts Institute of Technology, 350–377.

Jaye, Chrystal 2004: Talking around embodiment: The views of GPs following participation in medical anthropology courses. *Medical Humanities* 30 (1), 41–48.

Journal Citation Report. In: *Wikipedia: The Free Encyclopedia.* In: http://en.-wikipedia.org/wiki/Journal_Citation_Reports DE 06/2009.

Karlberg, Michael 2004: Discourse and culture. *Communication* 420, 1–21. In: www.-ac.wwu.edu/~karlberg/420/420DiscourseAndCulture.pdf DE 05/2008.

Keenan, Edward L. 1985: Passive in the world's languages. In: Timothy Shopen (ed.) 1985: *Language Typology and Syntactic Description.* Vol. 1: *Clause Structure.* Cambridge: Cambridge University Press, 243–281.

Kenny, Nuala P., Brenda L. Beagan 2004: The patient as text – a challenge for problem-based learning. *Medical Education* 38, 1071–1079.

Kestenbaum, Victor (ed.) 1982: *The Humanity of the Ill.* Knoxville: The University of Tennessee Press.

Kestenbaum, Victor 1982: Introduction: The experience of illness. In: Victor Kestenbaum (ed.) 1982: *The Humanity of the Ill*. Knoxville: The University of Tennessee Press, 3–38.

KIAP – Cultural Identity in Academic Prose: National vs. discipline-specific. 2006. In; www.uib.no/kiap/index-e.htm DE 07/2008.

Kirmayer, Laurence J. 1988: Mind and body as metaphors: Hidden values in biomedicine. In: Margaret Lock, Deborah Gordon (eds.) 1988: *Biomedicine Examined*. Dordrecht: Kluwer Academic Publishers, 57–93.

Kleinman, Arthur 1973: Medicine's symbolic reality: On a central problem in the philosophy of medicine. *Inquiry* 16, 206–213.

Kleinman, Arthur 1980: *Patients as Healers in the Context of Culture*. Berkley: University of California Press.

Kleinman, Arthur 1988: *The Illness Narratives*. New York: Basic Books.

Knorr Cetina, Karin D. 1981: *The Manufacture of Knowledge: An Essay on the Constructivist and Contextual Nature of Science*. Oxford: Pergamon.

Knowles, Murray, Rosamund Moon 2006: *Introducing Metaphor*. London: Routledge.

Kopytko, Roman 2007: Philosophy and pragmatics: A language-game with Ludwig Wittgenstein. *Journal of Pragmatics* 39, 792–812.

Koskela, Merja 1997: Inference in science and popular science. In: Anna Duszak (ed.) 1997: *Culture and Styles of Academic Discourse*. Berlin: Mouton de Gruyter, 343–355.

Kövecses, Zoltán 2005: Metaphor and metonymy in cognitive linguistics. In: Kamila Turewicz (ed.) 2005: *Cognitive Linguistics. A User-friendly Approach*. Szczecin: Wydawnictwo Naukowe Uniwersytetu Szczecińskiego, 13–34.

Kress, Gunther 1985: *Linguistic Processes in Sociocultural Practice*. Geelong: Dedwin University Press.

Kress, Gunther 1995: The social production of language: History and structures of domination. In: Peter H. Fries, Michael Gregory (eds.) 1995: *Discourse in Society: Systemic Functional Perspectives*. Vol. 1: *Meaning and Choice in Language*. Norwood: Ablex, 115–140.

Kress, Gunther R., Robert Ian Vere Hodge 1981: *Language as Ideology*. London: Routledge & Keagan Paul.

Kumagai, A. K. 2008: A conceptual framework for the use of illness narratives in medical education. *Academic Medicine* 83 (7), 653–658.

Kyper, Albert 1654: *Institutes of Medicine*. Amsterdam: [no indication of publisher.].

Labov, William 1979: *Language in the Inner City: Sudies in the Black English Vernacular*. Philadelphia: University of Pennsylvania Press.

Lakoff, George, Mark Johnson 1980: *Metaphors We Live by*. Chicago: Chicago University Press.

Langacker, Ronald W. 1987: *Foundations of Cognitive Grammar*. Vol. 1: *Theoretical Prerequisites*. Stanford: Stanford University Press.

Langacker, Ronald W. 2000: *Grammar and Conceptualization*. Berlin: Mouton de Gruyter.

Langacker, Ronald W. 2002: *The Cognitive Basis of Grammar*. Berlin: Mouton de Gruyter.

Lella, Joseph W., Dorothy Pawluch 1988: Medical students and the cadaver. In: Margaret Lock, Deborah Gordon (eds.) 1988: *Biomedicine Examined*. Dordrecht: Kluwer Academic Publishers, 125–153.

Lingard, Lorelei, Catherine F. Schryer, Kim Garwood, Marlee M. Spafford 2003: 'Talking the talk': School and workplace genre tension in clerkship case presentations. *Medical Education* 37, 612-620.

Lock, Margaret, Deborah Gordon (eds.) 1988: *Biomedicine Examined*. Dordrecht: Kluwer Academic Publishers.

Logan, Michael. H. 1975: Selected references on the hot-cold theory of disease. *Medical Anthropology* 6, 8–14.

Lopez, Jose Julian 2007: Notes on metaphors, notes as metaphors: The genome as musical spectacle. *Science Communication* 29 (7), 7–34.

Luhmann, Niklas 1990: Complexity and meaning. In: Niklas Luhmann (ed.) 1990: *Essays in Self-Reference*. New York: Columbia University Press, 80–85.

Lupton, Deborah 1994: *Medicine as Culture. Illness, Disease and the Body in Western Societies*. London: Sage Publications.

Luzón Marco, María José 2000: Collocational frameworks in medical research papers: A genre based study. *English for Specific Purposes* 19, 63–86.

Lynch, Michael 1985a: Discipline and the material form and images: An analysis of scientific visibility. *Social Studies of Science* 15, 37–66.

Lynch, Michael 1985b: *Art and Artifact in Laboratory Science*. London: Routledge and Kegan Paul.

Lynch, Michael 1990: The externalized retina: Selection and mathematization in the visual representation documentation of objects in the life sciences. In: Michael Lynch, Steve Woolgar (eds.) 1990: *Representation in Scientific Practice.* Cambridge MA: MIT Press, 153–186.

Macdonald, Alexander 1984: *Acupuncture.* London: Allen and Unwin.

Macnaughton, Jane R., Martyn H. Evans 2004: Medical humanities and medical informatics: An unlikely alliance? Is there a role for patients' voices in the modern case record? *Medical Humanities* 30 (2), 57–58.

MacWhinney, Ian R. 1975: Family medicine in perspective. *The New England Journal of Medicine* 293 (4), 176–181.

Margotta, Roberto 1996: *History of Medicine.* London: Hamlyn.

Marshall, P. A., J. P. O'Keefe 1995: Medical students' first-person narratives of a patient's story of AIDS. *Social Science & Medicine* 40 (1): 67–76.

Martinez, A. Iliana 2001: Impersonality in the research article as revealed by the analysis of the transitivity structure. *English for Specific Purposes* 20, 227–247.

Mathiasen, Helle 1997: Literature and medicine: The human experience. *The American Journal of Cardiology* 79, 1222–1225.

Matthews, Janice R., Robert W. Matthews 2008: *Successful Scientific Writing.* Cambridge: Cambridge University Press.

Mattingly, Cheryl 1994: The concept of therapeutic `emplotment'. *Social Science & Medicine* 38, 811–822.

Mattingly, Cheryl 1998: *Healing Dramas and Clinical Plots. The Narrative Structure of Experience.* Cambridge: Cambridge University Press.

McCarthy, J. 2003: Principlism or narrative ethics: Must we choose between them? *Journal of Medical Ethics* 29, 65–71.

McCullough, Lawrence B. 1989: The abstract character and transforming power of medical language. *Soundings* 72 (1), 111–125.

McEwen, Irene 2009: *Writing Case Reports. How to Manual for Clinicians.* Alexandria, Virginia: American Physical Therapy Association.

McKee, Alan 2003: *Textual Analysis: A Beginner's Guide.* London: Sage.

McKenna, Bernard 2004: Critical discourse studies: Where to from here? *Critical Discourse Studies* 1, 9–39.

Mead, Nicola, Peter Bower 2000: Patient-centeredness: A conceptual framework and review of the empirical literature. *Social Science & Medicine* 51, 1087–1110.

Méndez-Cendón, Beatriz 2009: Combinatorial patterns in medical case reports: An English-Spanish contrastive analysis. *The Journal of Specialized Translation* 11, 169–190.

Miles, Steven H., Kathryn M. Hunter 1990: Commentary. *Second Opinion* 15, 60–63.

Miller, Carolyn R. 1994: Rhetorical community: The cultural basis of genre. In: Aviva Freedman, Peter Medway (eds.) 1994: *Genre and the New Rhetoric*. London: Taylor & Francis Publishers, 67–78.

Mishler, Elliot 1984: *The Discourse of Medicine: Dialectics of Medical Interviews*. Norwood, NJ: Ablex.

Myers, Greg 1990: *Writing Biology: The Social Construction of Popular Science*. Madison, Wisconsin: University of Wisconsin Press.

Neumann, John [Johann] 1959 [1928]: On the theory of games of strategy (English trans.) In: Albert W. Tucker, Robert Duncan Luce 1959: Contributions to the Theory of Games, Vol. IV., Princeton University Press, Princeton, N.J. (Annals of Mathematics Studies 40), 13–42. [Zur Theorie der Gesellschaftsspiele. *Mathematische Annalen* 100 (1): 295–320].

Neumann, John von. 1928: Zur Theorie der Gesellschaftsspiele. *Mathematische Annalen* 100, 295–320.

Newman, C. 1957: *The Evolution of Medical Education in the Nineteenth Century*. London: Oxford University Press.

Nijhof, Gerhard 1998: Naming as naturalization in medical discourse. *Journal of Pragmatics* 30, 735–753.

Nowell-Smith, Harriet 1995: Nineteenth-century narrative case histories: An inquiry into stylistics and history. *CBMH/BCHM* 12, 47–67.

Nwogu, Kevin Ngozi 1997: The medical research paper: Structure and functions. *English for Specific Purposes* 16 (2), 119–138.

Ochs, Elinor 1992: Indexing gender. In: Alessandro Duranti, Charles Goodwin (eds.) 1992: *Rethinking Context: Language as an Interactive Phenomenon*. Cambridge: Cambridge University Press, 335–358.

O'Halloran, Kieran. 2003. *Critical Discourse Analysis and Language Cognition*. Edinburgh: Edinburgh University Press.

O'Toole, J. 1995: The story of ethics: Narrative as means for ethical understanding and Action. *The Journal of American Medical Association* 273, 1387–1390.

Paivio, Allan 1979: *Imagery and Verbal Processes*. Hillsdale: Lawrence Erlbaum.

Palmer, Frank Robert 1994: *Grammatical Roles and Relations*. Cambridge: Cambridge University Press.

Parker, Ian 1992: *Discourse Dynamics*. London: Routledge.

Pasveer, Bernike 1989: Knowledge of shadows: The introduction of X-ray images in Medicine. *Sociology of Health & Illness* 11 (4), 360–381.

Pellegrino, Edmund D. 1976: Philosophy of medicine: Problematic and potential. *Journal of Medicine and Philosophy* 1 (1), 5–31.

Pellegrino, Edmund D. 1979: *Humanism and the Physician*. Knoxville: University of Tennessee Press.

Pellegrino, Edmund D. 1982: The humanities in medical education. *MOBIUS* 2, 133–141.

Pellegrino, Edmund D. 2001: *Physician and Philosopher*. Charlottesville, VA: Carden Jennings Publishing.

Pereira, M. Graca, Thomas Edward Smith 2006: Evolution of the biopsychological model in the practice of family therapy. *International Journal of Clinical and Health Psychology* 6 (2), 455–467.

Pettinari, Catherine Johnnson 1988: *Task, Talk, and Text in the Operating Room: A Study in Medical Discourse*. Norwood: Ablex Publishing Company.

Phillips, Nelson, Cynthia Hardy 2002: *Discourse Analysis. Investigating Processes of Social Construction*. London: Sage Publications.

Pickering, Neil 2000: The use of poetry in health care ethics education. *Medical Humanities* 26, 31–36.

Pigeaud, Maurice Jackie 1988: Literary style as a constituent element of medicine. Trans. Faith Wallis. Paper presented at McGill University, Mar. 1988. [Unpublished ms.].

Plato 1975 /1793/ *The Cratylus, Phaedo, Parmenides, Timaeus, and Critias of Plato*. Translated from the Greek by Thomas Taylor. Minneapolis: Wizards Bookshelf /(Verbatim with the original edition of 1793; with new material. Edition limited to 500 copies) London: Printed for B. and J. Whit,/.

Plato 1998 [ca 390 B.C.] Cratylus. Translated, with introduction & notes by C. D. C. Reeve. Indianapolis: Hackett Pub. Co. [Κρατύλος].

Poirier, Suzanne, Daniel J. Brauner 1988: Ethics and the daily language of medical discourse. *Hastings Center Report* 18 (4), 5–9.

Pomme 1796 [1762]: *Traite des Affections Vaporeuses des Deux Sexes*. Vol. 1. Lyons: Duplain.

Porter, Roy 2003: *Blood & Guts. A Short History of Medicine*. London: Penguin Books.

Potter, Jonathan 1996: *Representing Reality: Discourse, Rhetoric and Social Construction*. London: Sage.

Quill, Timothy E. 1983: Partnership in patient care: A contractual approach. *Annals of Internal Medicine* 98, 228–234.

Rabinowitz, Stanley, Benjamin Maoz, Michael Weingarten, Riva Kasan 1994: Listening to patients' stories: Storytelling approach in family medicine. *Canadian Family Physician* 40: 2098–2102.

Radley, Alan 1997: What role does the body have in illness? In: Lucy Yardley (ed.) 1997: *Material Discourses of Health and Illness*. London: Routledge, 50–67.

Rawlison, Mary C. 1982: Medicine's discourse and the practice of medicine. In: Victor Kestenbaum (ed.) 1982: *The Humanity of the Ill*. Knoxville: The University of Tennessee Press, 69–85.

Reiser, Stanley Joe 1981: *Medicine and the Reign of Technology*. Cambridge: Cambridge University Press.

Roberts, Celia 2006: Continuities and discontinuities in doctor-patient consultations in a multilingual society. In: Maurizio Gotti, Françoise Salager-Meyer (eds.) 2006: *Advances in Medical Discourse Analysis – Oral and Written Contexts*. Bern: Peter Lang, 177–195.

Rosenberg, Charles E. 1985: The therapeutic revolution: Medicine, meaning, and social change in nineteenth-century America. In: Judith Walzer Leavitt, Ronald Numbers (eds.) 1985: *Sickness and Health in America*. Madison: University of Wisconsin Press, 39–52.

Rosenberg, Charles E. 1989: Discourse in history: Frames and framers. *Milwaukee Quarterly* 67, 1–15.

Rowley-Jolivet, Elizabeth 2007: A genre study of *If* in medical discourse. In: Kjersti Fløttum (ed.) 2007: *Language and Discipline Perspectives on Academic Discourse*. Newcastle: Cambridge Scholars Publishing, 176–201.

Rundblad, Gabriella 2007: Impersonal, general, and social: The use of metonymy versus Passive Voice in medical discourse. *Written Communication* 24 (3), 250–277.

Sacks, Oliver 1983: *Awakenings*. New York: Dutton.

Salager-Meyer, Françoise 1994: Hedges and textual communicative function in medical English written discourse. *English for Specific Purposes* 13 (2), 149–170.

Salager-Meyer, Françoise, G. Defives, C. Jensen, M. de Filipis 1989: Communicative function and grammatical variations in medical English scholarly papers: A genre analysis study. In: Christer Laurén, Marianne Nordman (eds.) 1989: *Special Language: From Humans Thinking to Thinking Machines*. Philadelphia: Multilingual Matters, 151–160.

Salager-Meyer, Françoise, Nahirana Zambrano 2001: The bittersweet rhetoric of controversiality in nineteenth- and twentieth-century French and English medical literature. *Journal of Historical Pragmatics* 2 (1), 141–173.

Salager-Meyer, Françoise, Maria Angeles Alcaraz Ariza, Maryelis Pabon, Nahirana Zambrano 2006: Paying one's intellectual debt: Acknowledgments in scientific conventional and complementary/alternative medical research. In: Maurizio Gotti, Françoise Salager-Meyer (eds.) 2006: *Advances in Medical Discourse Analysis - Oral and Written Contexts*. Bern: Peter Lang, 407–430.

Sapir, Edward 1929: The status of linguistics as a science. In: David G. Mandelbaum (ed.) 1951: *Selected Writings of Edward Sapir in Language, Culture and Personality*. Berkeley: University of California Press, 160–166.

Sarangi, Srikant, Celia Roberts (eds.) 1999: *Talk, Work and Institutional Order: Discourse in Medical, Mediation and Management Settings*. Berlin: Mouton de Gruyter.

Sayers, Gwen. M. 2002: Of pipes, persons, and patients. *Medical Humanities* 28 (2), 88–91.

Scambler, Graham 2003: *Sociology as Applied to Medicine*. Edinburgh: Saunders.

Schiffrin, Deborah 1994: *Approaches to Discourse*. Oxford: Blackwell.

Schneider, Carl E. 1998: *The Practice of Autonomy*. New York: Oxford University Press.

Schryer, Catherine F. 1994: The lab vs. the clinic: Sites of competing genres. In: Aviva Freedman, Peter Medway (eds.) 1994: *Genre and the New Rhetoric*. London: Taylor & Francis Publishers, 125–132.

Schryer, Catherine F., Lorelei Lingard, Marlee Spaford, Kim Garwood 2003: Structure and agency in medical case presentations. In: Charles Bazerman, David R. Russell (eds.) 2003: *Writing Selves/Writing Societies: Research from Activity Perspectives. Perspectives on Writing*. Fort Collins, Colorado: The WAC Clearinghouse and Mind, Culture, and Activity, 62–96. In: wac.colostate.edu/books/selves_societies/ DE 6/2008.

Scientific thought-styles: The evolution of English medical writing. In: www.helsinki.fi/-varieng/domains/scientific%20thought.html DE 06/2008.

Semino, Elena 2010: Descriptions of pain, metaphor and embodied simulation. *Metaphor and Symbol* 25 (4), 205–226.

Shorter, E. 1985: *Bedside Manners*. New York: Simon and Schuster.

Skelton, John R., J. A. A. Mcleod, C. P. Thomas 2000: Teaching literature and medicine to medical students, part II: Why literature and medicine? *The Lancet* 356, 2001–2003.

Smith, Carlota S. 2003: *Modes of Discourse. The Local Structure of Texts*. Cambridge: Cambridge University Press.

Sontag, Susan 1991: *Illness as Metaphor and AIDS and Its Metaphors*. London: Penguin.

Souba, Wiley W. 2002: Academic medicine and the search for meaning and purpose. *Academic Medicine* 22 (7), 139–144.

Speed, Ewen 2006: Patients, consumers and survivors: A case study of mental health service user discourses. *Social Science & Medicine* 62, 28–38.

Staiano, Kathryn Vance 1986: *Interpreting Signs of Illness. A Case Study in Medical Semiotics*. Berlin: Mouton de Gruyter.

Statistica (data analysis software system), version 8.0. PL. 2007. StatSoft, Inc. (http://www.statsoft.com).

Stubbs, Michael 1997: Language and the mediation of experience: Linguistic representation and cognitive orientation. In: Florian Coulmas (ed.) 1997: *The Handbook of Sociolinguistics*. Oxford: Blackwell Publishing, 358–373.

Suchman, Anthony L., Dale A. Matthews 1988: What makes the patient-doctor relationship therapeutic? Exploring the connexional dimension of medical care. *Annals of Internal Medicine* 108, 125–130.

Swales, John (ed.) 1985: *Episodes in ESP*. Oxford: Pergamon Press.

Swales, John 1990: *Genre Analysis. English in Academic and Research Settings*. Cambridge: Cambridge University Press.

Sydenham, Thomas 1742: *The Entire Works of Dr Thomas Sydenham, Newly Made English from the Originals*. London: Edward Cave.

Taavitsainen, Irma, Päivi Pahta 1998: Vernacularization of medical writing in English: A corpus-based study of scholasticism. *Early Science & Medicine* 3, 157–185.

Taavitsainen, Irma, Päivi Pahta. 2000. Conventions of professional writing: The medical case report in a historical perspective. *Journal of English Linguistics* 28 (1), 60–76.

Taavitsainen, Irma, Päivi Pahta, Noora Leskinen, Maura Ratia, Carla Suhr 2002: Analyzing scientific thought-styles: What can linguistic research reveal about the history of science? In: Helena Raumolin-Brunberg, Minna Nevala, Arja Nurmi, Matti Rissanen (eds.) 2002: *Variation Past and Present: VARIENG Studies on English for Terttu Nevalainen*. Helsinki: Societa Neofilologica, 251–270.

Takakuwa, Kevin M., Nick Rubashkin, Karen E. Herzig (eds.) 2004: *What I Learned in Medical School. Personal Stories of Young Doctors*. Berkeley: University of California Press.

Talmy, Leonard 2001: *Toward a Cognitive Semantics*. Vol. 1: *Concept Structuring System*. Cambridge, MA: Massachusetts Institute of Technology Press.

Temkin, Owsei 1968: The history of classification in the medical sciences. In: Martin M. Katz, Jonathan O. Cole, Walter E. Barton (eds.) 1968: *The Role and Methodology of Classification in Psychiatry and Psychopathology: Proceedings of a Conference Held in Washington D. C., November 1965 under the Auspices of the American Psychiatric Association & the Psychopharmacology Research Branch, National Institute of Mental Health*. Washington: U.S. Department of Health, Education, and Welfare, National Institute of Mental Health, [no pages].

Torode, Brian 1984: *The Extra-ordinary in Ordinary Language*. Rotterdam: Instituut Preventieve en Sociale Psychiatrie, Erasmus University (Konteksten 5).

Trautmann, Joanne 1982: The wonders of literature in medical education: The role of the humanities in medical education. *MOBIUS* 2, 23–31.

Valle, Ellen 1997: A scientific community and its texts: A historical discourse study. In: Britt-Louise Gunnarsson, Per Linell, Bengt Nordberg (eds.) 1997: *The Construction of Professional Discourse*. Edinburgh: Pearson Longman, 76–98.

Van Dijk, Teun A. 1980: *Macrostructures. An Interdisciplinary Study of Global Structures in Discourse, Interaction, and Cognition*. Hillsdale: Lawrence Erlbaum Associates, Publishers.

Van Naerssen, Margaret M. 1985: Medical records: One variation of physicians' language. *International Journal of the Sociology of Language* 5, 43–73.

Van Oosten, Jeanne 1984: The nature of subjects, topics and agents: A cognitive explanation. [Unpublished Ph.D. dissertation, University of California, Berkeley].

Van Rijn-Van Tongeren, Geraldine W. 1997: *Metaphors in Medical Texts*. Amsterdam: Rodopi.

Van Valin, Robert D. 2001: *An Introduction to Syntax*. Cambridge: Cambridge University Press.

Van Valin, Robert D., Randy J. Lapolla 1997: *Syntax: Structure, Meaning and Function*. Cambridge: Cambridge University Press.

Ventola, Eija, Anna Mauranen 1992: Non-native writing and native revising of scientific articles. In: Eija Ventola (ed.) 1992: *Functional and Systemic Linguistics. Approaches and Uses*. Berlin: Mouton de Gruyter, 457–492.

Vihla, Minna 1998: Medicor: A corpus of contemporary American medical texts. *ICAME Journal* 22, 73–80.

Wade, Derick T., Peter W. Halligan 2004: Do biomedical models of illness make for good healthcare systems? *The British Medical Journal* 329, 1398–1401.

Wallis, Patrick, Brigitte Nerlich 2005: Disease metaphors in new epidemics: The UK media framing of the 2003 SARS epidemic. *Social Science & Medicine* 60, 2629–2639.

Walsh, Stephen, H. 2004: The clinician's perspective on electronic health records and how they can affect patient care. *The British Medical Journal* 328, 1184–1187.

Warren, Kenneth S. 1984: The humanities in medical education. *Annals of Internal Medicine* 101, 687–701.

Warter, John Southey 1865: *Observation in Medicine, or the Art of Case Taking*. London: Longmans, Green, and Co.

Wąsik, Elżbieta 2007: *Język narzędzie czy właściwość człowieka? Założenia gramatyki ekologicznej lingwistycznych związków międzyludzkich* [Language a tool or a property of man: Towards an idea of ecological grammar of human linkages]. Poznań 2007: Wydawnictwo Uniwersytetu im. Adama Mickiewicza (Seria Filologia Angielska Nr 28).

Watts, M. S. 1985: Some side effects of science and technology on medical practice. *Western Journal of Medicine* 142 (4), 545.

Wear, Delese, Julie M. Aultman 2005: The limits of narrative: Medical student resistance to confronting inequality and oppression in literature and beyond. *Medical Education* 39, 1056–1065.

Werner, O. 2001: Sapir-Whorf Hypothesis. In: Rajend Mesthrie (ed.) 2001: *Concise Encyclopedia of Sociolinguistics*. Amsterdam: Elsevier, 65–73.

West, Gregory K. 1980: That-nominal constructions in traditional rhetorical divisions of scientific research papers. *TESOL Quarterly* 14, 483–489.

Whorf, Benjamin Lee 1956 [1940]: Science and linguistics. In: Benjamin Lee Whorf, *Language, Thought, and Reality*. Cambridge, MA: The M.I.T. Press, 207–219.

Whorf, Benjamin Lee 1956 [1941]: Language, mind, and reality. In: Benjamin Lee Whorf, *Language, Thought, and Reality*. Cambridge, MA: The M.I.T. Press, 246–270.

Whorf, Benjamin Lee 1956 [1941]: *Language, Thought, and Reality*. Cambridge, MA: The Massachusetts Institute of Technology Press.

Williams, Ian A. 2010: Cultural differences in academic discourse. Evidence from first-person verb use in the methods sections of medical research articles. *International Journal of Corpus Linguistics* 15 (2), 214–239.

Wittgenstein, Ludwig (Johan) 1958 /1953/: *Philosophische Untersuchungen. Philosophical Investigations*. Trans. Gertrude Elisabeth Margaret Anscombe, Rush Rhees (eds.). 2nd. ed. Basil Blackwell & Mott /Oxford: Basil Blackwell & New York, Macmillan/].

Wodak, Ruth 1996: *Disorders of Discourse*. Harlow, Essex: Longman.

Woods, Nicola 2006: *Describing Discourse*. London: Hodder Education.

WordSmith Tools 5. Lexical Analysis Software Ltd. In: www.lexically.net/wordsmith.

Young, Allan 1982: The anthropologies of illness and sickness. *Annual Review of Anthropology* 11, 257–285.

Yoxen, Edward 1990: Seeing with sound: A study of the development of medical images. In: Wiebe. E. Bijker, Thomas P. Hughes, Trevor Pinch (eds.) 1990: *The Social Construction of Medicine*. Edinburgh: Edinburgh University Press, 281–303.

Zeiger, Mimi 2000: *Essentials of Writing Biomedical Research Papers*. [no place of publication]: McGraw-Hill.

Primary sources

B1 Hicks, N. R., M. Dawes, M. Fleminger, D. Goldman, J. Hamling, L. J. Hicks 1999: Chlamydia infection in general practice. *The British Medical Journal* 318, 790–792.

B2 Jones, Ian R., Gary Sullivan 1998: Physical dependence on zopiclone: Case reports. *The British Medical Journal* 316, 117.

B3 Parker, Martyn, J. 2000: Managing an elderly patient with a fractured femur. *The British Medical Journal* 320, 102–103.

B5 Mulrow, Cynthia D. 1998: Helping an obese patient make informed choices. *The British Medical Journal* 317, 266–267.

B6 Buckley, Graham, Nicholas Setchfield, Richard Frampton 1999: Two case reports of possible noise trauma after inflation of air bags in low speed car crashes. *The British Medical Journal* 318, 499–500.

B7 Vause, Sarah, Mary Macintosh 1999: Use of prostaglandins to induce labour in women with a caesarean section scar. *The British Medical Journal* 318, 1056–1058.

B8 Graham, Anna, Tom Fahey 1999: Sore throat: Diagnostic and therapeutic dilemmas. *The British Medical Journal* 319, 173–174.

B9 Bligh, J., R. Farrow 2003: A 66 year old woman with a rash: Case progression. *The British Medical Journal* 326, 640.

B10 Ash, Samanta, Jo Beardsley 1999: Sciatica: Which intervention? *The British Medical Journal* 319, 302–303.

B11 Gareth, Thomas, Alastair Gascoigne 1997: Coma induced by abuse of {gamma}-hydroxybutyrate (GBH or liquid ecstasy): A case report. *The British Medical Journal* 314, 35.

B12 Bullock, Nigel 1997: Impotence after sclerotherapy of haemorrhoids: Case reports. *The British Medical Journal* 314, 419.

B13 Chaudhry, Rama, Shyam Bala Lall, Baijayantimala Mishra, Benu Dhawan 1998: A foodborne outbreak of organophosphate poisoning. *The British Medical Journal* 317, 268–269.

JA1 Straif-Bourgeois, S., T. Sokol, A. Thomas, R. Ratard, K. D. Greene, E. Mintz, P. Yu, P. Vranken 2006: Two cases of toxigenic vibrio cholerae O1 infection after hurricanes Katrina and Rita – Louisiana, October 2005. *The Journal of American Medical Association* 295 (10), 1118–1119.

JA2 Mak, Ryan, G. C. Gray, M. D. Malasig, L. N. Binn, L. V. Asher, D. Cute, S. C. Kehl, B. E. Dunn, J. Zablocki, A. J. Yund 2001: Two fatal cases of adenovirus-related illness in previously healthy young adults – Illinois, 2000. *The Journal of American Medical Association* 286, 553–556.

JA3 Barakat, Lydia A., Howard L. Quentzel, John A. Jernigan, David L. Kirschke, Kevin Griffith, Stephen M. Spear, Katherine Kelley, Diane Barden, Donald Mayo, David S. Stephen, Tanja Popovic, Chung Marston, Sherif R. Zaki, Jeanette Guarner, Wun-Ju Shieh, H. Wayne Carver II, Richard F. Meyer, David L. Swerdlow, Eric E. Mast, James L. Hadler 2002: Fatal inhalational anthrax in a 94-year-old Connecticut woman. *The Journal of American Medical Association* 287, 863–868.

JA4 Meyers, H., G. Inami, J. Rosenberg, J. Mohle-Boetani, D. Vugia, J. Yuan 2007: Brief report: Foodborne botulism from home-prepared fermented tofu – California, 2006. *The Journal of American Medical Association* 297 (12), 1311–1312.

JA5 Garde, Vinaya, David Harper, Mary P. Fairchok 2004: Tertiary contact vaccinia in a breastfeeding infant. *The Journal of American Medical Association* 291, 725–727.

JA6 Tucker, M., B. Eichold II, K. Micher, J. P. Lofgren, J. Schier, M. Belson, M. Patel, C. Rubin 2005: Brief report: Acute illness from dry ice exposure during hurricane Ivan – Alabama, 2004. *The Journal of American Medical Association* 293 (12), 1585–1586.

JA7 Cordell, William H., Gordon Berry 2004: Faux Pox: 2 case reports. *The Journal of American Medical Association* 292 (13), 1554.

JA8 Kopko, Patricia M., Carol S. Marshall, Malcolm R. MacKenzie, Paul V. Holland, Mark A. Popovsky 2002: Transfusion-related acute lung injury. Report of a clinical look-back investigation. *The Journal of American Medical Association* 287 (15), 1968–1971.

JA9 Kellenberg, J., S. Buseman, K. Wright, J. F. Modlin, E. A. Talbot, J. T. Montero, E. Abernathy, J. Icenogle, R. Plotinsky 2005: Brief report: Imported case of congenital rubella syndrome – New Hampshire, 2005. *The Journal of American Medical Association* 295 (5), 492–493.

JA10 Ofner, M., M. Lem, S. Sarwal, M. Vearncombe, A. Simor 2003: Cluster of severe acute respiratory syndrome cases among protected health-care workers – Toronto, Canada, April 2003. *The Journal of American Medical Association* 289, 2788–2789.

JA11 Kenyon, C., K. Ehresmann, D. Boxrud, P. Cassiday, G. N. Sanden, K. M. Bisgard, K. Kiang 2004: Fatal case of unsuspected pertussis diagnosed from a blood culture – Minnesota, 2003. *The Journal of American Medical Association* 291 (13), 1557–1558.

JA12 Rooney, J., K. McCombs, B. Pavlin, J. Sinclair 2005: Two cases of hantavirus pulmonary syndrome – Randolph County, West Virginia, July 2004. *The Journal of American Medical Association* 293 (4), 416–418.

JA13 Landgraf, J., M. G. Stobierski, G. Stoltman, M. Boulton, S. Wiersma, J. R. South, D. Neitzel, H. Hull, K. Smith 2001: Malaria deaths following inappropriate malaria chemoprophylaxis – United States 2001. *The Journal of American Medical Association* 50, 597–599.

LA1 Tuohy, Kathryn A., William J. Nicholson, Fred Schiffman 2003: Agitation by sedation. *The Lancet* 361, 308.

LA2 Woodman, A. M., J. F. Douglas, J. A. Jefferson 2004: Recurrent hyperkalaemia cured by amputation. *The Lancet* 364, 908.

LA3 White, J. M., R. D. Barker, J. R. Salisbury, A. J. Fife, S. B. Lucas, D. C. Warhurst, E. M. Higgins 2004: Granulomatous amoebic encephalitis. *The Lancet* 364, 220.

LA4 Libman, Richard B., Barry L. Menna, Sandeep Gulati 2005: Consequences of ephedra use in an athlete. *The Lancet* 366, S22.

LA5 Carroll, D. N., P. Kamath, L. Stewart 2005: Congenital viral infection? *The Lancet* 365, 1110.

LA6 Lo, Steven, Jeremy Noble, Ian Bowler, Brian Angus 2004: Dysuria and a headache. *The Lancet* 364, 1554.

LA7 Wroe, Stephen J., Suvankar Pal, Durrenajaf Siddique, Harpreet Hyare, Rebecca Macfarlane, Susan Joiner, Jacqueline M. Linehan, Sebastian Brandner, Jonathan D. F. Wadsworth, Patricia Hewitt, John Collinge 2006: Clinical presentation and pre-mortem diagnosis of variant Creutzfeldt-Jakob disease associated with blood transfusion: A case report. *The Lancet* 368, 2061–2067.

LA8 Robertson, David, Emily M. Garland, Satish R. Raj, Nicholas Demartinis 2005: Marathon runner with severe autonomic failure. *The Lancet* 366, S13.

LA9 Kong, Marie-France, Rajesh Jogia, Stephen Jackson, Mary Quinn, Paul McNally, Melanie Davies 2005: Malignant melanoma presenting as a foot ulcer. *The Lancet* 366, 1750.

LA10 James, R. F. 2005: Rectus sheath haematoma. *The Lancet* 365, 1824.

LA11 Keenan, Niall, Waljit S. Dhillo, Graham R. Williams, Jeannie F. Todd 2006: Unexpected shortness of breath in a patient with Cushing's syndrome. *The Lancet* 367, 446.

LA12 Sheridan, E. A., J. Cepeda, R. De Palma, M. M. Brett, K. Nagendran 2004: A drug user with a sore throat. *The Lancet* 364, 1286.

LA13 Chapman, Roddy, Adrian Tully 2004: A life-threatening sore throat. *The Lancet* 364, 112.

LA14 Lindley-Jones, M., D. Lewis, J. L. Southgate 2004: Recurrent tetanus. *The Lancet* 363, 2048.

LA15 Bernstein, R., S. Futterer 2004: Venous unresponsiveness. *The Lancet* 363, 368.

NEJM1 Nierenberg, David W., Richard E. Nordgren, Morris B. Chang, Richard W. Siegler, Michael B. Blayney, Fred Hochberg, Taft Y. Toribara, Elsa Cernichiari, Thomas Clarkson 1998: Delayed cerebellar disease and death after accidental exposure to dimethylmercury. *The New England Journal of Medicine* 338, 1672–1676.

NEJM2 Vinetz, Joseph M., Jun Li, Thomas F. McCutchan, David C. Kaslow 1998: Plasmodium malariae infection in an asymptomatic 74-year-old Greek woman with splenomegaly. *The New England Journal of Medicine* 338, 367–371.

NEJM3 Bishai, William R., Neil M. H. Graham, Susan Harrington, Christopher Page, Kristina Moore-Rice, Nancy Hooper, Richard E. Chaisson 1996: Rifampin-resistant tuberculosis in a patient receiving rifabutin prophylaxis. *The New England Journal of Medicine* 334, 1573–1576.

NEJM4 Silber, Sherman J., Kathleen M. Lenahan, David J. Levine, Jorge A. Pineda, Kim S. Gorman, Michael J. Friez, Eric C. Crawford, Roger G. Gosden 2005: Ovarian transplantation between monozygotic twins discordant for premature ovarian failure. *The New England Journal of Medicine* 353, 58–63.

NEJM5 Rickman, Leland S., William R. Freeman, W. Richard Green, Sandy T. Feldman, Janet Sullivan, Valentina Russack, David A. Relman 1995: Uveitis caused by tropheryma whippelii (Whipple's Bacillus). *The New England Journal of Medicine* 332, 363–366.

NEJM6 Childs, Nancy L., Walt N. Mercer 1996: Brief report: Late improvement in consciousness after post-traumatic vegetative state. *The New England Journal of Medicine* 334 (1), 24–25.

NEJM7 Weisbord, Steven, Jeremy B. Soule, Paul L. Kimmel 1997: Poison on line – acute renal failure caused by oil of wormwood purchased through the Internet. *The New England Journal of Medicine* 337 (12), 825–827.

NEJM8 Srinivasan, Arjun, Carl N. Kraus, David DeShazer, Patrice M. Becker, James D. Dick, Lisa Spacek, John G. Bartlett, W. Russell Byrne, David L. Thomas 2001: Glanders in a military research microbiologist. *The New England Journal of Medicine* 345 (4), 256–258.

NEJM9 Bush, Larry M., Barry H. Abrams, Anne Beall, Caroline C. Johnson 2001: Index case of fatal inhalational anthrax due to bioterrorism in the United States. *The New England Journal of Medicine* 345 (22), 1607–1610.

NEJM10 Arioglu, Elif, John Doppman, Mario Gomes, David Kleiner, David Mauro, Carolee Barlow, Dimitris A. Papanicolaou 1998: Cushing's syndrome caused by corticotropin secretions by pulmonary tumorlets. *The New England Journal of Medicine* 339 (13), 883–886.

NEJM11 Hirshberg, Boaz, P. Michael Conn, Gabriel I. Uwaifo, Keith L. Blauer, Bradly D. Clark, Lynnette K. Nieman 2003: Ectopic luteinizing hormone secretion and anovulation. *The New England Journal of Medicine* 348 (4), 312–317.

NEJM12 Seckl, Michael J., Paul J. Mulholland, Anne E. Bishop, J. Derrick Teale, C. Nicholas Hales, Mark Glaser, Sylvia Watkins, Jonathan R. Seckl 1999: Hypoglycemia due to an insulin-secreting small-cell carcinoma of the cervix. *The New England Journal of Medicine* 341 (10), 733–736.

NEJM13 Sayegh, Mohamed H., Robert B. Colvin 2003: Case 8-2003: A 35-year-old man with early dysfunction of a second renal transplant. *The New England Journal of Medicine* 348 (11), 1033–1045.

NEJM14 Dodson, Thomas B., Noopur S. Raje, Paul A. Caruso, Andrew E. Rosenberg 2008: Case 9-2008: A 65-year-old woman with a nonhealing ulcer of the jaw. *The New England Journal of Medicine* 358, 1283–1291.

NEJM15 Haver, Kenan E., Christopher J. Hartnick, Daniel P. Ryan, Randheer Shailam, Eugene J. Mark 2008: Case 10-2008: A 10-year-old girl with dyspnea on exertion. *The New England Journal of Medicine* 358, 1382–1390.

NEJM16 Rubin, Robert H., Mary Etta King, Eugene J. Mark 2003: Case 7-2003: A 43-year-old man with fever, rapid loss of vision in the left eye, and cardiac findings. *The New England Journal of Medicine* 348 (9), 834–844.

Index: Names and terms from the main text

Author's note: While all the occurrences of the authors' names mentioned in the work have been listed here, some limitations have been introduced regarding the terms used. Due to their high frequence of occurrence in some chapters/sections, in some cases, e.g., *patient* or *case report*, primarily theoretical and methodological contexts where the terms occur have been listed or those which are key to the empirical part of the work.

Y

Z

Philologica Wratislaviensia
From Grammar to Discourse

Edited by Zdzisław Wąsik

The subject matter of this series is intended to cover a wide range of interdisciplinary research works on the *texts* or *text-processing* activities of humans embedded as communication participants into their social roles and culture. Within the scope of particular topics, the readers may find academic treaties pertaining not only to the structure and content of meaning-bearers materialized in the verbal behavior of people but also to their functioning in the domain of art and education. Respective contributions in the form of books and articles will be made by specialists of theoretical and applied linguistics, as well as the history of literature and intercultural communication engaged in the process of second language teaching.

Vol. 1 Zdzisław Wąsik / Tomasz Komendziński (eds.): Metaphor and Cognition. 2008.

Vol. 2 Elżbieta Magdalena Wąsik: Coping with an Idea of Ecological Grammar. 2010.

Vol. 3 Zdzisław Wąsik (ed.): Unfolding the Semiotic Web in Urban Discourse. In Scientific Cooperation with Daina Teters. 2011.

Vol. 4 Ryszard W. Wolny / Zdzisław Wąsik (eds.): Faces and Masks of Ugliness in Literary Narratives. 2013.

Vol. 5 Magdalena Zabielska: Searching for the Patient's Presence in Medical Case Reports. 2014.

www.peterlang.com